A SHORT HISTORY

OF CHRISTIANITY

Martin E. Marty

Fountain Books

WILLIAM COLLINS + WORLD PUBLISHING CO., INC.

Cleveland

MARTIN E. MARTY

Martin E. Marty is professor of the history of modern Christianity at the University of Chicago and associate editor of the Christian Century. *The author of eighteen books, he was awarded the National Book Award in 1972 for* Righteous Empire: The Protestant Experience in America. *Professor Marty is the recipient of nine honorary degrees and is a Fellow of the American Academy of Arts and Sciences. In addition to his scholarly and journalistic career he is a minister in suburban Chicago.*

A FOUNTAIN BOOK

Published by William Collins & World Publishing Co., Inc.
First printing March 1959.
Thirteenth printing November 1976.
Library of Congress Catalog Card Number: 59-7187
ISBN Number: 0-529-02078-5
Printed in the United States of America.

COLLINS WORLD

To Elsa

CONTENTS

CONTENTS

PREFACE AND ACKNOWLEDGMENTS

This short history of Christianity is intended to make its way between specialized monographs and ponderous general narratives of the past of this faith. Depending on a historian's distance from the subject, his perspective, and the time and space he would have to tell the story, he could theoretically write such a history in four lines or four thousand pages. The early Christians were not timid about reproducing digests of sermons which compressed a view of all world history into a few lines in the canonical Book of Acts. Yet they could look at the potential of expansion of one historical moment, the event of Jesus Christ, and say: "But there are also many other things which Jesus did; were every one of them to be written, I suppose that the world itself could not contain the books that would be written" (John 21:25).

I am to stand at the distance which will make possible a book of less than four hundred pages. Awed by my audacity at accepting the assignment, I should like to atone by fulfilling it with a modesty of method and intent. I shall try to strike a note somewhere between the prosaic positivism of syllabi for classrooms and the rhapsodic passion of uncritical religious histories. The entire book is an attempt at recovering the obvious, from its four chronological divisions (Early-Medieval-Reformation-Modern) to its principle for narration. That principle relies on "that which has been believed everywhere, always and by all" Christians, the four notes of the Church (one, holy, catholic, apostolic). The Church is one, according to its own profession, because it is the one Body of which Jesus Christ is the Head; holy because God has chosen it for His own and lives in it through His Holy Spirit; catholic because it is "spread throughout the whole world from one end to the other" and because it is all-embracing in intent; apostolic,

9

because it bears the impress of the teaching and discipline of the original witnesses. The disparity between this ideal and the historical reality makes up the plot of this story. This ideal of the Church is comprehensive, therefore the outline is not confining. It exists as an aid to historian and reader, as a disciplining agent. As we deal with the cluttered course of Christianity through history we confront what William James would call the rich thicket of reality. This thicket may have a single root in the divine self-disclosure of God in a historical person, but to find this root through its bewildering thorns and blossoms we shall welcome several main historical strands to grasp and examine.

It seems to me that a basic commitment to the general reader of this general history has been involved from the outset. I have not been conscious of writing particularly for the "intelligent" or "unintelligent" layman, cleric, academic, or historian; I have tried simply to take hold of a great story and then to attempt to stay out of its way as much as possible. This "general" commitment did necessitate, however, the removal of the masks and marks of erudition. Documentary reference is kept to a minimum. Since all footnotes are citations and none are expository or elaborative, they are placed at the rear of the book, along with chronological tables and a bibliography. Finally, it is helpful to the reader to know in advance the controlling assumptions of the historian. I shall go about this task critically but without deviation from the viewpoint which shall become so obvious: I believe in one holy catholic and apostolic Church.

Any "Christian" enterprise is inevitably a communal endeavor. While I am individually responsible to the reader for the character of this book, I am indebted to many people. A general history should include general thanks to the men at Concordia Theological Seminary, Chicago Lutheran Theological Seminary, and the University of Chicago, who led me by degrees from the history of the early Church, through medieval and Reformation times, to a final specialization in modern religious history. Specific thanks go to Professors Sidney E. Mead and Daniel J.

Boorstin, who were decisive in shaping my approach to history, and to those who had a part in producing this specific work.

I am flattered to hear from Marvin Pierce Halverson that the effort has fulfilled his expectations along the lines of his original conception. Most of the ideas here have been nurtured in dialogue in a shared office with Theodore A. Gill. F. Dean Lueking's reading of the manuscript produced helpful suggestions, particularly in the discussion of the "catholicity" of the Church. Jaroslav J. Pelikan, as editor and historian, could and did make stylistic suggestions along with his substantial criticisms. To preserve the integrity of his criticism, I should add that in my extension of interest in Paul's missionary activities and my necessary compression of Eastern Christian history the proportions did not fully satisfy him. Edward A. Dowey, Jr., is also to be thanked for his reading of the final draft. Cecilia C. Gaul, who regularly "translates me into English," was again most cooperative; Mrs. Florence Adam and Mrs. Lorraine Karp typed the manuscript under tne usual pressure of deadline.

Finally and most significantly, my father, Emil A. Marty, who painstakingly combed much of this manuscript, is most responsible for my interest in Christian history. This particular book, a response to an assignment, thus becomes an act of devotion, a thank-you card to my first and my best teacher.

M. E. M.

Chicago, Illinois
November, 1958

PART I: *The Matrix*

1

THE WHISPER AND THE THUNDER

Historic Christianity has worn many faces. A hymn-sing in a plain Methodist chapel in Iowa and high mass at St. Peter's in Rome; a peasant prayer and an Aquinian system; the percussive affirmation of a tribesman and a choral rendition of the B Minor Mass; the simplicity of a St. Francis and the pomp of a Renaissance pope; the withdrawal of an anchoritic monk and the involvement of a worker-priest or socialist Christian—all are somehow directly related to the Christian faith. To speak of these many things is, in some senses, to speak of one thing. The contrasts and disparities between them are understandable only in their common reference or loyalty to a historic person, Jesus Christ, who died in Palestine *c.* A.D. 30. To make sense, the narrative of the Christian movement must begin with Jesus of Nazareth.

From the first we are thrown into the midst of a mystery, the mystery of Christian life: the revelation of God in Jesus Christ and the relation of Christ to the Church, primitive and historic. This event cuts across time and eternity: when the creed declares the incarnation of God in Christ, the Catholic Christian kneels. And this event cuts across East and West: Christianity is an oriental religion, yet it shaped the Western world. The "many" in the Christian tradition would all insist that there is only "one" in Christ. The

15

theories as to the meaning and intention of Jesus vary, yet the historical reality of the Church seems to by-pass the theories. Many recent critics, from Adolf Harnack through Rudolf Bultmann, argue that Jesus did not intend to found a church; as Alfred Loisy put it: "Jesus proclaimed the Kingdom of God, but it was the Church that came." [1] The Catholic Christian, on the other hand, insists that Jesus came expressly to found the Church. Adherents of both views, however, would probably agree with a recent study of the Church:

> Scripture shows that what constitutes the Church as the Church is the presence in its midst of God through the living Christ in the fellowship of the Spirit. The existence of the Church arises directly out of the ministry of Jesus Christ.[2]

But underlying this and all the other mysteries is the mystery of Jesus. On one hand he is regarded as Pantocrator, the ruler of all things, represented in Christian symbolism as wearing royal robes and bearing in his hand the globe topped with a cross. Yet to the historian there is as much warrant for agreeing with Karl Barth: Jesus Christ is also the historically obscure Rabbi of Nazareth, whose activities, compared with those of other religious founders, are in many respects commonplace.[3] Faith in the "Pantocrator" does not explain the limitations of the Church in history; and the "commonplaceness" of the Rabbi does not explain the existence and durability of the faith.

This chapter deals with the birth in obscurity of that Mediterranean religion which was to inform the Western world. It takes its cue from a footnote in a modern study of these origins. Back in 1935 R. H. Lightfoot, delivering a series of lectures that dealt with the question before us, ended with this statement: "For all the inestimable value of the Gospels, they yield us little more than a whisper of [the Lord's] voice; we trace in them but the outskirts of his ways." Fifteen years later he inserted in his *The Gospel Message of St. Mark* a footnote replying to the criticism of this historical skepticism. Rounding out his original allusion (to Job 26:14), he wrote: "The last words of the verse, 'But the thunder of his power who can understand?'

show that the point of the passage lies in the contrast between that comparatively small knowledge which in Job's
view is all that is at present available to man, and the
boundless immensity which is quite beyond his grasp." [4]
A whole philosophy of Christian history is hinted at in that
footnote—a philosophy that is most apt for approaching
one who was so obscure to his family and contemporaries
yet is so grand to the eye of faith and Christian history.
The obscurity is the whisper; the grandeur is the thunder.

Happily for my vocation, Christianity is a historical
religion which rejoices in what it can see of the fringe of
God's garments and hear in His whisper. The historian who
traces what he can of the path of Jesus knows he is dealing
with a "divine incognito," with "the scandal of historical
particularity." Even so, he is dealing with a real and not
an ideal world. Now and again, whenever Christian discussion becomes too abstract and ideal, the historian is
called to stamp firmly on Palestinian soil. Yet there is
"thunder" in his choice of soil, for in choosing Palestine
he too is affirming a Christian view of history which puts
Jesus the Christ at the center, with events leading up to
and away from him, just as the calendar does.

The "events" which lead up to the event of Christ center
around the career of the people of Israel, whose days of
glory and defeat are chronicled in the Old Testament.
Jesus was born into the complex of the Graeco-Roman
world. The land of his birth was Palestine—a small, moun-
tainous terrain on the eastern shores of the sea. In this insignificant corner of the world, among a people who had
been a puppet of empires through most ages, a universal
kingdom was proclaimed and a universal Church was established. The events of the life of Christ centered in the north
of this area, in Galilee, a crossroads of the ancient world,
where he spent most of his years, and in Judea to the
south, where he was put to death in Jerusalem.

THE PEOPLE OF GOD IN THE
OLD TESTAMENT

As a son of his times Jesus appropriated much of the experience of his people, who had walked those roads and inhabited those villages for many centuries.

He certainly saw himself against the pattern of the promise and prophecy contained in their sacred writings, which recorded their dialogue with Yahweh in the long centuries before his birth. That dialogue in effect marked the development of a vision of mankind; in other words, of a view of history. On the basis of the writings of one of the original witnesses in the New Testament Scriptures, St. Paul (—c. 65)• (Gal. 3:6ff.; Rom. 9–11; 5:12ff.), Oscar Cullmann has summarized this view of history: After man who was intended to rule creation had fallen into sin, God chose one group, the people of Israel, for the salvation of the world. Out of this grew a smaller creative and redemptive community, the "remnant" or *kahal Jahve*. Finally, the remnant is summarized in and reduced to one man who assumes Israel's role. He is the suffering servant of Yahweh described by the Second Isaiah, or the Son of Man described by Daniel. He enters history in the Son of God, Christ. Through a vicarious death he completes the purpose of God. Now after this reduction from all men to the people of Israel to the remnant of Israel to the man of Israel, the process reverses itself, "to proceed from the One to the Many, but in such a way that *the Many represent the One*." [5] The way leads from Christ to those who believe in him, who are saved by faith in his death. And the community of believers forms the Church, the body of the One, which serves as the remnant in subsequent history.

If we remember that this summary is based not necessarily on Christ's own words but on St. Paul's, we can use it provisionally to help us understand the function of

• This usage, followed throughout the book, indicates date of death.

Old Testament events as preparation for the new age. Sayings of Jesus preserved in the Gospels suggest that he saw himself not as the destroyer of "the Law" or the religion of the past but as its fulfillment. The people who listened to Moses and the prophets would listen to him also. Many of the signs of the Old Testament pointed toward him. The Old Testament was one whose keystone, rigid monotheism, separated it from documents of most other ancient faiths. "Hear, O Israel, the Lord our God is one Lord." This one Lord is the creator and preserver of the world; but He is not aloof from human history. He entangles Himself in the career of His people, in events and times and places and peoples and mighty deeds. He is both wrathful and loving, and is served through praise and faithfulness. He will reward man for his good works and will not desert His righteous children. Service of the Lord, Yahweh, is not a guarantee of exemption from suffering, but trust in the Lord's continued care and revelation and a sense of openness to what the future under Him may bring sustains His children. This Lord, Jesus addresses as Father. The high theology of St. Paul's letter to the Colossians sees in Jesus the dwelling of the fullness of the godhead bodily, and the Fourth Gospel speaks of Jesus as the eternal word of God made flesh. But neither these writings nor the sayings of Jesus are intended to contradict the monotheistic pattern: "He who believes in me, believes not in me but in him who sent me" (John 12:44).

JUDAISM

The history of Israel centered in Moses, the kings, and the prophets. Between their times and the birth of Jesus a great deal happened, and we need more than ever the Old Testament to understand the events of Jesus' life and the disputes with his contemporaries. To put it more precisely, Jesus' proclamation emerges out of Judaism. "The proclamation of Jesus must be considered within the framework of Judaism. Jesus was not a "Christian," but a Jew, and his preaching is couched in the thought forms and imagery of Judaism, even where it is critical of traditional Jewish piety." [6] Historically this means that he appears in post-post-exilic Judaism, in a Palestine that had been conquered successively by the Ptolemies of Egypt, the Syrian Seleucids, the Greeks and, finally, the Romans. The Jews chafed under the foreign yoke and from time to time they revolted. Under the Maccabees, they even enjoyed reasonable independence (143–63 B.C.). But in 63 B.C. Pompey (—48 B.C.) took Jerusalem for Rome. Jesus was born into a Roman puppet state, ruled ostensibly (after 37 B.C.) by the Herods. By A.D. 6 the Emperor Augustus (—A.D. 14) tired of Herodian misrule and established a procuratorship in Judea under which the Jewish Sanhedrin and the high priest were partially independent. One of these procurators, otherwise obscure, finds himself embarrassingly prominent in history because of his inclusion in the Christian creed. His name: Pontius Pilate, Procurator A.D. 26–36. Outside Judea, Herod Antipas ruled in Peraea and Galilee (4 B.C.–A.D. 39), and Philip, another Herodian, ruled in the northeastern areas (4 B.C.–A.D. 34). Misrule, underproduction of food and overpopulation, the discontent of a proud people under foreign government, slave labor, and the historic sense of chosenness and promise: these problems and feelings haunted the land in the years of Jesus' lifetime.

The religious scene too had undergone great changes since the period described in the Old Testament. Jerusalem remained the hub of national life and piety, and, as the Gospels show, Jesus recognized Jerusalem's hegemony in his pilgrimages to the temple and his confrontations with religious leaders in the city. As to worship, the ancient priestly pomp of ritual and sacrifice had been largely replaced by routine readings and prayer in local synagogues. Several parties competed for attention in Jewish religious circles, and each of them becomes a foil to the claims of Jesus. There were, first, the Sadducees, a party of aristocrats who did not chafe under the Romans. It is no surprise to find this patrician group representing religious as well as economic and political complacency and conservatism. The Sadducees rejected the newer religious ideas associated with an apocalyptic piety; in the New Testament (Mark 12:18 and Acts 23:8) they appear in opposition to the doctrine of the resurrection. Two of this lineage, Caiaphas and Annas, are prominent in the trial of Jesus.

If the Sadducees are the right wing, then various Pharisaic parties represent the left. At the extreme were the activists, called Zealots, who were ready to take up arms for God and nation. Less impetuous were the more popular parties made up of men who rigorously observed the ritual demands of legal religion. In the times of the Maccabees the pious and concerned Jews who revolted were called the Hasidim, and out of them had come the Pharisees. Within this group were the "scribes" or professionals who often allied themselves with the Pharisees in opposition to Jesus. Little is known of them.

Parallel with the legalistic piety of the popular parties and the ritual piety of the Sadducees there developed a distinctive religious literature for a people whose hopes were disproportionate to their condition—a literature of often fantastic imagery known as apocalyptic, or revelation, for it purports to unveil the future and describes cosmic struggles and victories. Jewish apocalyptic literature, making its first appearance between 200 B.C. and 100 B.C., points to the end of the existing world order and the establishment of a new one. Perhaps the Book of Daniel begins this line, for many scholars date it during the period of Antiochus Epiphanes (175–163 B.C.), but similar strains are evident in the prophetic literature—in Joel, Isaiah, Amos, and Ezekiel. Many of the apocryphal books are of this genre, and not only the canonical Apocalypse but also many passages in the Synoptic Gospels suggest the pervasiveness of apocalyptic imagery (see Mark 13; Matt. 24, 25; Luke 21; I Thess. 4; I Cor. 15). Indeed the language of apocalypse helps to mold Jesus' own image.

THE GRAECO-ROMAN WORLD

In the background of Israel's later life and religion lies the complex called the Graeco-Roman world. While the Gospels seem to picture Palestine as an isolated land suspended in the remote Empire, the course of Christianity in its first generation makes it plain that the world of Hellas and Rome colored the faith from the start. Much of the early Christian literature suggests parallels to a Hellenized Judaism: the Fourth Gospel and the writings of Philo (—c. A.D. 50) come to mind immediately. In this literature emphasis has shifted from the Old Testament's heavy-handed tracing of God's judgment to a Grecian interest in God's wisdom. The concrete earthiness of the Hebraic gives way to a soaring Hellenic expression. Not only in the intellectual, but also in the civil realm the earliest years suggest the involvement of Palestinian Christianity in imperial life.

To speak of the Graeco-Roman world at the beginning of the Christian era is to speak of a soul and a body, for the body of Greek institutional life was senescent while its spirit still informed the intellectual world. Rome never succeeded in reaching the philosophical and cultural heights the Greeks had scaled. But Rome excelled in the institutional realm. She was the world's political master, and the virtues of the political life—a sense of order, reasonableness, compromise, and legal grandeur—aided her in coloring and transforming the Greek heritage.

JESUS' LIFE

To spiral to an eccentric center from the grandeur of this world: after the years of the republic and in the early years of the Roman Empire (31 B.C.–A.D. 192)—the years when Caesar Octavianus, later named Augustus, was Emperor; when Herod the Great was ending his reign in Judea; when Roman procurators ruled the Jews; when writers of the Augustan Age (like Ovid, Horace, and Livy) were flourishing—there was born in Palestine to a girl of Nazareth named Mary a man-child who seemed destined to obscurity in the carpenter's shop of her husband Joseph. He was given a name common in the period, Jesus. Little is known of his early years. When, at about the age of thirty, he began preaching, he was rejected by his townspeople as a carpenter's son and by the urbanites to the south as an upstart from Nazareth. In two or three years he was to die. And out of his ministry and death was to come a transformation of the old faith in the midst of new empire that would change the world. Out of those years which in a Christian perspective form the midpoint of history came the Christian Church. Every student who has studied the many strands that made up the one Church and the one faith and has seen how they are all strained through the career of one man has asked with that man's contemporaries: What manner of man is this?

The Gospels answer by beginning his story with reference to an earlier prophet, John who was called the Baptist. In the early literature John assumes the function ascribed to him by the painter Gruenewald in the Isenheim altarpiece: he points to Jesus the Christ. He made his appearance c. A.D. 27 in the wild and deserted country along the Jordan, attracting attention by his outlandish dress and manners and by the power of his message which had one theme: repent and be baptized for the advent of the Kingdom of God. The ritual of baptism with water had its parallels in other religions and there are evidences of its existence in earlier Judaism; however, there seems to be no question but that the people of John's day regarded the rite as something new. Among those drawn to it were Jesus (who had himself baptized) and at least three of the men who were later to become Jesus' own followers. While John's influence persisted for a time (see Acts 18:25; 19:1–7), his star receded as Jesus' rose, and before John was arrested for his rebuke of Herod Antipas he deferred to Jesus as one mightier than he. John was the hinge to the new age; his slightly younger contemporary was the door.

The account in the earliest Gospel is forthright: "In those days Jesus came from Nazareth of Galilee and was baptized by John in the Jordan. . . . Now after John was arrested, Jesus came into Galilee preaching the gospel of God, and saying, 'The time is fulfilled, and the kingdom of God is at hand; repent, and believe in the gospel' " (Mark 1:9, 14–15).

Another early record throws Jesus' ministry into a cosmic

dimension from the first. In this account Jesus came on the Sabbath, to the synagogue in his old home at Nazareth, and read these words in Isaiah:

> *The Spirit of the Lord is upon me,*
> *because he has anointed me to preach good news to*
> *the poor.*
> *He has sent me to proclaim release to the captives and*
> *recovering of sight to the blind,*
> *to set at liberty those who are oppressed,*
> *to proclaim the acceptable year of the Lord.*
>
> (LUKE 4:18–19)

Then he closed the book and sat down. But he added: "Today this Scripture has been fulfilled in your hearing." From here there would be no retreat. To assist in his work he gathered a group of intimates—the Gospels fix the number at twelve; this lends weight to the idea that in them was to be the founding of a new people of God, in place of the chosen people as founded in the twelve tribes of old. Within the circle of the twelve three stood out, Peter, James, and John. The twelve men, for the most part common folk—fishermen, tradesmen, tax-collectors—were initiated into the mysteries of the Kingdom and imbued with a sense of urgency. They were to gather the new people of God.

Throughout Jesus' ministry there was a double-sidedness reflected in our symbol of the whisper and the thunder. Many of those near him were deafened by the whisper; they turned their back on the commonplaceness of it all. Others were attracted by the thunder, responding to the magic of this mystery in the authority of Jesus' words and the loving manner of his life. Inevitably such a movement attracted the notice of the established religious leaders and the semi-established political figureheads, who refused to surrender to this strange proclamation of a new age that would supersede and transcend their own. Not long after, hate and violence and sporadic mob-action hardened into a countermovement. Annas and Caiaphas and Pilate and Herod became the agents of the people who opposed Jesus. By their fiat he was put to death like a common criminal, by crucifixion, on a Friday, 14 or 15 Nisan, around the year

A.D. 30. Most of his followers had retreated in the face of his unpopularity. To an observer on a windswept hill outside Jerusalem on that night of his burial it would certainly have looked as if the story were over.

THE NEW PEOPLE OF GOD

Yet out of this death and its sequel came the Christian Church. True, references to a "church" are to be found in Jesus' recorded teaching. The term "church" (*ekklesia*) occurs only three times in the Gospels, once in Matthew 16:18 and twice in Matthew 18:17. Scholars have long regarded all three occurrences as editorial additions made by the church of the second and third generations, though some scholars from the most critical school (among them K. L. Schmidt) are now prepared to argue their authenticity. Be that as it may, few critics today are still reluctant to find evidences that, despite his own eschatological views, Jesus had some regard for the continuity of his proclamation in succeeding years, and most critics discern in the records of his ministry an intention to provide for a new society. The pictures vary: the twelve, the flock, the Messianic remnant, the people implied by the Son of Man concept, the men of the new covenant.

Of all these pictures, two stand out. While Jesus apparently did not speak much of "church," he spoke a great deal of "kingdom"—the Kingdom of God which was revealed in his person—and of himself as the "Son of Man." His "Kingdom of God" was not a realm but a reign, a sovereign saving activity on the part of God. Here was a reminiscence of the covenant of old, with its recognition of the power of God and of His concern in history. *Now,* now when His people were in straits, when the days were evil, now He would help them; yet "now" did not exhaust the announcement: there was always an openness to the future that this Kingdom would bring. Similarly the title "Son of Man," which appears approximately seventy times in the Synoptic Gospels, drew its greatest weight from Daniel 7:13–14. If Jesus applied this title to himself it means that he saw himself as a leader of the people of God, the center of the revelation of God's activity. From this proclamation of the Kingdom by one who seems to have preferred to be known as the Son of Man, the young Church caught its concentration on fulfillment in his person. The crisis of this conception is clear from a story which succeeds the account of John the Baptist's imprisonment. John sent some of his disciples to inquire whether Jesus was really the anointed leader: "Are you yourself the coming one, or must we wait for another?" The answer of Jesus is the turning-point of the gospel tradition:

> *Go and tell John what you hear and see:*
> *the blind receive their sight and the lame walk,*
> *lepers are cleansed and the deaf hear,*
> *and the dead are raised up,*
> *and the poor have good news preached to them.*
> And blessed is he who takes no offense at me.
>   (MATT. 11:4–6)

This proclamation which centered in his person implied a new community that was to become the Church. No matter, then, if this message was to undergo a transformation, for the early church apprehended well what this signified. Out of the focus on the person of Jesus came the birth of the young Church.

> [Jesus'] claim that the destiny of men is determined by their attitude to him and his word was taken up by the early Church and expressed in their proclamation of Jesus as "Messiah"—particularly in their expectation that he was to come on the clouds of heaven as the "Man," bringing judgement and salvation. His preaching was thus taken up in a new form, thus becoming specifically "Christian" preaching. Jesus proclaimed the message. The Church proclaims *him*.[7]

The Church, then, was born in the offense of the whisper of the voice of God in His Word, Jesus the Christ. The mark of Christian particularity is this offense, this "scandal." So decisive was the experience of those who were in contact with the bearer of this revelation that: "the gospel of Christ replaced the gospel of the kingdom because by His death He became the Kingdom, becoming all that the Kingdom contained." The New Testament is a book of one theme in this respect, and the exegete Hoskyns is correct in his reference to the Fourth Gospel:

> The flesh of Jesus was the place where men did, and still do, believe and disbelieve; where the division between those who believe and those who do not believe becomes an ultimate division between the children of God and the children of the Devil. Any relative distinction between faith and unbelief is unthinkable.[8]

If the concentration in the New Testament writings is on the person of the proclaimer, so too, the emphasis falls on the last weekend of his life among men, the days remembered by the Church as Good Friday and Easter. Good Friday meant his death, seen to be vicarious, *for* others, for the newly gathered community of disciples and, by extension, for the whole world. When emphasis falls here, the Church is properly seen as the extension through history of Christ's atonement.

> Before the crucifixion Jesus Christ came as the Son of Man who joined Himself to the many in order to give Himself for them, the One representing the Many, but after Pentecost and on the ground of the work on the Cross the Church was sent out as the Many to represent the One Son of Man, the Saviour Lord. Thus the relation of the One to the Many carries with it and begets the relation of the Many to the One. The One and the Many is the doctrine of Christ. The Many and the One is the doctrine of the Church, the body of Christ.[9]

With the crucifixion, the other transforming event of the same weekend was the resurrection of Christ—a moment in history, but one across which historical science must draw a veil to leave as an issue, *the* issue between faith and unfaith. "They took him down from the tree and laid him in a tomb. But God raised him from the dead. And for many days he appeared to those who had come up with him from Galilee to Jerusalem" (Acts 13:30–1). "Heaven must receive [him] until the time for establishing all that God spoke . . . from of old" (Acts 3:21). The Church that was implied in the Old Testament, by the proclamation of the Kingdom, and by the person of Christ, was born in the universal Christian witness to his death and resurrection. "All that went before appears in a new light—new since the *Easter faith in Jesus' resurrection* and founded upon this faith." [10]

THE EARLY WITNESSES

To trace the beginnings of the Church in the career of Jesus we are dependent upon the witness of his followers and the record in the writings of the New Testament. In a work of history the proper question at this point is one of sources: who tells us of the founder, and how reliable is the substantiating document? Here, again, the thunder of God's power in Christ begins with the whisper of His voice and the outskirt of His way. The sources are all internal. Outside the New Testament reasonably contemporary references to Jesus are negligible. Josephus in his *Antiquities* (*c.* 93—a late date!) has two references, one casual and the other probably a Christian interpolation, tweezered into the book for apologetic reasons. Pliny, *c.* A.D. 112, has an oblique reference to the singing of hymns "to Christ as a god." Tacitus, perhaps three years later, tells us that Christ was killed in the reign of Tiberius by Pontius Pilate—but this reference is as far removed from the event as the end of the Second World War was from the American Civil War. A reference from this same period by Suetonius (—*c.* 138) is too garbled to be of worth. The apocryphal and agraphic references to the founding of the Church and the life of Christ have too much of an admixture of fancy and fantasy for the Church itself to take seriously. The earliest references in the Christian tradition are from the hand of St. Paul, whose epistles make up much of the New Testament. His earliest writing begins, around A.D. 49 or 51, with the letter to Thessalonica. The period between the death of Christ and the beginning of this literature is a period equal to the interim between the two world wars of our century; the letters are from the hand of an unlikely eyewitness who seems unconcerned with preserving the record of the life of Christ, though he was familiar with details (I Cor. 7:10, 11:23ff., 15:3ff.). Of great value are the sermons in Acts, which probably grew out of sources informed by Jerusalem, but decades also elapsed before their writing. Still later are the references in the letter to the Hebrews. For the most part we rely upon a literary type peculiar to the growing Church, the Gospels.

A full generation had elapsed before the maturation of this gospel tradition. Recent scholarly efforts to account for its rise in the vicissitudes of the growing community have complicated simple Christian acceptance of these documents. Yet, as someone has remarked, in the crucial generation across which the curtain seems to be drawn, the Church was no Rip van Winkle. Eyewitnesses lived on throughout the period of gospel formation from the sixth through the eighth decade of the first Christian century. The oral tradition was sufficiently cross-certified that it soon took on stereotypical character in sayings, parabolic stories, miracle accounts, and simple narrative. Perhaps as early as A.D. 50 a source which can be reconstructed out of the synoptics and usually known as "*Q*" was being written. It stands behind the earliest Gospel, Mark, written *c.* 65–70, behind Luke and "Matthew," who also bring to their work separate sources and who complete their work around A.D. 70, so far as the record of those years as reflected in their Gospels can be traced. A Fourth Gospel seems to be later, from a different world of thought. Though it consciously elaborates on the events of Christ's life, it is the most serious about its grounding in history. The existence of the Gospels from the hands of men who had first heard only the whisper and ran from its offense is, with the existence of the Church itself, a suggestion of the thunder of God's power revealed in the love of Jesus as he walked among men. Their gospels provide a more complete and generally accurate account of Jesus than we could expect of most other figures of the ancient world. Yet they "prove" nothing, for their own claim, while rooted in historical events, is made entirely by the hand of faith to the eye of faith: they call more for decision than for assent. Like Jesus himself, they both conceal and reveal the wonder of God because of the nature of the mystery.

A summary of the apprehension of that mystery in the

voice of the Church's early proclaimers can be reconstituted from condensed sermons in the Book of Acts from the hand of Luke. C. H. Dodd has put together a serviceable outline of the proclamation or *kerygma*:

> The prophecies are fulfilled, and the new Age is inaugurated by the coming of Christ.
> He was born of the seed of David.
> He died according to the Scriptures, to deliver us out of the present evil age.
> He was buried.
> He rose on the third day according to the Scriptures.
> He is exalted at the right hand of God, as Son of God and Lord of quick and dead.
> He will come again as Judge and Saviour of men.[11]

This was enough for the early Church's needs. This was the one faith in the one Lord that set it in motion for the task to be described in succeeding chapters: to spread throughout the world, to encounter the world, to shape its message for life in the world. We complete this picture by reference to the two early and decisive witnesses who most fully elaborate on the significance of the one Christian Church at the onset of its dialogue with the world. One is St. Paul; the other is the writer of the Fourth Gospel. Both were writing during the period of the Church's transition. The earliest followers had not girded themselves and packed for a long trip; the ring of urgency of Jesus' promise that he would come again soon to usher in the fullness of the New Age was still in their ears. Yet as the decades were passing they adjusted to life in history; they were members of the new community that was there to stay.

ST. PAUL AND THE CHURCH

St. Paul, with whom we are to become more familiar as a missionary, was a convert to Christianity after the death of Jesus. He came to it with a zeal which could only accompany the penitence of one who had once persecuted the Church and who was now making up for time lost. His writings, letters to the young churches of the first Christian generation, point to the thunder of God's power in the cosmically significant Christ (having little emphasis on his life as a man among men); they also show the interest of a missionary who has seen a scattered and varied cluster of churches made one in their common loyalty to Christ. His task was complicated and then enriched by his background in the Greek learning of his day and his life as a Hebrew of the Hebrews. He was changed in his conversion. But Paul when he wrote reflects also the Saul who knew the thought world of both Pharisee and Stoic. He was preeminently a sensitive autobiographer; in detailing the problems and possibilities of the Christian life he pointed his finger at himself. All turned on the change from man without faith to man in faith; man apart from the community of life in Christ to man in this community, the Church. The death and resurrection of Jesus were keystones here: he was determined to know nothing else. And the Church was to extend this work. Paul described his own involvement: "I rejoice in my sufferings for your sake, and in my flesh I complete what is lacking in Christ's afflictions for the sake of his body, that is, the church" (Col. 1:24).

Paul uses several pictures for the Church as the people of God. It is the one *ekklesia,* an eschatological community of people called out by the gospel from the world through baptism into Christ. The members are the "called," the "elect," the "saints," those who "belong to Christ," are "in" him, are the "Israel of God." The term *ekklesia* reflects the "assembly" in the Greek city-state, but there is a new and significant twist by the New Testament's addition of *"ekklesia* of God or of Christ." Paul Tillich summarizes the turn: "The spatial *ekklesia* of Greece has been replaced by the historical *ekklesia* of Christianity, the bearer of historical consciousness in all periods and nations." [12]

As there is the historical picture that unites Old and New Testament communities for their course in history, so also Paul employs a spatial image. If he were asked to compress into several words his definition of the Christian Church he could, as his writings are a clue, do so unhesitatingly in the term "the Body of Christ." *"The spatial center of [Christ's] Lordship is the Church, which constitutes His Body upon earth."* [13]

No other picture has laid so much onus on a later Church which has not only been properly diverse (as are the members of a body) but improperly divided (as no body can be). Anders Nygren states it radically and baldly, for he merely echoes Paul: *"The body of Christ is Christ himself. . . . The Church is Christ as he is present among and meets us upon earth after his resurrection."* [14] This is an offensive teaching, even to many within the Church. Right or wrong, it is Pauline, and as such part of that web out of which the life of the Church has been spun. Paul had sufficient sense for the totality of man that when he spoke of the Church as the Body of Christ he did not thus make a division between its life as a community of the spirit and as an institution. The two were connected, and Paul could easily move from a soaring discussion of the heights of the Church to concern over some practical aspect of life in some one church. Paul reminded the Philippian congregation that their *commonwealth* was in heaven, from which idea was to flow every detail of their earthly life, their fellowship in the Body of Christ. Paul was looking for an idea to die for, and he found it—or, as he would put it, it found him: "There is one body and one Spirit, just as you were called to the one hope that belongs to your call, one Lord, one faith, one baptism, one God and Father of us all, who is above all and through all and in all" (Eph. 4:4–5). With such a measure of the Church's character and life, there could hardly be a more offensive sin in Christian history than to create wrongful division of this body, no greater neglect than to fail to work as Paul did for reunion and healing.

THE FOURTH GOSPEL AND THE CHURCH

Of comparable significance in shaping the ideal against which the reality of the later Church is to be judged is the Fourth Gospel. Critical ferment concerning questions of authorship and date does not obscure the central issue here, for the Church has chosen this basic document as a criterion of its ongoing life. The "Plot" of this Gospel parallels that of the Synoptics, but there are different accents. The author began with the assumption that the world which was created good had come under the judgment of God. But God sent His son, Jesus Christ, not to destroy or judge but to save the world. The stress is on the incarnation, on God's eternal Word made flesh. Such a proclamation is offensive, especially in the world colored by a Greek attitude which finds the flesh to be a prisonhouse for the noble soul. There is nothing soft about the leading sentences of the book which flow out of the idea of incarnation. In concentrating on the whisper of God's voice in a word made flesh, the author does not neglect the thunder of His power in the cosmic significance of the activity of Jesus Christ. He is the bearer of divine revelation, the revealer of what he has heard and seen in the bosom of God his Father. One with the Father, he indicates himself when asked to show the glory of the Father. The concern throughout is to show the signs and wondrous works of the one who, "if [he] be lifted up, will draw all men unto [him]self." The author adds editorial comment: "He said this to show by what death he was to die" (John 12:32–3). Before this death he promised the comfort of the Spirit of Truth, and after his resurrection he revisited the gathered disciples, breathing on them and offering the Holy Spirit. The second chapter of Acts retells the story of the wonderful day of Pentecost when the Spirit was bestowed: the Church was born.

Out of this gathering grew the very Church which produced the Fourth Gospel, a community of the spirit. In place of Paul's picture of the *ekklesia,* this work describes the one flock of sheep gathered under one shepherd. Instead of the analogy of the Body of Christ it presents the emblem of the vine and the branches: "I am the vine, you are the branches. He who abides in me, and I in him, he it is that bears much fruit, for apart from me you can do nothing" (John 15:5). Again, then, there is the pull of Christ's personality that gathers people and the power of his person that holds them. With a devotional grace that has informed the language of the spiritual life ever since, this Gospel presents the climactic view of the Church's unity in Christ's last prayer to his Father: "That they may all be one; even as thou, Father, art in me, and I in thee, that they also may be in us, so that the world may believe that thou hast sent me. . . . That they may be one even as we are one, I in them and thou in me, that they may become perfectly one. . . ." Because this links the Church's manifest unity with a reduced offense in Christianity's promulgation, it has inspired and shamed later generations which have had to contrast the reality of the Church in its divided mission with the ideal of the prayer.

By the end of the apostolic generation, the end of the first Christian century, and within the time of the writings of the New Testament canon, it is possible to see emerging an ideal for the Church and an outline of its shape and its life. A common initiatory rite of baptism identified the believers (at least in Paul's description) with the resurrection of Jesus. A common meal, the Eucharist, an extension of the eschatological meal which Jesus shared in the Passover season with his disciples, united them with each other and with him: "Because there is one loaf, we who are many are one body, for we all partake of the same loaf" (I Cor. 10:17). Church order begins to emerge in the functions of the *presbyteroi* and *episkopoi,* the elders and overseers of the local assemblies. There was still room for the charismatics, the freer spirits who spoke in strange tongues, guided, as they believed, by the Holy Spirit. According to the Book of Acts certain communities expressed their common life by sharing the property of the individuals who made them up; there was a common creed, *Kyrios Christos,* "Christ is Lord!" a warrant for worship incorporating the apostles' doctrine and fellowship and the breaking of bread and prayers. "Only those with a belief can share effective communication," writes Karl Jaspers in our time; in their time the patriarchs of the Church knew this. It was the belief in the sacrificial death of Christ and in his rising to new life that had oriented them, and they would not forget this. Whenever again the Spirit of God moved here individuals, there cells, and there again entire movements to recapture the vision, the divine purpose which Christians have always seen in the founding of the Church was again realized:

> The divine purpose of love, in so far as it achieves its end of bringing human persons back to the real meaning of their life, calls into being, and must call into being, a new order of personal relationships. It creates a new fellowship of men and women which is both the realization and the organ of its purpose in history—so far as that purpose, which in the end must transcend history, is realizable on the plane of history at all.[15]

The plane of history-writing also necessarily involves a quest for a realization that is always beyond grasp. But that has not dulled the purpose of historians in the Christian tradition, who have tried to keep their critical senses alert even as they are swept along by what the Church has always known: that in the revelation on Palestinian soil *c.* A.D. 30 there was not only the outskirt of God's ways, but also a hint of their inner precincts.

2

THE WORLD TURNED UPSIDE DOWN

In the beginning the fellowship was hardly more than a family affair. The followers of Christ remained near the places they associated with his career, the sites of his wonderful works. They measured the health of the churches by their degree of proximity to these centers. Members of his family were held in special esteem. There seemed to be little vision of a horizon beyond the Palestinian provinces he had honored in his humanity. The Synoptic Gospels, which reflect the condition of the Church in its early development, reproduce words which suggest this limitation of mission. They recall an original charge of Jesus to the twelve disciples:

Go nowhere among the Gentiles,
And enter no town of the Samaritans,
but go rather to the lost sheep of the house of Israel.
(MATT. 10:5)

As their Lord, in the years of his manhood, had worked only in the provinces that border the eastern shore of the Mediterranean, so these followers first refused to take roads that would carry them to the Samaritan towns or to Gentile lands. No doubt their hopes of Jesus' early return remained alive; their tradition recalled this goal for a localized mission: "Truly I say to you, you will not have gone through all the towns of Israel, before the Son of man comes" (Matt. 10:23). With such a limited concept of their mission and such an immediate goal (so soon to be seen as frustrating the very idea of a mission!) these followers could hardly have been expected to divert the course of world history or even to leave a mark on succeeding generations. Just as it must have looked when Jesus died, so too there must have been little prospect of a future in the eyes of observers of that early Church.

Within three hundred years the empire which at first neglected the Palestinian movement was itself to become nominally Christian. Within three centuries the faith realized what its adherents professed: catholicity. The term "catholic" meant general or universal; it appears frequently in the writings of pagan contemporaries, Zeno the Stoic and Polybius, among others. In the Christian lineage it first appears in St. Ignatius' letter to Smyrna early in the second century. While the word gathers more specific coloring as time passes, sometimes to mean "the great Church" as opposed to the sects, or to identify a specific church body, its core meaning is best defined by St. Cyril of Jerusalem: "It is denominated Catholic because it is spread throughout the whole world from one end to the other." Circling the Mediterranean, gathering strength in North Africa, Asia Minor, Greece, Rome, Spain, and Gaul, "the catholic church" numbered adherents in substantial circles within an amazingly brief period. The Church's own reflection of the world's conception is clear in the record of an incident at Thessalonica when two missionaries were involved in difficulties: the Jews and the wicked fellows of the rabble and a crowd shouted: "These men who have turned the world upside down have come here also" (Acts 17:6). Turning the world upside down, disturbing it with the proclamation of the good news and the establishment of local cells of followers, became the characteristic work of the Church not long after Jesus' death and resurrection.

JERUSALEM

We need a place to stand to view the world, and many accounts of the spread of the faith suffer from the absence of such a place in a narrative sequence. Jerusalem, scene of the last days of Jesus, is the logical city for such a view because here the disciples regathered, here was a center of power, here was the location of early councils—even the activity of Paul is first oriented in relation to Jerusalem rather than to Antioch or Ephesus. We know considerably more of the early history of the church at Jerusalem than we do of those in Ephesus or Rome, and a guided tour of Christian expansion best begins in the holy city.

The tight familial and apostolic hold in Jerusalem was soon expanded by a circle of Hellenists with a somewhat larger view; that in turn was enlarged drastically in the worldwide mission of Paul. The points of breakthrough of these circles can be associated with three names: Stephen, Philip, and Paul; and they are to play a role in that sequence in this narrative.

To begin, then, with the familial center gathered around the memory of Jesus. The Book of Acts pictures James, the brother of the Lord, as the first leader in Jerusalem—no doubt he was accorded this honor not because of native leadership abilities, for they are not evident despite his prominence in the early accounts, but because of a blood-tie. One early history says that a cousin of Jesus became James' successor and that even beyond this blood relationship suggested a warrant for authority. Perhaps this relationship did not produce the qualities necessary to head the group in Jerusalem, for the New Testament itself does not picture the greatness of Jesus rubbing off on his relatives. At any rate, certain elders and presbyters and most of all the apostles themselves assume a more prominent position. To recognize their part is still to move in what approximates a tight family circle, for these intimates of Jesus shared a brotherly relationship with him which was solidified by his death and their consequent regrouping in the consciousness of his presence. Out of the years of their sway comes the Gospel of Matthew with its recall of the prophecy of Jesus: "Truly, I say to you, in the new world, when the Son of man shall sit on his glorious throne, you who have followed me will also sit on twelve thrones, judging the twelve tribes of Israel" (Matt. 19:28).

John, the son of Zebedee, and Peter clearly stand with James as "pillars" of this church—Paul calls them just that (Gal. 2:9). They had charismatic authority and continued wonder-working as they had seen Jesus do. Now there were changes. The observance of Sunday, the day of the resurrection, in place of the Jewish Sabbath; the catholicizing tendency of the sacramental meal and the initiatory rite of baptism, the nascent ecumenicity in time and space suggested by the early creeds: *Marana tha* ("Come!"), coupled with messianic reflections—all these predisposed the apostles to loosen the bonds which a limited conception had placed on the hands of the church at Jerusalem. Not that it was easy. Peter rebelled at the idea of a mission to the Gentiles, according to a story in Acts. Jerusalem regarded itself as the guardian of orthodoxy and as such made tests before approving the younger churches.

THE HELLENISTS

A symbol of the first breakthrough occurs in the account of the Hellenists led by an amazing man named Stephen, who appears and disappears within a moment, as it were, in the biblical narrative, but who left his impress on the growing movement. The Hellenists were actually Jews, but they spoke Greek or they grew up in the scattered outposts of Judaism in the Greek world. They had come home. They refused to be seen as second-class citizens, and they certified their credentials in the further task of proclaiming the Kingdom of God, assuming the missionary task. Stephen was to die for the faith—the first such martyr of a noble line, according to the New Testament. The speech which Acts 7 preserves in association with Stephen shows him to have been a prophet of the larger vision, one destined to clash with the Jewish authorities for his activities in attacking their exclusivism.

Accused by a party of "the Freedmen" at the synagogue and by other defenders of the old faith, Stephen was put to test for saying that "this Jesus of Nazareth will destroy this place, and will change the customs which Moses delivered to us." In answer to the question of the high priest, "Is this so?" Stephen is pictured as leading his accusers in a tour through Israel's history which revealed moments of God's concern and the nation's wilfulness and rebellion. The Holy Land knew no right to an exclusive claim as the site of God's revelations: He had also unveiled Himself when they wandered and were captive in other lands. What of the Temple? In Stephen's radical view Isaiah 66 detracted from its significance, for God said: "Heaven is my throne, and earth my footstool. What house will you build for me . . . ?" Then came the shaken fist in their faces, the mark of the breach of synagogue and church:

> You stiff-necked people, uncircumcised in heart and ears, you always resist the Holy Spirit. As your fathers did, so do you. Which of the prophets did not your fathers persecute? And they killed those who announced beforehand the coming of the Righteous One, whom you have now betrayed and murdered, you who received the law as delivered by the angels and did not keep it.

Such a revision of history was not good public relations, nor was it capable of generating good-will. Stephen paid for his attack on Jewish chauvinism with his life. The writer of Acts adds a curious touch. A young man named Paul watched over the garments of Stephen's executioners. He had not yet been drawn into the redeeming circle. The Hellenists had begun to make their mark in the enlargement of that circle, and while Stephen could not further participate, his death made him a symbol and the presence of his "speech" in Acts indicates acceptance of the enlarging view on the part of the Christians. They too began to pay for their views; sporadic persecutions developed against the Hellenists. No doubt the relative security of the Palestinian Jews, who were less hostile to the temple worship, brought tension in the Jerusalemaic group.

Another Hellenist, Philip, chose Samaria as a frontier; his mission later was regularized by Jerusalem in the persons of Peter and John. Others carried the work to Cyprus, Antioch, and Phoenicia. The early records show Peter alone among the Twelve acting as a missionary, and his "foreign" missions consisted largely of inspection. The Hellenists in turning their back on temple worship did not at first go all the way. They confined their activities largely to Jews. But the first painful cut of the umbilical cord that attached the daughters to mother Jerusalem was soon to come at Antioch. There among the displaced persons of the day were Hellenists who began to preach to Gentiles (Acts 11:19ff.). "A great number that believed turned to the Lord." The surprising success inspired the extension of the Gentile mission. Jerusalem did not subtract itself from the emergent scene: it still sent ambassadors to test the quality of each extension.[1]

> In the original Christian consciousness, there was in fact only one single Church of "disciples" of the Lord; its locus was temporarily the earthly Jerusalem, until at the *parousia* [reappearance] of the Son of Man, the heavenly Jerusalem would come down and be the dwelling-place of those who belonged to Him. Those who were compelled to live outside Jerusalem belonged equally to the Church at Jerusalem; for all the far-flung hosts of Christians were branches of the one all-embracing central body . . . The structure of the Church depended upon [Peter, as the only active apostle] in the earliest period, and the grafting of the newly-arisen churches on the total organism depended upon his recognition of them. (See MATT. 18:18 and 16:19.)

THE CAREER OF PAUL

For the reality of a Gentile mission that could stand on its own, with all due respect for Jerusalem, the Church awaited a prophet greater than Stephen or Philip. He came, says Acts, from the circle of persecuters of Christians. If Jesus was the "hero" of the first chapter, this Saul called Paul emerges in the second as the catholicist, the missioner, the ecumenician *par excellence* in the Christian logbooks. Others were, later, to go farther. Paul did not have the opportunities to round Asia that Francis Xavier (—1552) had; he did not have an encompassable globe as did William Carey (—1834) and then the nineteenth-century missionaries, or the devices of the international commuters of the recent period. But if the sun still set on the Christian

Church in Paul's life, it was because he lacked, not vision or energy and will, but only knowledge and means and time. If he had horizons, they were the same as the Empire's. Not the distorter of Jesus' work (as the generation before us would have it) but its extender, he had to conquer his own prejudices to see a world in which there was neither Jew nor Greek, neither bond nor free, neither male nor female, but only oneness in Christ.

Most subsequent revitalizations of theology in the Church's history, whether enduring or not, whether good or bad, drew their life in no small part from Paul as a theologian. In the second century the heretic Marcion (—160) set out to out-Paul Paul. St. Augustine drew on Paul's teaching on grace and destiny to counter the Pelagian heterodoxy early in the fifth century. Hincmar (—882) and Gottschalk (—868) were to skirmish on the same battlefield in the ninth century; it was again Paul who was at issue. Calvinist could tangle with Arminian, Lutheran with Roman, Jesuit with Jansenist, Molinist with Thomist, and in each case Paul's ideas formed the matrix out of which later ideas were born. In our time the shapers of theological thought, men like Karl Barth and Rudolf Bultmann and Anders Nygren, all drink deep at the Pauline well. Yet it is not Paul the theologian so much as Paul the theological man who did mission work that comes to the front here. Paul was intensely active but was not an activist—all his work grew out of the profound vision he had known, a vision which molded his vocation in spite of himself.

As Saul, he was born in the dawn years of the new faith, of a family of Benjamite Jews who possessed Roman citizenship status, in Cilician Tarsus. Trained partly in Jerusalem under Rabbi Gamaliel, according to a reference in Acts, he was immersed in the Jewish Scriptures, whose Christian significance he was later to divine. He lived in the Law and he was supported by it. He made it his own, and was a Hebrew of the Hebrews, a Pharisee of the Pharisees. Because life in Cilicia was diasporate, he picked up much of an alien culture and was accomplished in Greek. What happens to men who must make a radical about-face, a breach which sunders them from all past values and forces them to swallow past and pride and progress and to begin again? In other words, what is a convert? Paul was converted from active aggression against the Church to fanatic participation in it, on a road to Damascus. A voice from heaven: "I am Jesus, whom you are persecuting," threw Paul to the ground. As he picked himself up, he had the vision of the Church from which he was later never to waver. To persecute the Church was to persecute Jesus; conversely, to serve the Lord meant service of the Church. The psychological depth of the Damascus-road experience is clear from the frequency of reference to the change it brought, both in the letters of Paul and in three retellings in Acts.

Paul was baptized, accepted by one Ananias of the Dam-ascene flock, and departed for Arabia, if we follow Galatians 1:17. Shall we picture him there as an anchorite, in loneliness piecing together the past and the prospects for new life "in Christ"? In three years he was back at Damascus, whence he escaped under threat. From this point it is particularly helpful to follow Paul's career by its reference to Jerusalem. Acts 15 and Galatians 1–2 are not completely reconcilable on this matter, but the attempt must be made. In the course of his career a shift in Jeru-salem's centrality appears, until finally it loses its orbit to new centers such as Antioch and Ephesus and, later, Rome. Still, we begin with Jerusalem.

PAUL AND JERUSALEM

In what follows the primary source is Paul's own account in his letters and the secondary testimony of the Book of Acts, which at most points coincides and at all points adds color. To the degree to which we follow Acts we shall also become pilgrims to Jerusalem, for it is there that every effort is made to suggest the holy city's continued promi-nence. From Paul's writing we see much less stress upon the original center as well as less contentment with the authority of the Twelve there and throughout the Church.

Thus Acts shows that Paul, despite his gifts, is inferior to the original disciples, a witness of the Resurrection through their own witness, not directly called to the ministry but ordained by the laying on of their hands. Paul in turn lays stress on his direct involvement as a witness, with more casual reference to the Twelve. The sharpest clash between the two narratives comes over the question of the locale of Paul's earlier operations as a persecutor—was he a resident of Jerusalem, as Acts implies, or a visitor, perhaps from Damascus, as he seems to imply? [2]

> When he had come to Jerusalem [after his conversion] he attempted to join the disciples; and they were all afraid of him, for they did not believe that he was a disciple. But Barnabas took him, and brought him to the apostles, and declared to them how on the road he had seen the Lord, who spoke to him, and how at Damascus he had preached boldly in the name of Jesus. So he went in and out among them at Jerusalem, preaching boldly in the name of the Lord.

Paul writes that after he was converted he did "not confer with flesh and blood." "I did not . . . go up to Jerusalem to those who were apostles before me," though Acts indicates that he did. Paul does all he can to dissociate himself:

> Then after three years I went up to Jerusalem to visit Cephas, and remained with him fifteen days. But I saw none of the other apostles, except James the Lord's brother. (In what I am writing to you, before God, I do not lie!) Then I went into the regions of Syria and Cilicia. *And I was still not known by sight to the churches of Christ in Judea* [Emphasis, of course, is ours.] (GAL. 1:18–22).

The clash, the oath, the concern in Paul all indicate how the question of the centrality of Jerusalem becomes itself a symbol of a clash over law and gospel, authority and freedom, tradition and renewal.

Involvement in this question is also necessary if we are to determine whether to approach the Pauline activity as it is conventionally patterned on the basis of familiarity with the account in Acts: as a sequence of three great missionary journeys with exclusive reference in Jerusalem. Or shall we see it as the letters themselves seem to suggest, that Paul as a universal emissary of the good news did not receive his impulse from one geographical center but from Jerusalem and Antioch and Ephesus and Corinth? In this view it would seem that Paul himself would not have known on which numbered missionary journey he was. We shall refer only to the three visits to Jerusalem that Paul himself recalls, and follow the chronological picture contingent upon this recollection. It would place Paul's conversion somewhere around A.D. 35, with visits to Jerusalem in three years, again for an apostolic council, around A.D. 51, and finally for deliverance of a monetary offering in another three or four years. With that outline in mind the details of the Acts narrative can describe the extension of the Church through the career of Paul.

PAUL'S MISSION

After his conversion Paul knew that he had been given grace to be a minister of Christ Jesus to the Gentiles; "for necessity is laid upon me. Woe to me if I do not preach the gospel" (I Cor. 9:16), both to the Greeks and to the barbarians, both to the wise and to the foolish. Because of this necessity he conceived the plan of offering hope to as many of the Gentiles as he could—not forgetting those who frequented the synagogues where he also preached, the Jews—so that the entire inhabited world could know Christ. No city was too formidable, no first reception too cold, no arena too forbidding for his tramp across the roads of Asia Minor or his voyages on the Mediterranean.

Paul's first center, then, was not Jerusalem but Damascus. Then came the visit to Jerusalem which Paul denominated his first. He was greeted with suspicion until his future companion, Barnabas, came to his rescue. Now he makes not Jerusalem but, most likely, Tarsus the focus. At any rate he worked in Cilicia near where he had grown up. Luke, the writer of Acts, shows little interest in this activity, which seems to be a diversion on the arrowline from Jerusalem to Rome. No doubt Paul met persecution here. The missionary Barnabas later recruited him from Tarsus.

back to Antioch that he might further the conversion of that newly prominent Christian center. His obvious intent was to harmonize the missionary work of Paul and the Antiochians, among whom the slightly less radical Hellenists were active. Paul convinced them of the worth of the radical mission to the Gentiles. Here no longer is the milieu Oriental and the language Aramaic: this is Mediterranean and Graeco-Roman.

Damascus, Tarsus, Antioch—but still not Jerusalem, were points of initiative for Paul: and Antioch, where men were first called Christians, most of all inspired him to go with Barnabas and (at first) John Mark to the island of Cyprus. Is there any earlier record of the catholicizing of the faith across the sea? Barnabas decreased that Paul might increase from this point. Together they went to Asia Minor, where Mark deserted them. Paul conventionally began his work at these places in the synagogues, making no secret of his desire to convert Gentiles. Trouble dogged the missionaries all the way, and they were soon to return to Antioch. After the council in Jerusalem which we shall shortly discuss, Paul was back on the road to recover the same territory for the cross. To his joy he was able to revisit the cities of Asia Minor and to confirm saints there. At Lystra he picked up Timothy; from there they made disciples of the Galatians. Barnabas was no longer a partner—they split over the issue of John Mark's constancy. Gradually they made their way to Troas, where the mission was to take a new and decisive turn: in response to a vision, Paul entered Europe. Within two decades of the death of Christ a second continent was being called to his name.

At Philippi Paul knew immediate success; at Athens he failed. To the Greek the message of the cross was characteristic foolishness, and the sermon attributed to Paul in Acts indicates the difficulty the apostle experienced in his attempt to apologize to Hellas. Corinth was a different matter. There Paul seems to have settled in what for him was a long pastorate of eighteen months. The New Testament as we know it began to be born from this time, with his writing of the letters to Thessalonica, dated between A.D.

49 and 51. After Corinth he seems to have made Ephesus the neural point. If we list Corinth in the cycle, this becomes the fifth such place; here Paul worked for two years, though he did make some journeys from Ephesus during that time. At Ephesus Paul ran into opposition from the silversmiths, who had mercenary reasons for opposing him. He visited Corinth and set out for Jerusalem with a collection for the saints. He was to be frustrated from further endeavor among the churches he loved in Asia Minor, Syria, and Greece.

After Jerusalem he was imprisoned, he appealed to Caesar, and set out for Rome, where Acts begins to lose his trail. It tells us that he was captive there for two years. Spain was still in his travel plan, but it is doubtful that he was ever given opportunity to go. St. Clement of Rome (*fl. c.* 96) tells us that Paul did reach the "limits of the Occident," and Cyril of Jerusalem and Chrysostom (—407) among others also place him there. Tertullian closed the book on Paul's life by reference to the apostle's execution by beheading in the Neronian persecution.

We have overleaped the Jerusalem visits, reserving them for the later comment which can bring into focus their importance. The three trips that Paul himself mentions had as their purpose, first, becoming aquainted with the leaders of the church there; second, an apostolic council; third, the delivering of a collection to the impoverished mother congregation. Luke, in Acts, for all his interest in shifting the burden of gospel preaching to the Gentile world, has greater concern for the prominence of the church at Jerusalem. What was the issue at the council; what was the intent of the monetary offering?

Paul had not been to Jerusalem, he emphatically writes, for at least thirteen years. He would interrupt his activity only for crucial matters. Such a matter had arisen in the question of observance of the Jewish ritual laws in the case of Gentile converts. The Gentile mission was waxing as Jewish Christianity assumed the defensive, and Gentile Christians were troubled. Paul, observing much of the ritual without raising the theological question, showed the Gentile world the idea that freedom from the law should be attractive. With Paul went Barnabas to face the pillars: John and, even more, James and Peter. Jerusalem held to its basic conservatism: though it would not go out to the Gentile world, it would tolerate the Gentile mission apart from close observance of the ritual law. A pagan who had undergone Christian baptism did not have to be circumcised. In return, the Gentile daughters were to give financial support to the ailing and oppressed mother (things were in a bad way in Jerusalem at this time).

As Paul and Barnabas returned, no doubt with joy, to Antioch, it did not perhaps register clearly in their minds that the council had but placed a plaster on a malignancy in Jewish Christianity. The basic issues had not been solved in the expedient council. It should be added, to Peter's credit, that when in Antioch he did as the Antiochians, accepting their local ways in ritual matters. But the Jamesians were more severe. No Jew born a Jew could ever turn his back on ritual Judaism. Peter withdrew from his more positive stand and Barnabas wavered. The one Church was two, even in its central supper. In one of the decisive "blasts" of Christian oratory Paul "opposed Peter to his face" (Gal. 2:11). The issue was not yet finally decided.

Harassed by persistent legalisms in the mother church, Paul went his own way, almost seeming to disregard restrictions of those who had been apostles before him. In his trail went "Judaizers" who tried to impose ritual requirements on converts. It was they, and not Paul, that kept the tie to Jerusalem alive. Evidently fearing further open encounter with the original church, Paul worked with a fervor that made its claim seem secondary. But to become catholic the Church, for the moment, had to pay the price of disunity. Is Lietzmann too extreme in his shocking statement? [3]

[Paul] therefore had to be content to combat in principle the influences issuing from Jerusalem, and to rebuke, as firmly as he could, the emissaries who were ruining his churches. He never wrote a single word about those who gave them authority; nothing about James in Jerusalem; nothing about Peter in Corinth and Rome. He ignored them. But looking more closely, and reading between the lines of his letters, we perceive behind the "servants

of Satan" the "false apostles," and the "spurious brethren," the shadows of the great figures in Jerusalem.

Whatever the degree of irritation, it provided Paul with his
foil, "the Law," which he countered with "the Gospel."
Similarly it suggests how theology was knotted with practice
in his mission.

Nowhere is this more clearly expressed than in the letter
to the Galatians, written in the heat of the controversy. It
reflects Paul's anger at the shadows that followed him,
Judaizers who were in his path bewitching the foolish converts with the message of Law. It is a personal document in
which Paul shows the divine warrant for his mission, the
divine necessity laid upon him not to change the gospel,
the apostolic stamp which Peter, John, and even James had
placed upon his efforts. To continue: there is no point in
attempting to live by a code, because man is justified by
faith and not by law. Abraham was justified by his faith
in the promises which were fulfilled in Jesus Christ. "For
in Christ Jesus neither circumcision nor uncircumcision is
of any avail, but faith working through love." "You were
running well, who hindered you from obeying the truth?"
he writes in anger in Galatians 5:6–7. "I wish those who
unsettle you would mutilate themselves." The tension is
most brilliantly brought out:

> I through the law died to the law, that I might live
> to God. I have been crucified with Christ; it is no
> longer I who live, but Christ who lives in me; and the
> life I now live in the flesh I live by faith in the Son of
> God, who loved me and gave himself for me. I do
> not nullify the grace of God, for if justification were
> through the law, then Christ died to no purpose (GAL.
> 2:19–21).

When this legalistic knot was cut, Paul was sure he
could convert a world to the power of God and the wisdom
of God in Jesus Christ. But he kept one eye on Jerusalem,
and there is little doubt that implicit in his concern to
make the trip to the mother church with the offering was
his hope that he might bring about reunion, to lessen tension in the universal Body of Christ as it expressed itself
in a torn visible community. The mystery of Israel's re-

jection always pained him; his writings leave no doubt of that. He knew he might lose his life and his freedom by going, but the reconciling activity was pre-eminent in his concerns.[4]

> That significance is clear: he hopes that this offering will have the effect of bringing peace to the church, of healing the terrible schism between Jerusalem and the Gentile churches (at least *his* churches) which has distressed him and has embarrassed and impeded his work for a long time.

If we leave Paul on his way to Jerusalem with the offering for the saints in need we leave him in the most favorable and loving light; with the triumphing gospel in its Pauline cast, there was active in him a new law more powerful than the old, the law of love, the new life in Christ.

Paul no doubt is the most impressive human figure in the history of the Church; there need be little apology for devoting such attention to but one phase of his activities. For while his work can be seen as a microcosm of future missionary work, there is an extra validity in this concentration because Paul emerges so early and because his *cosmos* is not at all *mikros*. He had arced the north and east of the Mediterranean; later generations merely had to pick up the motif and fill it in from there.

THE SUB-APOSTOLIC AGE AND
THE SECOND CENTURY

With the death of Peter, the confirmer of missions, and Paul in Neronian times (perhaps both in A.D. 64), the apostolic age ends and the sub-apostolic generation rises. By the end of the century the Church had spread first provincially from Jerusalem to Caesarea and Joppa, than forth to Samaria and Syria; and then, in a larger arc, to Asia Minor and Greece and Rome. This Church was poised to move in the second century to Egypt (probably late in the century) after it had swept the Roman outposts in North Africa. The sources for the second generation and the second century are, curiously, less satisfactory than those for the first. Despite this, we can ascertain the sense of outline. By this time the mission was predominately non-Jewish, and Jewish Christianity—partly because of national disaster and partly under the Pauline sting—begins to recede. The leaders at Jerusalem were called to die for their faith, beginning with James the son of Zebedee in the time of Agrippa (A.D. 44) through the destruction of the city (A.D. 70) and in later times of nationalist revolt as under Bar-Cochba, a messianic rebel around 132. (In the latter disturbance Christians, by now separated from Jewish national aspiration, seem to have been relatively less disturbed. They had fled to Pella, and the continuity of the mother church, the center of the earliest activity, was largely broken.)

Tradition more than satisfactory documentation details the sweep across the Graeco-Roman world. The second century implied the consolidation of earlier gains, for example in the push from urban centers to the surrounding countrysides. The third century saw the realization of the promise of Latin Christianity in North Africa, especially around Carthage. This was the church that produced Cyprian and Tertullian and Augustine; the Vandal and Moslem onslaught of later centuries so trampled the holy places of Christianity that in our time we tend to neglect the prominence of early Christian effort there. Little is known of the origins of the church at Rome, which was flourishing within the lifetime of Paul and Peter and seemed to be supplanting Jerusalem within canonical times. So with the north of Italy, where the faith made its way, leaving little record as to how this was accomplished.

Gaul, which was to become France, was Christianized from the East, largely through Greek colonization. In the Grecian centers of Vienne and Lyons the cross knew greatest stature, and the second of these cities produced Irenaeus, one of the great fathers who had come from Asia Minor to learn the vernacular that he might convert others. Spain showed Christian influence, at least in the south, by the third century. It survived the Moslem sweep more healthily than did its North African counterparts because of its remoteness more than because of the durability of the faith: the edge of the Occident was not noted for its degree of appropriation of a universal gospel.

These were the outposts. The earliest churches grew and prospered, rising in reasonably direct proportion to the decline of imperial fortunes. During the dialogue with the persecutors, the faith seemed to prosper both in advance and in withdrawal: it was attractive in advance and mysterious in withdrawal—the world could resist neither. The Athenians were qualified in their reponse; in general, Italy and Asia Minor were more enthusiastic than was Greece.

Typical of the later missionaries is Gregory Thaumaturgus (—c. 270), a disciple of Origen. Returning after his training to the city of his noble birth, Neocaesarea in Pontus, he became Bishop and swayed the pagans of Pontus toward Christianity. Could he move mountains and dry swamps? The legend-makers would not have it otherwise; they must have seen something in his make-up to prompt the name "wonder-worker." Adapting and accommodating the offense of Jesus Christ to the customs and backgrounds of potential converts, he was enormously reputed in his time, as he worked on the borders of the empire.

THE DEVELOPING MISSION

Beyond the empire we must content ourself with traditions that border on fancy. India claims to be the outgrowth of the missionary activity of the apostle Thomas. There were Christians in Arabia in the third century; Armenia knew mass conversions toward the end of the third century. The strategic political position of this area, a buffer between competitive nations, made it attractive to Christians who relished the idea of planting the cross at the crossroads, whatever the cost. Here we meet another Gregory, the Illuminator (—c. 332), a noble who was converted in exile. Converting the King, Tiridates, he thereby was able to denominate the entire country as Christian. The mass-conversion method became characteristic in the period.

With this shift in methods it becomes less fruitful to pursue the course of missionary activity; particularly, with the conversion of Emperor and Empire to Christianity early in the fourth century, it is impossible to follow the Pauline trail as the normative means for expressing the catholicity of the faith. It is beyond the imperial centers that one must look to see personal conversion taking place alongside the official activities. Ulphilas (—c. 383) worked among the Goths as a missionary bishop; it is significant that Bible translation accompanied his work. (Philostorgius [—c. 439] adds a note: Ulphilas omitted the Book of Kings from the canon for fear lest the belligerence of God's people inspire bellicosity among the barbarian Goths.) St. Martin of Tours (—397), a contemporary, transferred commissions from the Roman army to the Christian cause, setting a pattern for monastic missionwork around Tours after 372. Martin is remembered for his interest in the countryside, in the rustic folk that peopled what was one day to be France. We verge now on the period of work of Ambrose, Chrysostom, and Patrick, a story that need not be detailed. Merely to cite it suggests the swath Christianity scissored across the known world. The universal creed of Christian understanding was becoming a reality. In several short centuries the failure from Nazareth had won the powers of empire; the despised and rejected man of Galilee had, through faith in his name, won a world. The most disciplined historian breathes awe at the achievement. The antagonistic historian (a popular choice would be Gibbon) pays the faith a compliment for all he blames upon it. However cluttered the motives for the spread, however accidental and contingent many factors in its rise were, however limited the vision of the many, some in each generation learned from Paul that, despite failure and folly, the bearers of a message of reconciliation must transcend geographical lines. They were destined, they believed, to go into all the world. Beginning with Jerusalem—sometimes in spite of Jerusalem—they went: there was a new Jerusalem, now, to the eye of faith. Everything was changed: to turn the world upside down the Church had had to begin with itself.

3

THE DIALOGUE, THE CODE,
AND THE RETREAT

The early Christians had not packed their bags for a long trip. The End, they knew, was at hand. When Christ failed to reappear in the time of their hopes they found it necessary to come to terms with the world. Christianity was a religion of commitment: it called people from the world's preoccupation to life in a daring new dimension. It was a corporate reality, and thus it placed its adherents in difficult situations in the face of competing human fellowships. Responses by believers took several forms, perhaps none of them fully predictable. The religion of love soon came to be regarded in the Empire as the standard of people who were called enemies of the human race. The religion of an open-ended ethic of obedient response to a divine call tended to express its holiness through codes. The faith that would reconcile the world numbered among its followers those who tried the path of total withdrawal. In all three activities—the dialogue of church and state, the quest for holiness, and the pattern of monasticism—we see the Church and its individual disciples attempting to assert that the Church was in reality as in ideal, holy.

"CHURCH AND STATE"

In the beginning the new movement was not characterized by strife with the state, though trouble was implicit in one set of premises pictured in the New Testament. So long as it was still tenting under the national claims of the Jewish state it was relatively safe, for Rome's religious policy was inclusive and the national religions of most segments of the Empire were respected. When the Jews pulled in their stakes and when the Christians chose to remove themselves from such shelter, also by intruding in the Gentile world, trouble began. While the history of Christianity in the long run involved a "tremendous, continuous compromise between the utopian demands of the Kingdom of God and the permanent conditions of our actual human life," it was not always so.[1]

The New Testament does not concern itself very often with problems of the secular state. Paul, of course, urged loyalty to the temporal authorities because they were ordained of God. More characteristic, however, was his own attitude, shared with his colleagues, that the state was a proximate entity, one of the ephemeral affairs. Jesus refused to outline a political theory and seems to have pushed questions concerning tax-payment to the periphery of importance. He refused claims of temporal kingship for himself. He was embarrassed by attempts which would see him in opposition either to the effigies of state in Judea or the puppeteers who pulled their strings in Rome. The crucial aspect of his times and his message allowed for little distraction in a realm that was not his own but belonged, as Paul was to put it, to other principalities and powers. Was he not ironical in his comment: "The kings of the Gentiles exercise lordship over them; . . . but not so with you . . ." (Luke 22:25–26), and emphatic in his assertion: "My kingdom is not of this world"? His followers had a higher loyalty, and in momentary expectation of the end were to make their way in day-to-day existence in the earthly realm of authority. Paul's outline in Romans 13 goes somewhat further in its expression of temporal loyalty, and the late "Petrine" writings are fairly servile.

Simultaneously the apocalyptic cast of Mark 13 and Revelation 13 jars this uneasy resolution. Paul, too, may be hinting at distaste for the Empire in his early references to the anti-Christ in First Thessalonians. The competition of ideas between and within these writers provided no ready pattern; from the tension it created there emerged a dialogue of church with church and of church with world. The institutional form of this dialogue is the familiar picture of persecution. There were not ten persecutions, as Orosius counted them; local ferment was almost constant, and the universal picture is more fairly represented as latent storm and erupting storm in rhythm for over two centuries.

The Church has responded to this rhythm in every age. Tertullian called the tune with his adage: the blood of the martyrs is the seed of the Church. Martyrs in the arena, at the block, attached to the stake, did no doubt attract converts to so durable a faith. But if we look only at this side of the picture mysteries remain. Why did Rome oppose Christianity in the first place? Why did it not use its resources to sustain persecutions and stamp out the Church? Why did it succumb and become nominally or officially Christian in so short a period of time? There were leaks and letups, exceptions and failures of nerve. Policy changed with the passing of emperors; often the better emperors were the worst persecutors while the inefficient and less capable rulers let Christians pass unharmed. Before we can follow the progression from persecution not inspired by law, to persecution for which policy was provided, to the time of patent aggression for the faith by the state, it will be necessary to view the shape of Roman life with reference to religion.

ROMAN RELIGION

We should best compare Roman religion when the Church was young to the relaxed shintoism that colors many modern states. The metaphysical backdrop and the ceremonial support are assumed and implicit. The religion of the state was intended to undergird imperial claims, but this intention was rarely articulated because it was rarely challenged. In its inclusiveness this way-of-life religion could incorporate in syncretistic fashion most national faiths of the new additions to empire; when direct challenge came, this was customarily from vulgar and popular religion like, say, Christianity. Tradition and institutional conservatism played a much larger role than ideology (here we might compare the religion of democracy in the United States of the twentieth century); no one said it better than Cicero: (—43 B.C.). "In the days beyond our memory the traditional ways attached to themselves by their own appeal the outstanding men of the time; and to the ancient ways and to the institutions of their ancestors men of moral superiority clung fast." This was the world in which anti-traditional and world-upsetting Christianity was to make its way. It had to meet several tests: was it acceptable morally? was it safe politically? would it skew the cultic picture? The Church failed on all counts. Enemies had no difficulty in misrepresenting it; Christians often failed to communicate properly; the more ardent went out of their way to invite trouble. Trouble came. *Romanitas*, the Romanness that was the pride of empire and the totality of life under the banners of the imperial city, was diffuse, traditional, and lethargic. Perhaps a mark of Christianity's greatness was its ability to arouse attack.

PERSECUTION BEGINS

Christian memory instantly recalls the name of a foppish playboy Emperor, Nero, to begin this story. The fires that lit the Roman sky on July 19, A.D. 64, still inspire tales of martyrdom. The charge was arson; the intent was scapegoating; if we are to believe Tacitus: to get rid of rumors

Nero set up as the culprits and punished with utmost refinement of cruelty a class hated for their abominations, who are commonly called Christians. Christus, from whom their name is derived, was executed at the hands of the procurator Pontius Pilate in the reign of Tiberius. . . . Besides being put to death they were made to serve as objects of amusement; they were clad in hides of beasts and torn to death by dogs; others were crucified . . . (*Annales*, xv, 44).

Nero pulled the hand away from the dyke of toleration and floods of hate poured through the gaping hole. Peter and Paul no doubt met death at that time. The year that begins the post-apostolic age also marks the beginning of imperial troubles for Christianity.

Palestinian Christians had met difficulty much earlier, at the hands of the Jews as well as the Romans; but in this period with the flight of Christians and the destruction of Jerusalem (A.D. 70) the original impulse-center was waning and we can concentrate on Rome. The successors of Nero (he committed suicide) did not bother to have laws passed. The widely despised Domitian (—96) included Christians in his broadly irrational sweep; the canonical Book of Revelation undoubtedly reflects the difficulties of this time. From the viewpoint of apologetics, Revelation was unfortunate because of its subversive tone. Despite the fuel this form of literature must have added to the flames of martyrdom, Trajan (—117) in his letter to Pliny the Younger (112) took little offense or offensive. Suffering was localized in the period following this for some decades as Rome gathered impulse for another wave of conflict.

JUSTIN MARTYR AND TERTULLIAN

If we permit ourselves two more extended glances at two forms of the dialogue on the part of the Church, one of them should concentrate on Justin Martyr (—165). Coming from paganism down a corridor of philosophies—Stoicism, Aristotelianism, Pythagoreanism, and Platonism, he tells us—he became a confessor *c.* 130 and undertook to defend his new faith to philosophers and political leaders. The *First Apology* remains his most important work (*c.* 155). Later singled out and attacked, he sealed his apology with his life under Marcus Aurelius. He belonged to the "liberal" school in that he tried to build what bridges he could to the shores of paganism and philosophy; nor did he seek martyrdom. Incidental remarks in his ill-organized arguments all move from a consistent center:

The Lord said, "Pay to Caesar what belongs to Caesar; to God, what belongs to God." Therefore we render worship to God alone, but in all other things we gladly obey you, acknowledging you as kings and rulers of earth, and praying that in you the royal power may be found combined with wisdom and prudence (*Apology I*, XVII).

Justin saw Christianity beleaguered by its own heresies, by persistent Jewish attacks, and by Roman pagan and national worship which would suppress the faith. None of these were ultimate threats. The God of history will judge attackers of the faith—they can only destroy the body. But a threat to the body, while not ultimate, is still rather uncomfortable. So Justin replied to criticism. He reacted consistently to the hatred, mistreatment, and mistrust of Christians, resenting their chains and imprisonment, their torture and death. The mob, the officials, the Jews—all were responsible. This left hardly anyone blameless; Justin noted that Christians and their Lord were, indeed, hated by all men.

Jewish accusations were least difficult to meet; Justin despised the Jews for their failure to see Jesus Christ as fulfiller of their own dreams. Since he was grandstanding to the Romans, he could do so by playing off another mistrusted minority against Christianity in his own attempt to extricate the latter from unpopular identifications. Jews and Romans alike were inspired by demons, evil angels. He would face this formidable opposition with calm appeals to reason, philosophy and judgment, not wasting energy on the extremist attacks. From Justin's writings we can detail four ideas that were central in mid-second-century attacks: first, the name Christian carried a symbol of suspicion and drew odium; second, Christians are guilty of irreligion and atheism; they engage in brutal and sensual forms of worship; and finally, they are disloyal to the state. Group suspicion, guilt by association, and mass action angered him most. Let there be individual punishment of the individual offender: "we are hated only because of the name of Christ, and not because of injustice." Atheism was the most ridiculous charge in the catalog, inspired by refusal to worship the emperor of cultic gods:

> Thus we are even called atheists. We do proclaim ourselves atheists as regards those whom you call gods, but not with respect to the Most True God, who is alien to all evil and is the Father of justice, temperance, and other virtues.

Forms of worship played a curiously important part in accusations and defense: were these not cannibals when they ate their God? Justin was not ashamed to defend the faith against the charges of disloyalty: the kingdom which Christians seek is not earthly. The morality Christianity fosters should actually attract Romans. Justin aimed high, addressing his *First Apology* to emperors. He described and attacked the cult of emperor-worship, alleging that false witnesses were needed to testify to imperial divine acts and charismatic powers. In bursts of daring he reminded the emperors that their Procurator, Pontius Pilate, put Christ to death; but now Urbicus, the Roman Prefect and Consul under Antoninus Pius, was the villain. This mixture of good intentions, confused philosophizing, eagerness to be on the right side, and blustering counteroffensive did not dim Justin's bright perception of the more profound call in a crucial age; for all his moderation, he was to die a martyr's death.

Several decades later other voices spoke in the continuing dialogue. Septimius Severus (—211) was Emperor and a new and more effective kind of apologist was emerging. Most memorable of these was Tertullian (—220), a Carthaginian lawyer converted around 195. We shall revisit him as a church father and articulator of Western theology; now his *Apology* (c. 197) alone concerns us. Forgotten are Justin's bridge-building and liberal compromises. Philosophy was the subject-matter of the world's wisdom: "that rash interpreter of the divine nature and order." "What is there in common between Athens and Jerusalem? What between the Academy and the Church?"

Tertullian thundered. But in the *Apology* he was emphatic: Christians are loyal to the Empire as empire. Ignorance inspired attacks on Christianity. The Empire was the result not of the piety of Romans but of the power of God. Christians help the Roman cause by refusing to sacrifice to the emperor, for his "Genius" is demonic—such action would displease God. They do not wish to see the Empire fall, only to face the rise of a worse alternative. Were only one document preserved from all those that are known, this *Apology* of Tertullian's would best serve to describe with style, sarcasm, clarity, and point, the relation of the Church in its holiness to the Empire in its attack.

> Christians alone are not allowed to say anything to clear themselves, to defend truth, to save a judge from injustice. That alone is looked for, which the public hate requires—the confession of the name, not the investigation of the charge . . . (*Apology*, II).

> For we call upon God for the safety of the Emperor . . . (XXX).

> . . . We know that the great upheaval which hangs over the whole earth, and the very end of all things, threatening terrible woes, is only delayed by the respite granted to the Roman empire. Because we would not experience these things, we favour Rome's long continuance when we pray that they be delayed . . . In the Emperor we reverence the judgment of God, who has set him over the nations . . . (XXXII).

Tertullian, who could speak of the martyr's blood as the Church's seed, showed that he was part of its flowering. For in the ability to remain alive, without denial of principle, a fruitful alternative to the path of the Book of Revelation and the martyr-complexed confessors revealed itself.

FROM PERSECUTION TO FAVOR

The rhythms recurred, however, and emperors like Decius quickened persecution (*c.* 250) with the misguided fanaticism of leaders whose career and state were insecure. Valerianus (—260) struck a similar note: his successor

Gallienus (—268) was more mild. Diocletian (ruled 284–305), his motives obscure, renewed the scourge, for the last time with sustained effort. As late as 303 and 304 he was issuing severe orders against the faith. Then, in one of the more dramatic about-faces of Christian history, everything began to change. The persecuting Empire became the confessing state, and a new pattern of possibilities for the assertion of the Church's holiness in reference to the state was cut. Galerius, in 311, promulgated an edict of toleration; Maximin (—314), after delay, was coerced to participate. Constantine (—337) sharpened the change with a declaration of religious freedom for Christians as he accepted their faith.

Summary questions remain: who was to blame in the dialogue between church and world? Christians were not blameless for their agitation, their inflaming writings, their often unnecessary evocations of official wrath. Rome was guilty in the way it struck out from insecurity and bewilderment, in its refusal to understand the basic nature of the threat. Both sides should be faulted for frequent failure to make their points, for closing doors and then complaining that the voices of communication were muffled. What changed the picture? Rome had made way by permitting the camel's nose of popular mystery religion in its traditional tent. When Rome permitted this opening, this shaft of light and space between its view of state and religion, the opening would become wide and the fabric of *Romanitas* would tear. Christianity thus found its way. Progressively it could make its point more provocatively: it was not disloyal. With basic misunderstandings out of the way the reasons for opposition between the two realms tended to disappear and Christianity, storing up strength in its times of troubles, was poised for victory, poised to become the imperial religion that would displace others. As eschatology was unrealized and apocalypse obscured, Christians recognized that they were in the world to stay—at least for a while. It was no longer a mark of holiness to be persecuted. There remained only the spark provided by Constantine's conversion: the change in one Emperor made a change in all history. Claiming to see a monogram of

Christ in the sky, and hearing a promise of victory, he became a confessor of the name long despised by Rome. The Church had confidence and knew prestige; it had survived the scourgings and spanned the classes and nations. Well-organized, the Church held a vigorous faith to be lived for and died for—how could it fail? The hit-and-miss revivals of paganism under Julian the Apostate (361–63) did not reintroduce the rhythms. Christians called the tune: the hymn of holiness was now to be sung from books other than the one marked for martyrs.

Down into modern times the persecuted Christian has been pictured most colorfully; he has been remembered in the calendar of the Church's year. The poet Charles Péguy portrays God describing martyrs flaming like torches to earn their green palms; their blood glitters like diamonds. But single-minded concentration on this path of holiness fails to measure other and more durable ways. It is difficult to avoid exaggerating the part courage and color play; historians have perhaps contributed to the assumptions of popular piety that every Christian was in constant danger, that the only way to be holy was to face the lion's mouth or the torch. A reminder from the past pulls this into perspective. Writes Origen: "Those who have died for the Christian faith at different times have been few and are easily counted." But those who gathered in a communion of holy things and holy ones for worship and those who tried to express the separateness of Christian life have been many and no man can number them.

THE CHRISTIAN LIFE

Christian worship was the center of response; the risen Christ was the magnet of cultic attraction. Gathered around the proclamation of the good news associated with his mighty work were the faithful who knew his enduring presence in psalms and hymns and spiritual songs, in prayer and conversation and cross-witness, in the water of baptism and the bread and wine of the meal he had shared with them. The meal was considered the most dramatic and profound participation, in the second century. An order or ritual attached to this observance was discovered at Constantinople in the nineteenth century. This *Didache,* or teaching of unknown origin, urges first baptism "in the name of the Father and of the Son and of the Holy Ghost, in living water." The eucharistic meal is reserved for the baptized: "Give not that which is holy to the dogs." After thanks for the cup and the broken bread all are to be filled, and shall then rejoice in thanksgiving, according to this ritual. The mark of holiness concludes the rite: "Let grace come, and let this world pass away. Hosanna to the God of David. If any is holy, let him come: if any is not holy, let him repent. Maranatha. Amen." The ethical pattern attached to the meal was largely intra-Christian. Those who had differences were to settle them before they approached the table.

The form of the *Didache* was soon superseded by variants which express Pauline influence. The importance of the common meal waned; in its place bread and wine became part of the morning service with its preached word. In mid-century times Justin reports after the readings of Scripture and a sermon (forms which are reminiscent of the synagogue worship in which Christian rites were born), the faithful and only they remained for the blessing and the eucharistic prayer. Sacrifice and sacrament, divine spark and earthy participation, all these were fused in the observance.

This food is called with us the Eucharist, and of it none is allowed to partake but he that believes that our teachings are true, and has been washed with the washing for the remission of sins and unto regeneration, and who so lives as Christ directed. For we do not receive them as ordinary food or ordinary drink; but as by the word of God, Jesus Christ our Saviour took flesh and blood for our salvation, so also, we are taught, the food blessed by the prayer of the word which we received from him, by which, through its transformation, our blood and flesh is nourished, this food is the flesh and blood of Jesus who was made flesh.

Simultaneously with these developments, baptism was being crystallized into forms; no longer was the simplicity of repentance and the trip to the river the extent of initiation. While the *Didache* provides for nothing more than a brief ethical instruction, and Justin implies a somewhat more extensive orientation, we begin to understand the purpose of the trial period in the order of Hippolytus (around 225) which describes a three year probation: clearly the focus was on holiness of life and strength of profession. In baptism exorcism threw out the demons and the washing implied holiness in identification with the risen Lord.

Such worship which first continued the synagogue tradition of Sabbath gatherings very soon had been changed to Sunday, the day of the resurrection and the first day of the week. Bodily preparation for Sunday observance included fasting as an external mark of an internal separation to holiness. Certain days, the commemorations of the faithful departed and Easter in particular, were set aside for holy observance. Holy objects and pictures flourished: the Roman catacombs are the most familiar reminders of the association of art with Christian memory. Late Judaism had broken with the Old Testament's severe strictures against imagery, and from this source Christians openly portrayed the symbols of their faith and, with the fish, the cross, the shepherd, they had emblems of Christ himself.

ASCETICISM

So, too, it was with ethics. The Gospels show Christ breaking the codes of Judaic legalism in his casual disregard for ritual observance. The sons of the bridegroom were to rejoice in his presence. The asceticism of John the Baptist was overshadowed by the participation in banquets and wedding parties by Jesus and his followers. That ethic which St. Augustine outlined in one line: Love, and then do as you will, had been obscured in the early Church where more formal patterns of isolation from worldly pressures seemed necessary. As early as the canonical Epistle of James this predominates, and in the sub-apostolic period the Pauline emphasis on freedom of Christians from laws and codes was shadowed by attention to detail in observances and rules. This quasi-legalistic approach was moderate in the earliest times; most disciples were to continue the normal pattern of corporate life in home, congregation, and state. Paul, indeed, made it clear that celibacy favored the work of the apostolate, but this support did not canonize celibacy or make it a normative path to holiness in the Church.

Christians found many ways to express their separation. The Book of Acts portrays them sharing property as an example of commitment and fellowship. This was not regularized, however, and a customary expression in its place implied strictures against selfishness, hoarding, and wealth. The fathers could not agree on so relative an item. Tertullian was rigorously critical, while Clement made room for the rich in his ethic. While possession of charismatic gifts separated the pneumatics, and the apostolic vocation pulled others to abnormal extents of devotion, most of the nameless faithful ones continued in their callings, some of them reluctantly but others in a sense that the faith nurtured and deepened the conception of vocation. Acceptance of Christianity transected class distinctions, and by the third century many believers were highly placed in the councils of power. Ethical theory seems to have kept pace with this shift of standards: where once the meek and humble were the salt of the earth, it became a standard of achievement to attract the wealthy and influential: the conversion of Constantine was a culmination of this development. Christianity did not seem capable of transcending certain social patterns of the day, and slavery was accepted in the legal sense. Implied criticism of this bondage came through the indirect efforts of Christians to change the hearts of slaveholders and in urgings which prompted the release of slaves on a voluntary basis. Family patterns were similar in church and world, but it was assumed that Christian love was to pervade familial relationships.

It is difficult to discern a normative pattern in the early ethics. James and Tertullian in their centuries represented the right-wing response; perhaps Clement of Alexandria is typical of the rather legalistic main stream. Modern readers may still wince at the codification and attention to detail in Clement's complexities, but at the very least obedience to law did not exhaust the motivation of response. The goal of the Christian life was to be a progress toward the likeness to God:

> . . . on the righteous soul there steals a kind of divine power of goodness, through the divine visitation, revelation, and directing activity. This power, as it were of an intellectual radiance, like the sun's warm beam, stamps on the soul a kind of visible seal of righteousness, a light that is united to the soul through unfailing love, which bears God and is borne by God. (*Stromateis* VI. XII., 104, 1).

The main stream did not satisfy the more ardent swimmers. They could not be contented with the inevitable compromises with evil and the world which existence in the relativities of state, congregation, family, and affairs implied. From time to time this ferment broke out in heretical forms, as in Montanism, which joined ascetic response to spiritualistic excesses. Marcionism and Manichaeism professed abhorrence of the body. Subtle pervasion by Greek influences colored Christianity's view and led it toward an unbiblical despising of "the body." Not all rigorism was heretical, however. Catholic Christianity found room for the ascetic stream within its borders. For some, holiness was to be found in the attempt at complete isolation and removal from the "world."

MONACHISM

This approach is known as monachism or monasticism. An institution which to the modern mind is characteristic of "dark" middle ages was flourishing before the end of the third century in Egypt. There St. Antony (*c.* 251–356!) pioneered in eremitic withdrawal. By 285 he had made his way to the wildernesses where, if we follow the biography by Athanasius, he fought demons, wild beasts, and temptation. In a sense the withdrawal by Antony and his colleagues was self-defeating. Their achievement became attractive to others who followed them. Corporate life for hermits seems to be a contradiction in terms with which the pioneers were required to deal. Around 305 Antony deserted his attempt at achieving absolute isolation long enough to organize communities of hermits. They lived in proximity to each other but had little life in common. For the first time "monks" lived under a rule. Soon at centers such as Nitria, Cellia, and Scotis in Egypt there were cells of monks who came together only for worship and work. Extremism and eccentricity characterize the movement. It is best explained as a reaction against the secularizing of the Church in the years when it was poised to overtake the Empire.

Antony's anchoritism was not the only pattern. Pachomius (—346) is associated with "coenobitic" or communal monachism. His monastery on the banks of the Nile was attractive to many who were not prepared for the isolation of Antony's rule. Pachomius' personal holiness was the chief advertisement for Tabennisi, his community; from this grew other monasteries for men and women. Rules of holy living played a larger part in gathered monachism than they did in the eremetic forms. Pachomius established patterns which were accepted through long centuries: the most far-reaching of these was the totalitarian authority granted the abbots.

So radical a movement needs theological justification; the warrant for Egyptian monasticism is difficult to isolate for several reasons. The origins of Egyptian Christianity are obscure; Greek influence was minimal. Legend, subjectivism in reporting, and fantasy obscure the ideological picture. But certainly at its heart was a belief in demons and the demonic at the center of life in the world. The monastic community prepared one for battle with demons by denying property, sexual intercourse, or interest in worldly matters. The cross of Christ seems to have been of interest only in exorcism of demons; speculative and dogmatic theology did not concern them. Yet monks were the shock troops of orthodoxy when the creedal controversies developed later. They memorized huge portions of the Bible. All this appeared in such a legal cast, however, that some scholars, among them Hans Lietzmann, will grant to this monasticism but one distinctively Christian mark; the conviction that sin separates man from God and that prayer to God overcomes alienation. But even this became obscured by legal attention to detail, a magical view of the sacrament, the eagerness to report visions of God and miracles. The virtuosos of holiness had established a new and difficult course. Only later could they be drawn into service of the Church in its main flow.

Such service came not from Egyptian monasticism so much as from its daughters. In Palestine Jerome (—420) was distinguished for his regularized asceticism. For him service was marked by Bible translation and comment. In Syria the athletes of God, among them Simeon Stylites (—459), distinguished themselves upon their pillars where intercession and curiosity attracted converts. Even more sensational was the approach of the *acoimetai* or sleepless ones, who would awaken every three minutes throughout the day to sing praises.

The chart of monastic expansion includes Basil in Asia Minor (—379), Martin of Tours in Gaul, and nameless adherents of the Pachomian ideal in Italy, Spain, Africa. From the counsels of perfection in the Sermon on the Mount of Jesus, the prophetism of John the Baptist, and the biological harshness of Paul (I Cor. 7), apologists for the movement provided a rationale. Of the varied types of response to the call for holiness, retreat drew the smallest minority. But out of this minority there were to come men who in worldly churches would preserve learning and culture, ideals of holiness and pace-setting piety. The bane of those who would work out salvation in the broader avenues of daily life, they provided the Church with a note of judgment and of conscience that cannot be dismissed. They had picked up a strand in the authentic fabric; their mistake came as they pulled at it with such strength that it twisted the whole garment. This distorted the question of Christian vocation, complicating it for those who chose not to go to the desert or the cell. The martyr and the monk, then, each had a place, but each in his color detracts from the pastel and gray response of holiness in congregational life and daily calling. Perhaps it was most difficult to be holy there where no beasts roared or fire flamed, where no demons fluttered around the ears of saints—but where the structures of evil pervading life called for higher witness to the way of the cross. The varying hopes for holiness were like ropes. They bound some in misery to stakes. They corralled others in cells. But for most they were stretched across poles of church and world: it is never easy to walk a tightrope.

4

THE SHAPE OF APOSTOLIC DOCTRINE

No feature of the development of the Church in the first Christian centuries has been more maligned by moderns than the process which shaped its teaching. Since the Western Enlightenment it has been fashionable to caricature the efforts of theologians in that time: they split hairs in whirlwinds, argued doctrines while their comrades were being martyred, or obscured the simple teaching of Jesus of Nazareth. This view fails on at least three counts. It refuses to analyze a period from within; it does not recognize that shaping the Church's teaching *was* a life-and-death matter; it burlesques the process of formulation. For Christian teaching was neither first of all philosophical, though it employed philosophy; nor was it speculative, systematic, and anticipatory. It was economical, elaborating existing teaching on a minimal basis.

The Church began not with a Gnostic body of esoteric teaching, in which all the mysteries were knotted; it began with the loose ends of witness from many eyes and hands; these ends led not to a teaching but to a person. At the center was the redemptive activity of God in His son and servant Jesus Christ. While there was less disparity between the "theology of Jesus," of Paul, of John, and of the church fathers than was implied in the scholarship of recently passed generations, variety did characterize the early witness. This chapter concerns itself with the attempt at formulating a doctrine acceptable to the whole Church.

It will serve us well to practice dealing with threes in the time of trinitarian concerns. A trinity of institutions developed during the second century, each making its contribution to the task of shaping doctrine: the canon of Scripture, the early canons of doctrine, and the historic episcopate. All were developments. None were instituted by fiat or action of committees. Each reflects the pressures on the Church in its fight for survival, as well as its creative response.

THE CANON OF SCRIPTURE

The canon of Scripture, a catalog of the books which "belong" in the sacred writings of Christianity, was in part an inheritance from Old Testament times. The Old Testament itself developed until the later decades of the first century A.D., when its canon or "rule" was closed. Certain books called the Apocrypha had uncertain status then and they still do. Christians early accepted the Old Testament canon. But the process in respect to the New Testament is what concerns us. From what has been told here it should be obvious that most weight fell on the epistles of Paul and the four Gospels; these seemed to have met general respect as early as the middle of the second century. Perhaps by A.D. 200 they were as broadly accepted as was the Old Testament among Christians. Other included books were more controversial; Eusebius' list cast doubts on two Johannine epistles, Jude, Hebrews, II Peter, and the Apocalypse. The "Muratorian Canon" of the second century presents all but four of the New Testament books (Hebrews, James, I and II Peter), though it adds others. Isolated churches clung to sub-apostolic writings such as the Shepherd of Hermas and the Epistle of Barnabas. The canon in its present form was detailed completely for the first (preserved) time by Athanasius in A.D. 369. The Church regarded this body of inspired writings as qualitatively different from all others. It helped constitute doctrinal authority, and made clear a path of salvation.

The formation of the canon reflects the need of the Church to keep pure the chain of witness and to provide an internal principle for criticizing teachings. Several questions were asked of the books: Did they carry their own spiritual and theological weight with the ring of inner authenticity? Did they claim justifiably the warrant of apostleship? This second question was a test of tradition and history—efforts were made to connect each book with the name of an apostle of the first generation who could be regarded as the receiver of authentic teaching from the lips of Christ. Papias (—130) and Irenaeus (—200) provide some of the earliest indications of this process. Several decades had elapsed from the time of the later writings and the earlier glimpses of canon-formation. This was just enough time to leave questions of authorship open down to our own time.

No single external pressure seems to have forced the Church's hand, necessitating the closing of the canon; but the canon provided by the heretic Marcion for his disciples accelerated the development in marked fashion. Similarly, the Gnostic heresy necessitated the selection of an authentic body of tradition about the years of Christ's humanity such as was seen in the Gospels. The heresy's reliance on secret tradition had to be exposed. Fear that the tangle of apocryphal writings would be smothering also contributed. When pneumatics embarrassed the Church catholic by their extreme claims to inspiration, they were answered with a body of writings that claimed a different and higher kind of inspiration. Finally, as the church fathers and respected theological leaders repeatedly quoted from the same writings, these attained a prestige which their fanciful competitors never knew.

Drawing together the loose ends of scriptures into a canon did not, of course, solve everything. The "closed" canon remains perpetually open because it is a product of the Church it helped produce. The diversity of teachings based upon the same scriptures also suggests enduring difficulties. "The New Testament canon, as such, is not the foundation of the Church's unity. On the contrary the canon, as such—i.e. as a fact as it is available to the historian—is the foundation of the multiplicity of confessions." [1] Yet the canon should not be blamed for the misuses Christians have made of it. Difficulties on this front simply recall the problems which result from the central Christian affirmation: that somehow the Infinite broke through in the times and places associated with Jesus Christ. The great contribution of the canon in its positive sense was this: it assured the simplest possible access of later generations to the original proclamation concerning the Kingdom of God and the suffering servant.

THE CANON OF DOCTRINE

A second institution was a nascent canon of doctrine. Like the canon of Scripture, this also grew in the period when personal witness to an event was necessarily being translated into correct teaching about that witness. So long as the apostles could meet face to face in council they could assume that the sense of the meetings with their Lord would be transmitted. Passage of time made this impossible, and a mark of correct doctrine as opposed to heterodoxy or heresy was necessary for the survival of the basic core of Christian witness. Here the apostles came into their own: "The apostles we accept as the Lord," wrote Serapion c. A.D. 200. In the missionary period the church at Jerusalem was concerned that "the teaching of the apostles" would not be diffused. Just as they became the decisive factor in judging Scripture, so now they were determinative for the core of doctrine within the scriptures. In the first process the apostles were the post-planters around the scriptural corral; in the second they were the guides to greenest pastures within the corral.

In the face of heresies, of Gnostic secrets, and various winds of doctrine, there developed a need for a brief and open rule of faith, a compact guide and judge. It is grossly inaccurate to picture the apostles or their sons sitting down to formulate such a rule. It grew. Its seed is evident in little liturgical passages in the New Testament, such as the Christ-hymn of Philippians 2. Its germination came with the development of brief baptismal formulae. The Apostles' and Niceno-Constantinopolitan creeds which most Christians still accept date from the end of the period to be covered by this chapter, but it will provide the reader with a place to stand if at the outset we reproduce an early extant creed from Rome, c. A.D. 340.

> *I believe in God almighty.*
> *And in Christ Jesus, his only son, our Lord*
> *Who was born of the Holy Spirit and the Virgin Mary*
> *Who was crucified under Pontius Pilate and was buried*
> *And the third day rose from the dead*
> *Who ascended into heaven*
> *And sitteth on the right hand of the Father*
> *Whence he cometh to judge the living and the dead.*
> *And in the Holy Ghost*
> *The holy church*
> *The remission of sins*
> *The resurrection of the flesh*
> *The life everlasting.*

This brief outline of faith is properly sketchy: it serves to remind that no settled canon of doctrine matched the relative authority of Scripture in the earliest centuries. To determine the part creeds and rules played at this time we must now concentrate on the third institution, entrusted with custodianship of doctrine and life, the historic episcopate.

THE EPISCOPATE

The question of the episcopate has flashed into prominence in recent ecclesiastical conversation, and new scholarly light is constantly being shed on its origins. Much of the defense of the institution has come from Roman Catholic, Orthodox, and Anglican bodies which seek a traceable line of succession to the apostles of the first generation; this question divided and divides world Christendom whenever it discussed polity. Defenders of the succession point to the New Testament for primitive warrant, while critics refuse to see what the placing of someone's hand on someone else's head in the first and second centuries has to do with authority today.

Paul in his epistles gave various pictures of early life in the churches he founded, but his testimony on the question of apostolic authority is understandably ambiguous. The very terms he uses are open to a double interpretation. In his time the apostles and the pneumatics were still active. In Romans 12 he speaks of prophets and teachers, but he shows no formal concern with the office of bishop. The Book of Acts also pictures early church life, wherein bishops and presbyters assume what might seem to be "secular" functions, overseeing finances and serving tables.

The first post-apostolic source is Clement of Rome in his letter written to Corinth just before the end of the first century. His letter has a definite Pauline cast; in making episcopal claims it does not distinguish between bishops and elders; but its very existence and character make clear the implication that Clement as head of the Roman Church should have something to offer in a churchly quarrel elsewhere. This is, by the way, one of the earliest traces of that parallel development, the rise of Rome. Irenaeus lists Clement in a succession with Peter, Linus, and Anacletus in the bishop's chair at Rome. More decisive is the writing of Ignatius of Antioch, who wrote early in the second century. To the historian the thundering weight of Ignatius' work is the absence of apology for the bishop's office—he simply assumes the institution, he elaborates on what already exists. His view is "high":

> All of you follow the bishop as Jesus Christ followed the Father, and follow the presbytery as the Apostles; and respect the deacons as the commandment of God. Let no man perform anything pertaining to the church without the bishop. . . . Wherever the bishop appears, there let the people be, just as, wheresoever Christ Jesus is, there is the Catholic Church (EPISTLE TO THE SMYRNEANS, VIII).

If Ignatius is first to use the term Catholic Church, Hegesippus (c. 160) is first to speak of the succession of apostles. In Lyons, Gaul, c. 180, we find Irenaeus detailing the role of church, tradition, and succession in the historic episcopacy. It was he who put his witness to the adjective "historic" by providing a list of the Roman bishops as a guarantee of the all-important continuity of orders. Though he was Bishop himself, his deference to Roman authority is apparent. Irenaeus came from Asia Minor where Montanism, Marcionism, and some Gnostic heresies rose; they may explain his emphasis on episcopacy. For the bishop was now a guardian of orthodoxy.

Later glimpses find Victor of Rome implying his right as Roman Bishop to interfere in local disputes; Tertullian arguing the importance of succession and tradition; the "high"-churchman Cyprian (—258) arguing that the bishop is integral to the very existence of that Church apart from which there is no salvation. In this whole development we see a trend toward formalization of religious life, the development of stewardship for orthodoxy and authority, and a centralization of power, all under the rubric of apostolicity and continuity with the disciples on whom Christ himself first placed his hands.

With this trinity now assumed: canon of Scripture, canon of doctrine, authority of bishop, we can move on to another. We have mentioned that no other negative pressure was as fruitful for the development of the orthodox Church's life as was heresy. The early Church had to pick and choose its way between variants and denials of certain basics. The variants can be classified as heterodoxy, the denials as heresies. Theological errors which cut at the very vitals of Christian witness were attractive to parties within the Church from earliest times and demanded most vigorous counter-activity. The early heresies prefigure most later authentic perversions of the faith; for this reason they deserve emphasis.

THE HERESIES

Heresies were at least as complex as orthodoxy; competing teachers within them make classification difficult. But if we deal with a triad of such heresies in a simple and

direct fashion it will make the attention to creedal statement more intelligible later. We shall by no means exhaust
the catalog by reference to Gnosticism, Marcionism, and
Montanism, but these three supplement each other as
decisive versions of denial. Gnosticism denied one half of
the witness to Christ: his authentic humanity. Marcionism
denied one half of the authority of the word of God: His
law. Montanism denied one half of the working of the
spirit of God: His anchorage in Scriptures. At least so the
early Church thought, and the catholic church of later times
has followed in its repudiation.

GNOSTICISM

Gnosticism was the most pervasive, persuasive, and diffuse
of the heresies—it remains the most difficult to grasp or
contain in brief survey. D'Arcy has summarized it well:[2]

> Gnosticism seems to have been one of those unfortunate
> forms of thought for which human beings have a
> chronic appetite. That is to say, it was a syncretistic
> philosophy and religion: it made an apparent lofty unity
> out of the various systems known, and by picking out
> what it liked and eviscerating the doctrine of its true
> meaning within the original system, it pretended to be
> the highest and most spiritual of religions and the key
> to all others. . . . Gnosticism at its best represents the
> ever-recurring thought of humanity outside the startling
> good news from on high of the Christian revelation.

At the heart of Gnostic systems is a different view of
time and history than Christianity knows: the record of
God's revelation in the life of the people of Israel must
be repudiated. That involves denial of the Old Testament,
or its allegorical transformation. Second, it denies the
true humanity of Christ. Christ only seemed to have a human body; God only seemed to be really human and
involved in history. History has no immediate *telos* or
goal. For Gnosticism the Kingdom of God or the End can
never be at hand. Fusing a pagan ancestry with Christian

deviations, it knew many of the words but little of the music of the song of Christian redemption. It could be at home simultaneously with paganism, late Judaism, philosophy, and Christianity.

The Gnostics scorned ordinary Christians who walked by faith: they walked by sight, they knew, they had access to secret bodies of knowledge. Their god moved within a formless void such as that which characterized the earth in creation; he emerged in creative conflict. In this emergence God emanated aeons and out of them, man. But man was himself part of the chaos and evil that inhered in the aeons, and thus a new aeon, Christ, was sent. Christ came to Jesus; when Jesus died, Christ did not. In some versions of the Docetic heresy as reported by Irenaeus, Christ did not die because Jesus did not. Simon of Cyrene was actually crucified while Jesus watched and laughed at the Jews in their delusions!

Out of the crucifixion came a purification through holy living and initiation into the Gnostic corpus of knowledge. Perfection was the goal. Various mythologies clothed pseudo-theological structures such as these. Certain canonical writings reflect critical concerns with these views in their inchoate forms. The epistles of John oppose a Cerinthian heresy in which Christ only seemed to be a man. Paul's letter to the Colossians has a similar cast. Irenaeus countered the Christianity-of-the-backward-glance, commonly known as Ebionitism, which fused the faith with Judaizing and Gnostic wisdom. This father provides a more extensive picture of the heresy than any other. What Gnostic literature is extant largely substantiates his version.

By the beginning of the second century the Cerinthian stirrings found parallels in the writings of Dion of Brussa, who had developed a mythology of dualistic views which centered in a confusion and mingling of gods. The Leyden Cosmogony, another mythology, suggested a similar syncretism of the gods of Egypt, Iran, and Greece. In all these fantasies the stress lay on the processions of the gods, on mysteries and cultic observance. Eventually, as in Justin's Baruch, they bridge from pure paganism into the life of Jesus the son of Joseph and Mary. By this time there is predilection for scriptural rootage, though the Bible is used allegorically and in admixtures of Greek mythology. The New Testament never comes through clearly, no doubt because of the obvious stress on the humanity of Jesus. Gnostic syncretism was seductive to second-century Christians who could find in it an evasion of the offense of the cross. Like all seducers, it was sufficiently wily to attract Christianity at the points of insecurity.

In the writings of Basilides and Valentine the brush with the faith and the threat are most apparent. Valentine's was the more extensive system. He came from Egypt to Rome where he hoped to become a bishop; this was between 160 and 170. Irenaeus vehemently protested his enticements. Basilides lived in Egypt in the time of Antoninus Pius (—161). He wrote commentaries on the Gospels, fragments of which remain, but as with Valentine we gain a full picture from his opponents. In all the Gnostics the central threat to the faith was not in the distortion of the Gospels nor even in the new Christology which they fostered. The doctrine of God was really at issue—it is in all heresies. Christians resisted by remaining monotheists, worshipping a God in whom there is tension between wrath and mercy. Gnosticism is dualistic, halving God. When this is done, mystery disappears even in a religion of mystery.

Adolf Harnack called Gnosticism an acute Hellenization of Christianity; Hans Lietzmann saw it as a re-orientalization of the faith. In Gnosticism the Father of Jesus Christ met challenge in mythic oriental deities of human inventions, while it took expression in Greek terms. The church that would follow it would certainly have been schizoid! Yet to survive as long as it did as a heresy, Gnosticism had to be attractive; it infiltrated the normative expression of the Church catholic and forced critics to adopt some of its terminology. Thus when Christianity had finished asserting its own path of salvation in the face of heresy, it was involved in inevitable Hellenizations and orientalizations that were long a-dying.

MARCIONISM

If Ebionite Christianity looked backward, and Gnosticism looked east and west, in Marcionism heretics looked ahead, denying the past, denying continuities with the Old Testament and with the Law. It is not entirely unfairly described as an attempt to out-Paul Paul in its emphasis on new life and gospel. Marcion was evidently a son of a bishop in Pontus who arrived in Rome, eager for churchly status, c. 140. Organizing his own cult, he began to remove himself from the orthodox circle and was summarily excommunicated in 144. His movement spread in wildfire fashion. The heresy was plausible and attractive. Even after its founder died, c. 160, the movement lived on. Marcion's single writing has not survived but it is not difficult to piece together its gist.

This heresy halved Christianity on the issue of law and gospel: the new gospel of love would have nothing whatever to do with the law in any form. As with Gnosticism the basic issue was a doctrine of God: and the God of the Old Testament, the Creator, also was done away with. Here there was cleavage between creation and redemption in God's order. In Marcion's eyes, the evangelists and epistolary writers of the New Testament, because they wore Jewish masks, divined only the outlines of Christianity, with one exception: St. Paul. His most creative contribution to catholicity was in the pressure his own canon (Pauline writings and edited Luke) created to force the orthodox canon. Since his Christology bordered on the Docetic view—Christ only seemed to be fully human—it is easy to place Marcion with the Gnostics, but his rejection of allegory and myth and his rigorous ethic place him in an altogether different camp. His followers had no easy time of it. Despised as they were by catholic Christians, they set out also to do battle against persecutors, and they frequently became martyrs along with their more conventional brethren. As late as A.D. 200 Tertullian looked out from Carthage and feared that the Marcionite sweep would devastate the Christian world. But the movement was in reality a one-man force. So overpowering was the man Marcion that he was able to cast a shadow for another generation beyond his death; he had no first-rate successor and eventually catholicism, shaken to the roots, shook off Marcion's approach to Law and to God.

MONTANISM

A third heresy, Montanism, assumed entirely different forms. Christians have always believed that the Spirit like the wind blew where it pleased, but orthodoxy always refused to identify the Spirit with the lo here! and lo there! of individual claim. To avoid a free-floating concept of inspiration and Spirit-involvement it looked in the revelation of Christ, the witness in the Scriptures, and perhaps in certain holy signs, for this Spirit. Montanism stressed one half, the freedom of the Spirit and the claim of individual possession. In the first generation the Church, nurtured by Pentecost, tolerated in its midst pneumatics, charismatics, speakers in tongues, and spirit-mad prophets. But with the waning expectation of the End and the settling of relative normality such manifestations were rejected. In the middle of the second century one Montanus, also of Asia Minor, rekindled the fires of inspiration. He was, he claimed, the Paraclete or Spirit of Truth promised in the Fourth Gospel.

His first disciples, Maximilla and Prisca, shared his speaking in tongues and claimed for themselves a hold on the Spirit. Developing an egocentric eschatology, these prophetesses convinced their hearers that the end of the age and the return of Christ were imminent. Curiously, such extravagant claims did not lead to ethical license. Instead, the spirit-filled heretics greeted the watch for the end with fasting, celibacy, and common property at their center in Pepuza. Like the Marcionites, these sectarians met persecution and martyrdom willingly; as a matter of fact, they felt that the executioner's sword would merely hasten the day of the End. But such a fire could not long flame nor could so great an excitement keep its verve. The energy was spent and the succession of apostolic Christians organized resistance, but not before such noted leaders as Tertullian in Africa had come under the spell. The quality of inspirations was always under debate; leadership, naturally, quarreled. By the fourth century most traces of this heresy had disappeared. But Montanism joined with other perversions to help shape Christian dogma by the enforced attention it brought to problems of eschatology and ethics and the definition of the Divine Trinity and the Holy Spirit.

THE FATHERS

This is not intended to be a catalog of heresies or a handbook for witch-hunts; it is time to return to the quest for apostolicity and to approach the consensus of faith and doctrine that was the glory of the young Church. Here the danger persists that we content ourselves with a chronicle of councils and congresses of nameless theologians and rulers, of lists of dogmas and dull developments of abstractions. Actually the process was touched by the genius of as great a gallery of thinkers as the Church has known. There are few better ways to face the question of the shaping of apostolic doctrine than by looking at these men who were responsive to the New Testament, conscious of their involvements in culture and catholicity, learned men conversant with the academic discourse of their time. Some of these men we have already met, though not always by name: first, the subapostolics like Clement, Hermas, Ignatius, Polycarp, Barnabas, and "Peter," who seemed to be obscuring the freshness of the new vision in return to new law and reinforcement of new institution. Nor would we be content merely to mark the apologists, Aristides, Tatian (—160), Athenagoras, Theophilus, and most notably, Justin Martyr (—165), most of whom flourished at mid-second-century. The difficulties of their task and the mediocrity of their talent marked them for second-best status. They tried to fight off heresies within Christianity, to fight off persecutions, and to relate themselves to the

Hellenic world, to Rome, and to the memory of Jerusalem. This was a three-handed task for two-handed men. Philosophical discourse played a somewhat larger role in their thinking than in that of their predecessors; thus certain seminal ideas which bridged the canon and Greek thought were prominent, for example the *Logos* or eternal word. Christianity was itself a philosophy, qualitatively different from other philosophies because it is based on divine revelation. Theirs was a highly moralistic system, for they were involved in rational justification of their faith to a world which was suspicious of Christianity. In many respects it lost some of the incisiveness of the new Christian claim because it granted too much to the presuppositions of its enemy. But through the "New Law" of which they spoke there broke out the rays of the brighter gospel.

After them came the bright cluster of giants: Irenaeus (—200), the biblical theologian; Origen (—254), the genius of the early Church; the legal-minded Tertullian (—220); and the greatest of the fathers, Augustine (—430). All but Augustine are the precursors of the age of ecumenical councils, and we do well to think of them as ecumenical theologians. For while each stood in a separate tradition in Gaul, Alexandria, Carthage, or Rome, they represent, beyond individual personalities and expressions, a reasonable consensus of that tradition of the apostles which was to be braided from tangled strands into one whole. It is as unfair to these men to overstress their differences as it is to underplay the basic unities of their thought.

IRENAEUS

Irenaeus (—*c.* 200) of Lyons in Gaul was probably from Asia Minor; he fought off the heresies that originated in his homeland. The faithful guide of his flock through persecutions, he was rewarded with the bishop's chair. His work centered in attacks on Gnosticism and Montanist eschatology, but it is a measure of his greatness that despite his polemical interests his contribution is largely positive. For Irenaeus was not content to rival Gnosticism with

Christian Gnosticism: he countered with the appeal to apostolicity in the episcopacy and pre-eminently in the Scriptures. The first of the great ecumenical theologians, he is in the first rank among biblical thinkers. From the first he repudiated speculative theology in favor of scriptural documentation and intuitive perception of the meaning of the mysteries. With his doctrinal conservatism and churchly concern, Irenaeus represents a mainstream of churchly theology for his time, and many later doctrinal discussions are luminously prefigured in his writings. But the religious life that grew out of his theology and the pastoral care he evidenced have commended Irenaeus to the reverence of later Christian generations which have seen him in the spiritual line of the apostles.

TERTULLIAN

The faith that spread to Africa only to wane from that continent's northern shores within six centuries before the Moslem onrush found much of its most explicit definition there. As with the origins of the church of Gaul, so in Africa the outlines of beginnings are obscure. But as it emerged the church of Africa taught the entire West. Roman colonies there freshened lines of communication in the Empire, and cultural life incorporated much that was Greek. Out of this shore of Christians came Tertullian, a Montanist of Carthage. With his juridical background he was capable of presenting a quasi-legal case for Christianity. His writings suggest the richness of particular Christian witness; how far removed he was from the apologists in his constant rhetoric! Ridiculing philosophy, he enjoyed sharpening the offense of the faith. From his place in Carthage he squared his shoulders against the world of Hellas and helped place the faith decisively in the western stream through his love of order, institution, and tradition. The world of ancient culture could follow him only through an about-face.

A native of Carthage, Tertullian flourished at the turn of the century, and was active until about A.D. 220. So legalistic and ascetic was he that he found Montanism compatible, and probably spent his last dozen years with that sect. A voluminous writer, he was as noted for apologies, for polemic, for ethics as for orthodox formulations. A jurist, he was not comparable to a corporation lawyer, but an involved barrister who pleaded his case with emotion and drama. Travelling light intellectually he was more nearly capable of reaching his destination. Many of the terms that became part of the ecumenical debate—person, substance, Trinity—first appear in these contexts in his writings. His theology falls short on legalism and moralism, in its stress on human merit at the expense of divine grace. But the faith of the West needed an advocate and found one in the Carthaginian.

Tertullian had a colleague and successor in Carthage, cut of a different cloth, Cyprian, the "highchurch" Bishop of that city. Concerned with the holiness of the Church and the faithfulness of witness, Cyprian was involved in problems that dealt with Christians who weakened during the Decian persecution. His stand was controversial as it evolved from strict rigidity to penitence: it was not severe enough to please those who had suffered and not concessionist enough for those who had "lapsed." These practical problems led him to preoccupy himself with the doctrine and practice of the Church: "it is not possible to have God as Father without having the Church as mother." Apart from the Church, there is no salvation. The Church is a unity, centering in the episcopacy as apostolic witness to Christ. No sin looms so large as schism in the Church. Here we see a bishop in the line of Ignatius on the authority of the Church. Cyprian's final years were made stormy by partisans within the Church and enemies without; he died a martyr.

ORIGEN

Alexandria, to the east, was an entirely different story, for here apostleship bowed to Athens more than elsewhere, in direct contrast to Carthage's example. Here an exciting

thought-world competed with the Christian. Out of obscure origins the Church flourished by the end of the
second century in the persons of catechists like Clement
of Alexandria (—215). Clement tiptoed as far as he could
to the edges of Gnosticism before offering a Christian
replacement for the heresy. He is hidden in the shadows
cast by the towering father Origen. Origen (—254) inspires
a gasp of awe for his breadth and depth of thought; he was
a universal genius, a theological Leonardo da Vinci at home
in philosophy, dogma, apology, polemics, exegesis. Though
he was later repudiated by some in the East, he is the
eastern church's greatest teacher and, more than others,
formed the idea-patterns in which Christian creedalism
grew. Schoolboys remember him for the rigor of his response; he had himself castrated as an aid to asceticism
and for denial of the flesh. If he was consciously influenced
by Clement, he was careful to scuff the trail to his source.
Before him no other Christian, not even Justin Martyr,
had been in so close a brush with the philosophical schools
as Origen was with the Platonists of Alexandria to whom
he related Christianity. His *Hexapla,* a six-column version
of the Bible in many languages, suggests his biblical interests; his theology places him in the first rank as the
first authentic systematician of the faith. For him the decisive work of Christ was his mediation from a realm
beyond the time that is our time and the space that is our
space as the eternally begotten son of the Father. He
transformed the *Logos* concept in harmony with an allego-
rized view of Scriptures. Few can challenge Origen's depth
of divination in biblical waters; if he was one-sided in
approach, this inheres in the nature of the mysteries with
which he dealt and in the limits of genius. Let Origen
symbolize genius more than limitation. If we need one
guide to the ecumenical age and its spirit, let it be Origen.

THE COUNCILS

The forces, the heresies, the giants out of the way, we
come face to face with that perplexing and complex mo-

ment in Christian history when witness crystallized into creed and hit-or-miss apology became theological systems roughly acceptable to the whole Church in bowed consensus (though not without preliminary scuffling and infighting). Between 325 and 451, in councils at Nicaea, Constantinople, Ephesus, and Chalcedon, theologians achieved more by way of consensus on basic Christianity in terms acceptable in their day than they have in any similar span in ecclesiastical history. Throughout the Middle Ages there would be other councils: at Constantinople and Nicaea, and the succession of western meetings at Rome four times, Lyons twice, and in a final burst at Vienne, Constance, Basel before the Reformation. Later there were meetings at Rome, Trent and in the nineteenth century at the Vatican. Some of the later councils were strategic; some merely tried to heal schisms; others dealt with easily isolatable issues. But the fourth century was given two momentous tasks: to hold to the monotheism that Christianity professed, and yet make room for the work of the Father, Son and Holy Spirit (the trinitarian solution) and for a divine and human nature in Christ. Finite minds in relative situations in compromising moments of history were expected to grasp from below the idea of the wholeness of the Godhead and satisfy themselves that they were apostolic and the world that they were respectable. For all the snarling, the gnarling, and the knotting of their speculations, they attained an impressive height in their formulae.

It has long been fashionable to scorn the creedalists, to accuse them of failing in the one thing they set out to do. This line of argument suggests that the thunder of God's power and the whisper of Jesus' voice were forgotten in the deliberations on person and substance and essence; that the mark of apostolicity was shrouded by the masks of speculation and distance from the earthiness of the walk through Palestine. Harnack put this baldly: men gave up brotherliness and condemned others to chains and death for the sake of a *nuance* in asserting a Christology. Matthew Arnold thought trinitarian talk was fairy-tale telling. The arrogance of some formulators has antagonized many: thus Eunomius, Bishop of Cyzicus (—395): "I know God as well as He knows Himself." Orthodoxy was seen to be confining; as recently as 1941 Martin Werner could argue that orthodoxy substituted for primitive Christianity a Hellenistic-syncretistic mystery religion that promenaded about in Christian apparel, but was musty with the decadence of post-classicism and its religious forms. Of course, all these critics are partly correct. Seldom has the humanness and inhumaneness of the Church been as patent as in confessional controversy.

But recently men have become more sympathetic with the intent and often with the achievement of the ecumenical councils. The light achievement of similar attempts in our own day has bred patience with the faltering of another time and place. Many have begun to see again that the creeds were not arbitrary edicts but, as Dorothy Sayers liked to remind her readers, statements of fact. Christianity depended upon holy living *and* holy teaching; it survived rival institutions *and* rival ideas; shaping the doctrine in the apostolic line was a life-and-death matter.

The pettiness of princes and the intrigues of ecclesiastics entered in at almost every point of the debate. But nobler defenders of the faith were there too—among the Alexandrians, with their bent toward the "high" preoccupations with the deity and glory of Christ, and the earlier Antiochians, from whom the human life of Christ received fuller attention. Arching over the specific creedal issues of the times in their catholic concerns were an even greater breed in the tradition of the apostles and the fathers: Ambrose (—397), Jerome (—420), Augustine, and later Leo the Great (—461). In the writings of these persons and the utterances of their councils are to be seen reflections of the tremors of Christianity's Great Debate.

The two aspects of this debate can be treated chronologically or topically, but the result is the same: Was Christ fully divine? If so, how did he relate to the divine unity? This was the creedal discussion of the Trinity. Was he fully human? If so, how did his humanity relate to his divinity? Here Christology was central, the doctrine of the two natures. The first needed Nicaea (325), the second Chalcedon (451).

THE TRINITY

Trinitarianism is not referred to explicitly in the canon of Scripture. The post-apostolic fathers regarded Christ as God's son but did not concern themselves with detailing the relationships of persons in the deity. The apologists related Father and Son through the *Logos*-idea. Irenaeus urged men to perceive that Son and Spirit share the divine substance. Tertullian used the term "Trinity." Origen verged toward explicit formulation. All the thinkers of the Church flirted with an issue that demanded resolution in an uneasy time. Agitation came from one side among the Monarchianists, those who would place all the weight on the unity of the Godhead. But it amounted to a swing of the pendulum to the right, a failure to do justice to the Son in his independence in Christ. One cluster of these rigid monotheists was known as Modalist: God moved through a sequence of modes or operations in His self-revelation, wearing the successive masks of fatherhood, sonship, and spirit-ness. Sabellius headed this school. Somewhat different were the Dynamists or Adoptionists, led particularly by Paul of Samosata, who argued that Jesus was of the Godhead only in that a power from his Father invaded his humanity, or that the Father adopted the man Christ Jesus —in any case, he was not fully God. Then came Arius, who picked up the line of Paul of Samosata. Not a systematic theologian, he taught by compressing his teachings into verselets; yet his viewpoint was quite complicated. The text with which I grew up put it this way: "Arius was opposed to modalistic monarchianism, and strongly in favor of hypostasianism of the subordinationist type"; let the reader thank me for the cue! What it all means is that Arius saw the Son to be subordinate to the Father; there was a real and essential difference between them. The Son or Logos was finite and made divine, a god junior grade. One report summarizes Arius: "If the Father begat the Son [as also his opponents contended], he that was begotten had a beginning of existence; hence it is clear that there was [a time] when the Son was not. It follows then of necessity that he had his existence from the non-existent."

Arius went out to win the Christian world, and he nearly succeeded. He emerged around A.D. 319 as the Goliath of the subordinationists, working his way east. Constantine's legate, Bishop Hosius, was to head him off and reach compromise, but Arius would not settle. So it was that in the summer of 325 the Emperor Constantine called a council at Nicaea in Bithynia. The informal atmosphere soon became electric with cross-charges between parties. Constantine wanted unity more than apostolic concern for purity. A David had risen among the orthodox, one Athanasius (—373), a deacon of the Bishop of Alexandria. Over three hundred leaders heard the debates which resulted in the condemnation of Arius and his party: "it was unanimously decided that his impious opinion should be anathematized."

Nicaea actually represented a minority viewpoint; the settlement was uneasy and was unacceptable to many who were not Arian in outlook. Athanasius himself became an artful dodger as well as an accurate fencer; his popularity rose and fell and he was exiled so often that he virtually became a commuter. At Sirmium in 357, while Athanasius was in exile, a council voted to move resoundingly with Arian voice. But these "blasphemers" carried matters too far and the ultimate resolution lay with the Athanasians: "We believe . . . in one Lord Jesus Christ, the Son of God, begotten of the Father, only-begotten, that is, of the substance of the Father, God of God, Light of Light, true God of true God, begotten, not made, of one substance with the Father, through whom all things were made . . ."

The Arians were not easily put down; they remained to plague the Church, and in their missionary successes among the barbarians then rising to power they almost conquered. Not until the conversion to orthodoxy of the Franks after 496 was the ultimate victory of the Athanasian safeguard of the Trinity made sure.

THE DIVINE AND HUMAN IN CHRIST

If the apostolic witness to Christ's deity was thus assured in the trinitarian formulae, the problem remained to safeguard his authentic humanity. As it turned out, this became a knottier problem, picking up as it did all the attractive heresies from Cerinthus (c. 100) through Docetism and Gnosticism. The true humanity was frequently asserted: the witness of the Gospels was unambiguous in its picture of the Jesus who suffered, wept, hungered, and died. But whenever this human life was related to the divine essence, its earthiness and vital touch with common life was damaged in effect. Associated with this slighting of the humanity is the name of the somewhat obscure Apollinarius (—392), a vehemently orthodox anti-Arian in the earlier controversy and a friend of Athanasius. In his attempt to assert the unity of God and the humanity of Christ he avoided reference to a human *mind* in Christ; this had been replaced by the Logos. His attempt was noble, but astute theologians spotted the weakness in the formula: such a God-man could not fully redeem all of human nature, for he did not fully appropriate all of human-ness. Apollinarius was condemned at Constantinople in 381.

Within decades after that council the controversy flared again, this time from the other or Antiochian side among the Nestorians. Nestorius (—c. 451) was a Syrian monastic, reputed as a preacher and an ardent orthodoxist who would purge and exile heretics. Nestorius rejected reference to the Virgin as the *Theotokos* or God-bearer, for this implied a blending of humanity and divinity in her son. Cyril of Alexandria was quick to condem Nestorius, and in the Council of Ephesus of 431 this condemnation became formal. Nestorius was banished, but his emphasis lived on in a party and a church in Persia; it did mission work in the Far East and survives until today in certain provinces and rites.

After Nestorius the pole swung again from Antioch to Alexandria and the blunt extremism of a monk, Eutyches of Constantinople. At a synod in 448 he outlined his views and was condemned; a sequence of intrigues that need not occupy us here occupied the deliberators of the Church until the great council of Chalcedon in 451. This fourth ecumenical council was also held in Asia Minor, near Constantinople, and was again called by the Emperor to face up to Eutychianism. Almost all the bishops, over five hundred of them, were from the east. They cleared the air, repudiated the intrigues of the years preceding, and following Pope Leo's line of argument prepared the Chalcedonian Definition, a high-water mark of the ecumenical creedal period. It settled the issue of Christ's humanity and divinity in a justly famous sequence: in the name of Christ, Son, Lord, Only-begotten the Church recognized oneness, "in two natures, without confusion, without change, without division, without separation." Once again it was assumed that the apostles could rest well from their labors, that their mantles rested well on the conciliarists of the fifth century. In the defeat of Arianism, polytheism was avoided; in Apollinarianism, the humanity of Christ had been weakened but this did not triumph; nor did the opposite heresy in Eutychianism. God was one and the God-Man was one: this was the resolution of a responsive Church catholic. For the storms that were still to come the canon of Scripture, the growing canon of doctrine, and the concern of the bishops were to provide authorities and safeguards.

CONSENSUS

The ecumenical consensus, here denied and there disputed, often challenged, seldom resolved, was just that: a consensus, not an edict nor a law. But it had the prestige ascribed to that teaching which the Church regarded as truly apostolic, as in the words of Vincent of Lerins in 434: "Now in the Catholic Church itself we take the greatest care to hold that which has been believed everywhere, always and by all." With this confidence the Church was ready to face the long span of centuries in which Rome was dominant in the West; it was ready for new troubles from without and from within. As the greatest theologian of the day reminded: "The Church stands in darkness, in this time of her pilgrimage, and must lament under many miseries." But in this time of darkness the same Augustine could rejoice in the aspect of apostolicity, for through it he was near the Lord of the Church: "Christ Himself speaks through His disciples; his voice is heard through those whom he sends." Creedal orthodoxy to such fathers was not an awesome edict or an arbitrary resolution. It was a comforting fact, a guarantee of faith and life and nearness to the source and founder of the Church.

PART II: *The Span*

5

THE IDEA OF A CHRISTIAN SOCIETY

Popular fancy and historical extremism coincide in color-conscious descriptions of that long span of Christian history from the fifth to the sixteenth century. To one school, massively overextending the shadow that fell across a century, it is "The Dark Ages." To the other, nostalgically oversimplifying the twelfth century renascence and using the stereotype to describe a millennium, it is "The Golden Age" of Christian history. Protestant historians have tended to hop, skip, and jump from the glories of recent denominational history to the early years of Reformation, and then to the luster of the earliest Church. Roman Catholic historians, reminiscing about the days when the Church was assumed to be a monolith, have dilated the attention due the span. Recent convention demands that historians begin such an account as this by revising the colors: the dark ages were neither so dark, nor so aged as we were told; the golden age was neither so untarnished nor so long. Bowing to this convention as an acceptable if perfectly obvious picture of any historical period, we can set to work directly to describe several main colors of a prism that is neither dark nor golden.

97

A NEW SET OF ASSUMPTIONS

What stands out immediately in any review of these centuries is the changing set of assumptions concerning the relation of the Christian Church to the world around it. The dialogue between church and world continues, but on different terms. The code which prescribed patterns of daily life for Christians persists, but it is strengthened by the sanctions of a sacramental Church. The retreat from the world becomes a normative pattern of holiness for many more than it ever attracted in the ancient world. But the retreat is now considered to be not simple denial: it is also a tactic for approach to the world. The violent tenor of life that characterized the centuries would not allow an easy peace between the Church and its environment: there was always tension. But the tension now exists not between Christian Church and pagan world, but more between Christian Church and "Christian" state and society. This change constitutes one of the most radical revolutions in Christian institutional thinking in history.

What was new, or what became patent from the latency of early Christian apology, was the idea of a Christian society. The eschatological pull was still there: men envisioned an end to the age or to the world. But this was less imminent, the age could be more prolonged. The Church was here to stay. In the process, the Church became a "comprehensive, unifying, and reconciling social whole, which included both the sociological circle of religion itself and the politicosocial organizations." This hoary and still accurate description has come from Troeltsch:

> The interpenetration of the sacred and the secular, which was possible in the Middle Ages, cannot be explained as the result of intellectual dialectic impulses of development, but out of the actual pressure of events . . . here we have to do with the effect of the possibilities and necessities, which the actual course of affairs in the development of social life outside the Church brought into the ecclesiastical organization.[1]

We may argue with his depreciation of "intellectual dialectic impulses" and yet preserve the emphasis on the *actual pressure of events,* the *actual course of affairs*—the stuff of history-writing. What was necessary in order to produce that idea of a Christian society which Troeltsch argued was a specifically medieval creation, conceivable only in the historical conditions of that time, was a change in both institutional patterns and ideological assumptions. These occurred in the hinge period of the fourth century, to which point we have carried the story of church and society.

The edicts of Constantinian times which made the Roman Empire "Christian" (*c.* 313) were but the germ of what budded seven decades later in the Theodosian period. Theodosianism's distinctive character which made it "a significant point of departure in world history" [2] was its new religious policy. On February 27, 380, from Thessalonica, the Emperor issued it:

> We desire that all peoples who fall beneath the sway of our imperial clemency should profess the faith which we believe to have been communicated by the Apostle Peter to the Romans and maintained in its traditional form to the present day . . . And we require that those who follow this rule of faith should embrace the name of Catholic Christians, adjudging all others madmen and ordering them to be designated as heretics . . .

Sanctioned by the sword, this policy prevailed. A popular Fundamentalist tract suggests a modern Protestant reaction: "This was the WORST CALAMITY that has ever befallen the Church." [3] Rationalist history concurred; Gibbon was convinced that the genius of Rome died with Theodosius. In a way, he was right: Theodosius grasped for power beyond his reach, for past glory and future hope without being able to comprehend either. Disaster followed. But Theodosius did succeed, even as a wrecker, in achieving a positive result. He cleared the ground for that growth of a Christian society which appeared more naturally than his edict would have allowed. Out of this wreckage was to grow the constellation St. Augustine could telescope into a vision of the City of God.

We are dealing, then, with a new view of the relations of culture and Christianity. Orders of society, sacred and "secular," interpermeated each other; here was a quest for wholeness, for the organism, without denial of creative tensions. In the Apocalypse, in Tatian's rejection of legislation, in Tertullian's complaint over a Church persecuted, we saw tension without fusion, argument without synthesis, defensive apology. More is now claimed than St. Paul claimed in Romans 13 or than Justin was seeking. From apocalypse to apology to apodictic assumption: this is the movement to Augustine. The question was no longer whether society could be Christian, but rather how this was to be realized. This is the context of the development in the East (which occupies our seventh chapter) as well as in the relations of popes and emperors, prelates and princes in the West. The great rulers: Clovis, Pepin, Charlemagne, Otto I, Barbarossa; the great pontiffs: the Gregories, Innocent III, Boniface VIII—all would struggle for the strength and perhaps the supremacy of the body which they ruled. But the struggle occurred always within the context of a theocracy.

Thus when Henry IV protested after his humiliation at Canossa (1077) against Gregory VII as "no pope, but a false monk," it did not occur to him to set up a "secular" state or society. He simply tried to control the appointment and career of the next pope. On the other hand, after the papacy's "terrible day" at Anagni in 1303, when mercenaries, prompted by Philip IV of France, took Boniface VIII prisoner (the event is a symbol of pontifical weakness), the larger society was still not ready to listen to Marsiglio of Padua and other critics who came to prominence in the era of the papacy's nadir. When it did begin to listen we experience the beginning of the end of the medieval world.

Sometimes the idea of interpenetration and interpermeation was suffocating, and sectors of society took a gulp of air in the form of revolt, or sectarian withdrawal, of lyrical sensuality and even obscenity; but this was the exception and not the rule. The rule was a synthetic cultural expression: in cathedrals, in scholastic philosophy, in sculpture and hymnody. If the synthesis was later to break down in philosophical Nominalism, in reformative conciliarism, in nationalism and Renaissance esthetic paganism, it is interesting to observe that present-day attempts at synthesis on Christian terms still make their appeal to these partly mythical moments of vital fusion: neo-Thomism, Anglo-Catholicism, and neo-medievalism are evidences of this yearning.

THE HOLY ROMAN EMPIRE

In what follows we shall trace the idea of a Christian society in its medieval course along two lines. The first of these revolves around the theocratic question, the relations of popes to emperors in what has come to be called the Holy Roman Empire. The adjective "Holy" affixed to the imperial title in the time of Frederick I (1156) grew out of popular usage and old Roman reminiscence. The intention of its application in the original sense is uncertain. James Bryce in his classic work on the subject reviewed all the possibilities. Was it an extension of Roman and Constantinopolitan courtliness? Did it have religious significance in association with the prophecy of its dependence on the Pope's bestowal of the crown? Was it a defense by Barbarossa against charges of secularization? One strand of meaning does emerge with fair consistency:

> It was neither more nor less than the Visible Church, seen on its secular side, the Christian society organized as a state under a form divinely appointed, and therefore the name "Holy Roman Empire" was the needful and rightful counterpart to that of "Holy Catholic Church." [4]

It would be foolhardy to suggest a solution to this bewildering question of origins, but from Bryce's term "counterpart" we can derive a clue to the popular understanding of the imperial line: In these ages the Church was not to find its holiness by withdrawal and aloofness from the quasi-secular order. It was to express Christian holiness through its varied career of involvements. Another attempt aimed at expressing one side of the Church's holiness is monasticism. As background for both ways, as parallel to their record of "the actual pressure of events," St. Augustine's *City of God* is a creative point of departure.

AUGUSTINE

Augustine (—430) is one of those three or four figures of
Christian history that serve as a hinge between eras, and
in his greatness he belongs to all of them. Chronicles of the
ancient Church tend to culminate with the story of the
saint; medievalists begin with him. In Augustine's case, one
book out of an immense literary production serves as well
as the hinge between ages, this *City of God*. Written after
the fall of Rome under Alaric in 410 (writing seems to
have occupied Augustine from 413 to 426) as a rebuttal to
those who blamed the fall on Christian abolition of pagan
worship, it discussed contrasts between church and world.
While it turned out to be a cosmic and universal philosophy
of history, the work was put to more parochial use in succeeding centuries:

> St. Augustine's theory of the *Civitas Dei* was in germ
> that of the medieval papacy without the name of Rome.
> In Rome itself it was easy to supply the insertion and
> to conceive of a dominion still wielded from the ancient
> seat of government, as world-wide and almost as authori-
> tative as that of the Empire. The inheritance of the
> imperial traditions of Rome, left begging by the with-
> drawal of the secular monarch, fell as it were into the
> lap of the Christian bishop.[5]

This use illustrates the way in which a philosophical treatise
becomes part of "the actual pressure of events." A blend
of late Greek thought with a biblical line of history, the
book saw the revelation of God in Christ to be crucial and
central in the history of the world which began with creation and will end with a day of judgment. Instead of the
rhythms of Hellenic history, Augustine saw a linear development; along the line appear the cities of God and of man,
one created out of the divine love, the other out of desire
and love of self. Behind the two cities stand eternal kingdoms of angels and devils who act out their dramas in the
lives of men. The element which complicates the good of
creation is diverted desire, pride.

In this pride, man fell: therewith grew the earthly city. Culminating in Christ, the drama of life in relation between the cities would spin itself out over succeeding centuries until the time of judgment. It is not at all clear whether Augustine implied a neat overlapping of his picture of the City of God on the visible Christian Church, but their boundaries and avenues had much in common. Salvation, preparation for fulfillment in the heavenly city, was engendered and nurtured exclusively in the Church. But the men of the Church, as well as their "pagan" contemporaries, live out their lives still under the stigma of warping self-love. Therefore the state is necessary as a barrier against gross outbursts of evil that would disrupt human life in society. Pauline in his belief that civil powers were ordained by God, fearing chaos in temporal society, preserving a Roman feel for order, Augustine in both his realistic analysis of man and his conservative hopes for society was laying the foundations for a theocratic society in which the temporal rulers of the Church would play a bigger-than-life part in affairs of state.

How did Augustine come to this? First of all, he argued:

> The true God from Whom is all being, beauty, form and number, weight and measure; He from Whom all nature, mean and excellent, all seeds of forms, all forms of seeds, all motions both of forms and seeds, derive and have being; . . . it is in no way credible that He would leave the kingdoms of men and their bondages and freedoms loose and uncomprised in the laws of His eternal providence.[6]

This concern of God was expressed in revelation and in the life of the Church. The Church is not the transcendent Heavenly City in any full sense, but it represents that city before men. Augustine wanted secular power used against the Donatist heretics, not because the state had the right to interlope on ecclesiastical concerns but because the Church had a right to use earthly power to its ends. Obviously, in such a view the idea or function of an autonomous state is severely limited. He was looking "for a city that had foundations whose builder and maker is God."

THE THEOCRATIC DEVELOPMENT

So were the secular rulers of the succeeding centuries, but they also had to make a place for themselves under the sun. Here is the point of creative tension; here is the new kind of dialogue in medieval history. To discern it we must overleap the centuries following Augustine, the times of barbarian invasions of the Empire from north and east, the times of petty particularity and inchoate grasping for empire, and follow the characteristic Western development in the Holy Roman Empire. A turning-point toward this development came with the baptism of King Clovis (—511) in 496, fifteen years after he had become King of the Salian Franks. This conversion put him in an excellent strategic position: orthodox, he could battle the Arian barbarian; catholic, he could summon the power of Catholic bishops to his cause. No model of the Christian statesman, he was able to lay the ground for the model of the Christian state.

The development was abortive, however. In the sixth and seventh centuries, with the struggles of the Franks, the Germans, the Empire, and Islam casting such long shadows that these times more than any other deserve the description "dark," the church of the West which was to explode into glory after Charlemagne had to content itself with merely extending its life, with surviving—or, as Henri Pirenne says, with vegetating. That it succeeded in remaining intact to carry any sort of potential seems itself to be a mystery. It had a certain order in its hierarchy; it possessed great wealth in the territories of western Europe. A victim of barbarism, it was to be resurrected almost miraculously with the new stirrings of empire.

These stirrings again center in Frankish lands, particularly under Pepin III who inherited from his father, Charles Martel, a West unendangered by the Moslem (after the decisive battle of Tours in 732). Pope Zacharias agreed to Pepin's election in 751 and later papal sanction added more prestige. When he defeated the Lombards in 754 and 756 he gave their territories to the Pope and thus took on the mask of protector to Rome. Upon his death in 768 his son, Charlemagne, ascended: the hour for the renewal of "holiness," *"Romanitas,"* and the "imperium" was at hand. An empire involves land, and Charles set out during the first decades of his reign to follow the compass of conquest: to Lombardy, Bavaria, the Avars, Pannonia. With his other foot at the axis of the compass needle he consolidated his gains, bringing order to his government, reforming the social and encouraging the spiritual. If the age before him was dark, now came the dawn of the "Carolingian Renaissance," whose cultural aspects we shall have occasion to discuss in another context.

The symbolic climax of Charles' career came on Christmas Day in 800 when Pope Leo III crowned him Emperor with the titles reserved for the Roman rulers of the past. With imperial glory long removed to Byzantium, this meant that after a hiatus of three centuries the genius of imperial government breathed again in the West, though removed northward to the German, Frankish, and north Italian territories. But the new light of government was soon dimmed again; Charlemagne's successors were unable to keep it lit; by the time of the treaty of Verdun (843), which set up the outlines of the modern map of Europe, disintegration and division were evident. By the end of the ninth century Carolingian rule was eclipsed by the feudal society which found interplay with subsequent papal and imperial aspirations.

A detailed description of feudal society would divert us here from the dialogue in which the Church tried to assert her holiness *through* the state. But an aside is in place to this effect: the courtly belligerence of feudal society in which military virtues were exalted and central authority deemed inadvisable tugged at the guy ropes of the traditional Christian ethic. War was glorified; the turning of the other cheek was a sign of cowardice; capricious destruction of innocent life was the order of the day. In face of this the grey walls of the monastery attracted Christians as the only outlet for individual manly holiness. Here there need be no retreat from ethics—only retreat from the feudal milieu, the "world." Here was to develop the new resource for reform and holiness, for the Peace of God and the Truce of God among warlike men.

But the cloister called still the few. To return to pope and emperor and the more comprehensive quest for holiness: the dialogue now had to be carried on above the din of clattering swords and cluttering crowns; cities waned from significance. Wherever a man could hold land and power and fortress, he was king. Who was not king was knight or priest. The rest were at their mercy. Arab and Norman, meanwhile, besieged the imperium from without. Tensions in the search for holiness in the cloisters were torn without, where burlesque of these virtues was sung in courtly lyricism. Beyond the din, the enemy, and the lyre: the dialogue.

A new version was in the making; in the new situation the superficially cordial relations implied by the events of Christmas 800 were not to persist. In earliest Carolingian times church and "state"—we cannot invest the term with precision for the Middle Ages had no clear conception of this—are viewed best as cooperative entities. Charlemagne retained some of his power over the very Rome he was enhancing in his conquest and consolidation. In turn, he was deriving authority from the papacy and through a system of legation between the two powers. Coins of the time stamped the head of the pope on one side, the head of the emperor on the other.

Cooperation was thrown into imbalance first by the intrusions of later emperors who, though they still enjoyed papal coronation, strove to increase their supremacy over the city of Rome and the Empire. This is clear in the transition from the reforming Louis the Pious (ruled 814–840) to Lothair I (ruled 840–855), in whose time Verdun signalled the disintegration. Then followed internecine warfare; with both hands on this issue, no hand was free to attempt to control the papacy. This occasioned the opportunities for papal ascendancy toward its zenith under Innocent III. The popes were enabled to place their scepters over many lands of Italy that clustered around Rome, and were similarly enabled to bargain for and gain other more distant territories for the "patrimony of St. Peter."

In this period a skillful compiler assembled documents now known as Pseudo-Isidorean decretals (*c.* 850), which purported to show precedent for such papal activities. Nicholas I (reigned 858–867), perhaps knowing that they were for the most part forgeries of materials from ante-Nicene times down to the eighth century, used them to bring new authority to his chair. Throughout the Middle Ages these documents eluded the historical criticism which has since demolished their warrant. But even with these forgeries, the popes could not yet sound an all-clear. They were themselves too entangled with the feudal intricacies that also beset the emperor. Hierarchical offices had been dispensed through a system foredoomed to corruption in simony, the practice of permitting feudal lords to buy ecclesiastical appointments. The problem of the marriage of the clergy plagued the papacy. Church property was tied up with competing feudal claims. Both "state" and church were corrupt, evidently speeding toward doom.

Worst of all, the papacy was haunted by inner difficulties, by the harassments of factionalism, the frailties of the human nature of the popes, and the fiercely partisan hierarchical politics. A study of the papacy for almost a century until John XII (Pope after 955) seized power would find pontifical energies directed by force toward spiritual concerns, toward the salutary reforms in monasticism such as those associated with the order of Cluny (established 910). Whenever a pope's grasp exceeded his power to hold, disaster accompanied the action: John's voracity was not matched by veracity; his personally scandalous life and his political intrigues led to the slipping of his tarnished tiara. At the same moment monastic reform met happy confluence in a recovering imperial power: in the middle of the tenth century the dialogue that was smothered after Charlemagne was resumed with clarity. The symbol of this resumption was the coronation by the pope of Otto I (the Great) in 962. Otto began with an upper hand, deposing a pope, naming another, and forcing the pope to recognize the imperial right to a say in papal elections.

POPES VERSUS EMPERORS

A classic struggle between pope and emperor was in the making as honest and devout emperors like Henry II (ruled 1002–1024) and Henry III (ruled 1039–1056) persisted in reform and brought the imperial authority to its zenith. The Church was stunned for the moment by this climb; it experienced some decline while the bishops, themselves great landholders, were reduced to the status of lackeys and vassals of the king, often bringing bribes and homage even as the seculars. Monasteries were frequently placed under lordly protection. Simony had its day; investiture (the claim by secular rulers to the right to invest bishops-elect or abbots-elect with symbols of their office) was a nagging concern. The controversy between the powers came to be remembered as "the war of investiture."

Henry III, in his effort to set the papal house in order, succeeded in creating a rival for himself in Leo IX (reigned 1049–54), who not only reassumed rule over the bishops and abbots but also attempted to dominate royal powers. A popular pope, he insisted on being elected to office. He and his immediate successors pulled aside the curtain for one of the greatest of pontiffs, Hildebrand, Gregory VII (reigned 1073–85). His counterpart was Emperor Henry IV (—1106). Gregory delayed his own consecration in the hope that Henry would live up to the ideal of cooperation. But Henry conveniently forgot his part of the bargain. He expressed discontent over the existing solutions to the problem of lay investiture.

The Lenten Synod of 1075 and the Synod of Worms of 1076 represented the existing tug-of-war between the two rulers. Gregory chastened Henry and was in turn deposed by German bishops controlled by the Emperor. Turn-about was fair play: Gregory excommunicated Henry. The bishops came to their senses, seeing that their place in Christendom was dependent on their relation to Gregory. Under these pressures Henry tried to extricate himself in time from a tightening trap by a trip across the Alps in the guise of a penitent to Canossa (January 21, 1077), where Gregory, bested by this strategy, after three days absolved the Emperor. The victory of "holy" church in these intrigues was temporary. Both rulers resumed efforts at unseating each other and Gregory was to die disappointed in semi-exile, broken-hearted for his failure to complete his remarkable reforms or to absolutize churchly power. The issue of lay investiture was not resolved until the Concordat of Worms in 1122. The Emperor agreed to allow the Church to invest ecclesiastical lords, but elections were to be held before the king, who could also endow the church lords with secular powers according to his favor and purpose.

The investiture struggle was felt beyond the Empire, notably in England, which equally illustrates the difficulties of the papacy in its rise to political heights. There William I, the "Conqueror" (ruled 1066–1087) occupied himself with sweeping reforms of the church, particularly through his successful division of secular and sacred courts. This reform, of spiritual benefit to the church, implied a greater power for the king. Such a king, like Henry on the continent, would find it important to have a powerful hand in nomination of bishops and abbots if he wished to consolidate his kingdom. The situation was building up to the conflict that came with Henry I (ruled 1100–35) in his contest with Archbishop Anselm of Canterbury. Anselm was Gregorian in his stand on investitures; Henry paralleled his continental namesake in viewpoint. They came to terms in the Settlement of Bec in 1107, which in many respects prefigures the arrangements of the Concordat of Worms. But the struggle became rhythmic in England as on the continent: the limitations on the clerical courts in the Council of Clarendon (1164) show ways in which royalty did not take papal encroachments without effective counterattack.

The direct line of controversy again moves to the continent in the time of Frederick Barbarossa (ruled 1152–90). One of the great medieval kings, a man of noble character who fused Christian and military concerns into crusades, he saw himself in the line of the Caesars or of Justinian and Charlemagne. He was plagued by the two ageless hindrances to imperial claims: German particularism and papal resistance. In the face of reform and revolt under Arnold of Brescia in Italy he was forced to cooperate with the papacy, but the cooperation was temporary and somewhat reserved. To his successors was left the task of dealing with that most potent of popes, Innocent III (reigned 1198–1216), for whom the efforts of the centuries had seemed to be worth while: now the holy Church could express its holiness by informing all society. Innocent held as much political power as any pontiff before or since. He picked and chose among imperial aspirants until he cancelled the powers of each against the edge of the others. He was the virtual monarch of the West and his claims, backed by power, were recognized as far away as England, where King John encountered them. John resisted Stephen Langton (in 1207), the papal nominee to the See of Canterbury. Innocent replied to John's more drastic actions with an interdict (1208), that powerful weapon which would deprive John's subjects of spiritual participation in the life of the Church. (Innocent had used the same instrument against Philip Augustus of France in 1200.) Excommunication of John followed, and further papal artillery in the form of attempted enforcement of deposition brought John to surrender. One of the milestones of British legal development, the Magna Carta (1215), was forced from John near the end of his reign; it ratified the redress of clerical grievances of the years preceding.

What separated Innocent from most other popes was the obvious means he had to exert influence: he held power coextensive with his claims. The Fourth Lateran Council, held in his court, was attended by bishops and legates of kings; both religious and political issues could be treated in this arena of fusion *versus* tension. When Innocent died in 1216 he carried with him the memory of the highest point of earthly papal influence. Within twenty years the emperor was again supreme.

Only one aspect of the aftermath need pertain to a brief religious history: the burlesque of Innocent's power in the claims of Boniface VIII (—1303, Pope after 1294), whose appetites exceeded his reach. His fantastic secular claims were intended to obscure the fact of declining pontifical prestige. Local and national rulers were omnipotent in their spheres; when their interests merged, ecclesiastics were on the defensive. The stage was set for papal humiliation. It came when Edward I of England and Philip IV of France set out to tax the clergy, to the anger of Boniface. He demanded submission; they refused. His bull *Clericis Laicos* (1296) prohibited the payment of taxes by the clergy. By the time of the jubilee year 1300 Boniface only appeared to be head of the Christian world in the West. Almost all props had been pulled out from under him.

The overgrasp, now pathetic in character, is illustrated in the movement from Innocent to Boniface. Note the change in metaphor. Innocent spoke of two lights, the moon and the sun. Just as God appointed the sun to rule the day and the moon the night,

> He appointed two great dignitaries [for the firmament of the universal Church]; the greater to bear rule over souls (these being, as it were, days,) the lesser to bear rule over bodies (these being, as it were, nights). These dignities are the pontifical authority and the royal power. Furthermore, the moon derives her light from the sun and is in truth inferior to the sun . . . in the same way the royal power derives its dignity from the pontifical authority . . .

In Boniface's bull of 1302 papal claims were further exaggerated:

> We learn from the words of the Gospel [Luke 22:38] that in this Church and in her power are two swords, the spiritual and the temporal . . . Both are in the power of the Church . . . But the latter is to be used for the Church, the former by her; the former by the priest, the latter by kings and captains but at the will and by the permission of the priest. The one sword, then, should be under the other, and temporal authority subject to spiritual.

Words so strong as this. needed a stronger sword than Boniface could carry. *Unam Sanctam* met resistance by Philip, ending in Boniface's disgraceful arrest and, a month later, death. Often named with Gregory VII and Innocent

III, he was less gifted than they at calculating the rise of national powers—he reached too far and fell farther. In his place followed confusion, pope *versus* anti-pope *versus* secular *versus* councils, but never again the power the papacy had known in the days of Innocent III. Schism was inevitable; the popes went into "captivity" and the bilateral attempts at institutional achievement of a Christian society could not possibly be resumed.

MEDIEVAL MONASTICISM

Our narrative to this point has suggested ways in which the confluence of "the actual pressures of events" with developing ideological claims tempted the papacy toward an attempt to bring the Church's holiness to bear on the ordering of society, and how inevitably this involved the Church in less than holy politicking and intrigue. The progress of the papacy not only did not exhaust the possibilities of assertions of the Church's holiness: they prompted attention to be drawn to an alternative less easily soiled by secular contact. We speak of monasticism, which played a contrapuntal theme to the papacy in the quest of holiness. For purposes of clarity a certain chronological backtracking will be necessary, beginning with a recall of ascetic impulses among early Christians, the rigorous retreat of Egyptian anchorites and coenobites, and the arc described by the spread of monasteries around the Mediterranean and into the west of Europe. Medieval monasticism, to the relaxed standards of contemporary luxury still often verging on the inhuman, was in the main a more moderate development than its predecessor had been. Its retreat was strategic: to provide resource for winning the world. Its withdrawal was more limited; its manifestations were many-faceted and manifold.

It is as difficult to approach the fellowship of the poor, chaste, and obedient of the Middle Ages as it is to come freshly to the papacy of the same period. The institution has been overpraised as the normative path to holiness, the standard against which other vocations must be measured.

The strategic value of monks as the papal storm troops has been overstressed, and their cultural significance as bearers of civilization and producers of art has an overlay of unrealistic and romantic glow. The alternative extreme has had an equal number of spokesmen. This is typical:

> There is, perhaps, no phase in the moral history of mankind of a deeper or more painful interest than this ascetic movement. . . . A hideous, sordid and emaciated maniac, without knowledge, without patriotism, without natural affection, passing his life in a routine of useless and atrocious self-torture, and quailing before the ghastly phantoms of his delirious brain, had become the ideal of the nations which had known the writings of Plato and Cicero and the lives of Socrates and Cato.[7]

Not surprisingly, realism will find its path somewhere between romanticism and rejection. It is usually fruitful to pursue the meaning of an institution in the intent of its professors. Typical of this is the description of the monastic ideal by Peter Damiani (—1072), a Benedictine.

> How is holiness to find expression? "We have renounced the world [and] have constituted God as our property and consequently we have become His property . . ." Whoever, therefore, as a monk hastens to attain the height of perfection, let him confine himself within the walls of his cloister, let him love spiritual quiet, let him have a horror of running about in the world, as he would of immersing himself in a pool of blood. For the world is more and more every day polluted by the contamination of so many crimes that any holy mind is corrupted by the mere consideration of it . . . And so there is nothing but the love of God and the mortification of yourselves . . . "Always bearing the dying of Jesus in our body." [8]

One may disagree with this picture of the unholiness of the world and, more particularly, with this pattern of reaction, but it is helpful to begin by understanding it. This summary will distinguish first Celtic and Benedictine responses; then the great Cluniac monastic reform; third, new orders such as the Cistercian and Carthusian; finally, new departures among Dominicans and Franciscans.

The term Celtic brings us to the earliest point of the medieval narrative, for it refers to the British church up to the time of the Augustinian mission from Rome in 596–597. The most familiar feature of this church is the gray-walled on green-isled monastic austerity; for the monks were themselves the chroniclers of this civilization. Holding sway until at least 600, this rule borrowed from the more rigorous East. Poverty was the broadest path to holiness; one must bar the door of reminiscence and of contact with the world. In the Celtic communities of the fellowship of monastics, communally observing the rule, the counsels of perfection were to be pursued most effectively. The most familiar figure of the movement is, of course, St. Patrick in Ireland, a symbol of the Celtic emphasis on education, mission, and the preservation of learning. Severity characterized the cloistered life. Prayer, fasting, reading, and work made up the rule. The monk "must go to bed so tired that he will fall asleep on the way, and he must rise before he has had as much sleep as he wants." In the wild landscapes of the sea-surrounded northland physical labor was a necessity not only for strength of spirit but also for survival.

Destined for longer, broader influence was the Benedictine Order, founded by St. Benedict (—550) of Nursia, who took his encaved community from Subiaco to Monte Cassino, the Order's central house. When Lombards devastated Monte Cassino some spiritual sons of this father of the monasticism of the West brought its patterns and his rule to Rome. Through Gregory I it received papal authority and through Augustine of Canterbury it spread to Britain, where it clashed with more severe rules. The keynote of Benedict's system was not reproduction of the Egyptian pattern but a new ideal of service in holiness to God. The abbot was a spiritual father, not the tyrant he seemed to become in Celtic rules. When a house accepted a monk, his peregrinations were to end: he had to spend his life there in the routines of that house, in peasantlike simplicity and saintly piety. The canonical hours marked his day; mass highlighted the Sundays and holidays. The houses became schools for literacy, but were hardly successful as centers for preparation for vocation in the world. Gradually the Benedictine way prevailed over the less attractive Columban rule with which it competed, and in its maturing stages produced many of the great missionaries to the northland.

Monasticism was to have been the ideal for the few and, through a sort of osmosis or capillary action as well as by means of intercessory prayer, a boon to the many. But in its one-sided stress it was destined to decay and was a bloated target for abuse. Reform was often imposed by the pressures of "secular" reaction, but this was less effective than the new starts it received from occasional inner impulses. The most famous of these in the Middle Ages was the Clunic reform. Against the background of cloistered immorality, clerical intrigue, overinvolvement of the Church in political affairs, and the nagging aspects of the feudal tug, one cell of new life spread throughout the Christian organism.

Cluny, the name of a spot in Burgundy, otherwise obscure, was to become a symbol of much that was good and true and pure in the middle Middle Ages. A sign of reform, of restatement of intention and reintention, its ferment came at the moment when Europe and Christendom needed it most. As usual, there were several creative men who brought about the new situation in monasticism. First of all, William of Aquitaine, "the pious," who was persuaded beyond his reluctance to release his dogs from a hunting lodge. The persuader was Berno of Baume, the year 910. The lodge lay on a pilgrim route to the Holy City, and was so located that it was relatively safe from the plunderous men of the north. One innovation sparked the movement: the monks were permitted to elect their own abbot; no one could interfere with this process. Secondly, the protection of the pope rather than of the local bishop introduced a revised concept of authority. After Berno came one greater, St. Odo (—942), who has rightfully received greater acclaim for the strengthened rule. The Benedictine rule was his guide, depth in devotion his goal and in no small measure his attainment. With the revival of worship there was a relaxing of demands for physical labor.

Soon the ideas of Cluny made their way in other nearby communities. Odo trekked to Fleury on the Loire where the bones of Benedict of Aniane, a Benedictine organizer, lay neglected in the midst of monastic dishevelment. The Bishop feared that threatened monks at Fleury would pounce upon a reputed reformer: they pounced, but with embrace, not with weapons. A new day was appearing in Benedictinism. This newness was sealed with the efforts of Odilo (—1048), the fifth Abbot of Cluny, who lifted the intellectual standards of the movement; as for the central house, out of which the rule was spreading to others, "from wood it became marble," according to Odilo.

The abbots, backed by popular sanction and protected by their declination of high hierarchical office, inspired the seculars and were moving forces behind the attempt at raising clerical standards of morality and celibacy as well as halting abuse in ecclesiastical office. They found a willing instrument in the most noted Cluniac of them all, Gregory VII. The influence spread to England, where St. Dunstan (—988) of Canterbury reinforced the Benedictine rule and reintroduced order into British monachism. Awed islanders spread his name: he was counsellor to statesman, artist, craftsman, musician, intellectual leader. On the continent and in England the reformatory honing of these monks sharpened the edge of the Church's contact with the state; in its quest for holiness it enriched the dialogue of church with world, of pope with emperor. If it needs an epitaph or a monument, let it be "The Peace of God" or "The Truce of God," interruptions imposed by Christian men on a warring and violent age (c. 1000).

A century after Cluny's prime, new movements rose, the Carthusian Order after 1084 and the Cistercian after 1098. They came to maturity in the time of renascence in the twelfth century, a time of revitalization in which they played no small part. At the monastery of the Grande Chartreuse in the Dauphine Alps a spirit reminiscent of Egyptian traditions stressed meditation and contemplation—the solitary life still associated with Carthusianism. The pilgrimage to holiness through withdrawal detracted from any possibility of drama in the Order's history, but through austerity and saintliness, through the example of individuals like the

English St. Hugh of Lincoln, it infiltrated its age with new ideas of spiritual aspiration.

Larger, more prominent was the Cistercian Order, mothered at Citeaux by Benedictine Robert of Molesme. If Cluny chose the houses by the side of the road, Cistercians sought the inaccessible locations. They would be friends to men not through political involvement and ecclesiastical reform but through intercession and love shown in worship. In undyed fabrics and barest halls and cells Stephen Harding of England and Bernard of Clairvaux found richness in devotion to the wounds of Christ. Their lay brothers recited simplified prayers; they tended the sheep and built up the agricultural arts in each community. Built-in safeguards prevented the gradual relaxation of the rule; the weakness of most reform movements thus disappeared. With the voice of prophecy its sharp tongue judged Europe, with its devotion to grace it wooed the church beyond its borders.

Early in the thirteenth century two parallel but differing orders grew to climax medieval monasticism; Dominicans and Franciscans competed for attention in ways hardly typical of monks before them. In place of withdrawal, here was reinvolvement, concern for the lives of the common people in their common vocations, the cost of discipleship spelled out in sacrifice. At the head of the first was Dominic de Guzman (—1221) of Spain, who cut his theological teeth against the Albigensian heresy which plagued the Church catholic at the time. Unlike many misguided persecutors of the heretics, his tactic was an earnest attempt at reclaiming the errorists. Out of these concerns he developed an Order which has come to be known for its intellectual and homiletical interests; followers are known after their saint as Dominicans or, popularly, as friars.

Dominicans saw to it that each friary became an educational center, that all teaching conformed to the rule of Rome, that all friars were willing to serve as propagandists for papal projects, most notably the Crusades. We shall see evidence of their intellectual stature in a later review of scholasticism and that towering friar, Thomas Aquinas. The Franciscans (called "gray" in distinction from Dominican "black") organized under the gentler tutelage of Francis of Assisi, perhaps the most haloed man of his age, still cherished in Christian memory. Here holiness found supreme expression in group poverty and simplicity, frantically followed by the "Spirituals" and more moderately practiced by the "Conventuals." Harassed from the first by inner controversies about the rigor implied in the rule and by external issues with the Dominicans, gray friardom made its way in medieval recognition for its direct and popular preaching and its zeal for missions. As Dominicans produced Albertus Magnus and Thomas Aquinas, Franciscans had their Occam, Bonaventure, and Duns Scotus. On the continent both orders were the saviors of a threatened Church and the right arm of papal power. In England, where heresy was minimal and antipapal sentiment late, the friars had more opportunity for positive work in the picture of poverty and the program of preaching. They stamped the Middle Ages with the last new seal of monastic reform until their own freshness also faded and a different kind of Reform became necessary.

PERSISTENT HOLINESS

Dialogues of popes and emperors, bishops and lords, were inevitably blurred by men's frailty; they were marked by the stammer of human faithlessness and lack of ability. Monastic orders after their ferment, crystallized and hardened into an unlovely edge (as in Dominicanism) or a fragmenting inclination (as in Franciscanism). None of these events, ideas, or movements seemed to embody the pure intent of the holy founder of the Church; each has invited and deserved historical criticism along with the other events and institutions of its day. But the lisp of the dialogue and the limp of the friar were human witness of human intent to follow the divine will. Always over the shoulder of the falterer came the kind of reminder kept alive in his own day by Francis himself, in a cry to God:

Hallowed be thy name: let the knowledge of thee become apparent to us, so that we may know how plentiful are thy blessings, how long thy promises, how lofty thy majesty, how profound thy judgments.[9]

What the historians and critics of the radical Reformation and the Enlightenment forgot was that the Church in every age is measured by its distance from the blessing and the promise, its neglect of the majesty and the judgment. Seen in this perspective, the unholiness of the Dark and Middle Ages suggests its own kind of exception, its own mark of achievement. The ideal remained.

6

THE DIMENSIONS OF CATHOLICITY

The idea of a Christian society, which was unveiled against the background of political tension and monastic participation, was not exhausted in these embodiments. The idea that the Christian faith could pervade social life meets simple extension in the idea that cultural life also can fall within the orbit of religious information. This quest for wholeness, this all-embracing intent, is one measure of the Church's catholicity. Few ages of Christian history provide better illustrations of its realization than do medieval times, when Western life was being determined.

Western life—hardly realizing it, we have come into the millennium in which the *theatron* of tension and fusion between church and world has been moved. Before *The City of God* the Church catholic circled the Mediterranean with the impressive achievement of early Christian missions. From Jerusalem and Antioch to Ephesus and Rome, to North Africa and Spain it was moving. But after the fifth century new names and places are prominent. Now it is Canossa and Chartreuse and Cluny; Franks, Germans, and Celts occupy the stage where once Jew and Damascene and Carthaginian had played. This change is an alert that we must heed, to follow the other dimension of catholicity, the horizontal expansion of the Church into its new environment.

THE NEW SETTING

As radical as the shift of assumptions about church and society was this medieval shift of milieu. For most of the long centuries of its history, the Christian Church has been associated chiefly with Western Europe. In its earliest life, St. Paul had been concerned that neither of the parties which constituted it would dominate: he urged equality in a life where there would be "neither Jew nor Greek" in Christ. When the faith survived these earliest decades it would still have seemed logical that either Jew—recalling the womb of the faith—or Greek—picturing its prospect —would prevail. Ironically, "neither Jew nor Greek" meant something else in the actual pressure of events.

Christianity was born at a time when the Jewish national destiny had declined and was disappearing. The mold, therefore, in which Christianity had been cast was largely Greek. The Hellenic mind which sometimes reacted against Christians' offensive witness to a "Word made flesh" found ways of responding and recasting it, making it congenial. Much of this congeniality of outlook which we have come to recognize in Clement of Alexandria and Origen was to live on in the Eastern church, an account of whose fate still lies ahead. But the dramatic development did not move east with the emperor in the fourth century. The historian who concentrates on the West is not necessarily provincial, not necessarily a captive of the near at the expense of the remote, as later portions of this book will have reason to make clear. From the fifth to the nineteenth century western Europe did dominate, and to this day the continent and the British Isles must be reckoned with first in any accounting of Christian significances.

When he was reviewing the elements that shaped Europe, Paul Valéry in *Homo Europaeus* recounted the successive emphases of Rome, Christianity, and Greece:

Then came Christianity. You know how it spread, little by little, through the whole extent of the Roman conquest. If we except the New World, which was not so much Christianized as peopled by Christians; if we except Russia, the larger part of which was ignorant both of Roman law and the empire of Caesar, we perceive that the bounds of the Christian church coincide almost exactly, even today, with the former limits of imperial authority. These two conquests, although so different in their nature, bear a sort of resemblance to each other, and this resemblance is important. The policy of the Romans, which became more ingenious and more supple as the central authority declined in power, that is to say, as the Empire grew in extent and heterogeneity, was responsible for a remarkable innovation in the system of the domination of peoples by one people.[1]

What Valéry was implying was the catholicity of Christianity in its Western development. Just as Rome conferred citizenship broadly and almost universally, so the Church by baptism conferred the new dignity of Christian on people; it assumed the forms of the Empire, borrowing from Rome, settling its capital there (not at Jerusalem), adopting Latin, shaping Europe.

THE MISSION IN THE WEST

The direct way to the heart of a story is usually the best. The direct way to the story of the shaping of Europe, the conquest of the northland for Roman Christianity, is to follow its mission in the tasks of conversion, occupation, and conquest. We are ready for the story of the Christian mission in one of its two millennia. If we take the long view of this mission we can see it assuming certain coherent forms. At the beginning, after the Empire had become nominally Christian—not long after Theodosius—it was beset, as was its new faith, by barbarian invasions which led to its decline and fall. The Church and the Roman ideal showed their resilience in the gradual recovery and extension of their joint province toward the north: here occurred the Christianization of the Franks, the English, and the Germans. Later the mission was identified with imperial and specifically Carolingian fortunes, and finally, beclouded by bad motives and sloganized Christian idealism, it made its way with sword toward the east in the attempt to cover lost ground in the Crusades.

Begin with the barbarians then, with the northmen who rolled back the day, obscuring the old empire and shadowing the "dark ages." The story of their invasions is part of church history because they represented both the great threat to the faith and, later, the great opportunity of the times. Early in the fifth century the sores of old Rome festered, but the civilization the city had fostered still held allure, its treasures still attracted. Men of the north and east saw in its decline fair chance for their own enrichment. From the east were to come Tartar and Scythian; from Britain, Pict and Scot; from the borders of the Black Sea, the East Goths and West Goths; from the north, Danes and Vandals, Angles and Lombards, Jutes and Burgundians. Their own religions were often but crude combinations of polytheism, reverence of ancestor, and reverence for nature.

Among them were the Teutons, an Indo-European or Aryan people of wandering bent, craggy face, and hardy character, who for all their crudeness had developed a quasi-democratic government. More feared than they in the south were the Goths, the first invaders of the Empire. Why did they come? If we let the cinema and the stereotype have their way, the one motive was rape and "vandalism"; but the facts are more complicated. The internecine warfare of poorly organized parties (to be pictured much like some of the American Indian tribes in their boundaryless warriordom) on occasion forced one or the other to make its way into the Empire. On other occasions there was the matter of mere survival. Depending upon grazing and pasturage, they were constantly forced to seek new lands when the old produced less. Not least, in the storied riches of the southland and in the wealth of empire they dreamed of better life in better climate.

The West Goths had crossed the Danube by the end of the fourth century, partly motivated by the invitation of Emperor Valens. Theodosius and some of his successors tended to favor this people. But when the Empire was divided, Alaric, one of these Visigoths, captured Rome (410). Many monuments of the Roman Christian past were destroyed in the sack of the city which followed, and an honored civilization was on the verge of crumbling. Forty-five years later Vandals overran Rome and pushed on to the outposts of Roman civilization in North Africa. Then came the Burgundians and the feared Huns, a Mongoloid people who seemed to fill the enduring popular image attached to them, an image of lust for power and plunder. Attila, "the scourge of God," led these wild warriors; his defeat by Aetius at Chalons in 451 marked the high-water point of raw barbarianism. Clovis, the converted Frankish King, symbolizes the new look among the conquerors. Old look or new, old Rome had fallen; the critics are correct: Christianity had contributed to the fall as it displaced religions of imperial loyalty, as it encouraged asceticism and detracted from military ideals.

Not the fall of Rome but the heterodoxy of the rising barbarian Christendom was the most profoundly disturbing feature of the fifth-century religious scene in the West. Arianism, repudiated at and after Nicaea in 325, was the court religion at the time Vandals and Goths were becoming part of the Empire and as they conquered imperial cities. Whatever the barbarians undertook they did passionately: so they clung passionately to the Arian creed and persecuted adherents of the theologically triumphant catholic faith. In the East this theological defeat in the councils had been decisive; Arianism's survival for another half-century in the West was almost purely a military matter. The creed was common among the Franks, masters by the early sixth century; among the Ostrogoths in Italy, the Spanish Visigoths, the Burgundians, and most of the North African Vandals. Not until the overrun and latent orthodoxy of loyal catholics had an opportunity to be renewed and the fanatic conquerer himself been won to orthodoxy was the threat cut off. In this context Clovis' acceptance of the Nicene formula can hardly be over-estimated. As Arianism fell under military fortunes of a different cast, Europe began to reclaim a cultural unity with

Rome at its symbolic and often, both politically and religiously, its real center.

As Arianism plagued in the fifth and part of the sixth century, so Islam was a limiting factor in the catholic intentions of the seventh. This new world religion which swept westward across North Africa, decisively stamping out the Christian heritage of much of the West, indirectly assisted the Christian mission elsewhere. Its terror threw isolated Christian groups into common need and common thirst for the unifying word of the mission. Concurrently, the growing strength of the papacy served the expansion of the Church well: it provided an impulse and a center.

THE CONVERSION OF THE NORTH

The first of the great missionary popes serves us well to introduce the second phase of Christian expansion, beyond barbarism to the civility of the counterthrust, the conversion of the north. We speak of Gregory I (Pope 590–604), deservedly denominated "the Great." Like Augustine, he is a hinge-figure between ages; honored in Christian memory with Jerome, Ambrose, and Augustine as one of the "doctors of the Church," he molded the medieval papacy in its relations to the East, in its noble self-conception, in its administrative and liturgical life, and—most important here —in its missionary goals. A noble, he rejected a life of ease for the monasteries, and after his accession to the papacy distinguished himself first of all as umpire between victors and victims, between warring parties. A child of the city of Rome wasted by the Goths, he relished the monuments and memories of a greater age and incorporated much of its spirit in his ecclesiastical work.

We remember him here as the father of missions in their prime medieval sense: converting the uncivilized. His highest achievement was the work in England, where his emissaries succeeded in bringing the Christianity of the island safely into the Roman orbit. It is impossible to determine how the one who characterized himself as "servant of the servants of God" first was attracted to England. Bede preserves a twist in a pun: Gregory saw Saxons for sale in a slave market and punned with purpose: *"Non Angli, sed angeli."* So be it. At any rate he selected from one of his monasteries another Augustine (—604) and sent him off, in 596. With a company of forty and a bit of timidity in his heart, Augustine landed in Kent with credentials and encouragement of Gregory in his possession. A year later Gregory could report to another churchman:

> Whilst the people of the English, placed in a corner of the world, still remained without faith, worshipping stocks and stones, I resolved . . . that I ought with God's assistance to send to this people a monk from my monastery to preach . . . He and they who were sent with him are radiant with such great miracles amongst this people, that they seem to reproduce the powers of the apostles in the signs that they display (LETTER TO EULOGIUS OF ALEXANDRIA, 598).

Christianity had not fared very well in that corner of the world before this time. Roman troops remained in Britain for a century after the Empire had become officially Christian, but only in Wales did the faith seem able to develop loyalties. When the Christian invasion came, it confronted an heroic but ill-defined and uncreative Nordic religion.

The invasion took the form of a pincers. From the north came Aidan and Columba, from the south came Augustine as emissary of Rome. From the west, in Wales (the Christian "outpost"), there had been less initiative. St. Patrick had converted Ireland (432–61); from there Columba undertook missions to Scotland. Aidan moved from Scotland to Northumbria—but this more poised part of the pincers was actually later, almost forty years after Augustine's arrival. The Irish expression was monastic and somewhat "isolationistic"; it did not contribute much to the interpenetration of the realms of church and society. Saintliness, art in the illumination of manuscripts, a revival of learning, all these were there. But the catholic religion with its Roman "feel" awaited the Gregorian labors.

Kent seemed to be ready for Augustine; the wife of King Ethelbert was already Christian and a bit of wifely persuasion opened the kingdom to the Romans. It was there that Augustine established what remains the center of Anglican Christianity, the See of Canterbury. Beyond Kent the edge of the mission was blunted by persisting paganism and competing churchly claims. Northumbria and Mercia were attracted somewhat later; Aidan's monks from Iona by this time were achieving as much as were the Canterburians. But the successes of both brought new clashes between northern and southern expressions. The more or less imposed settlement at Whitby in 664 threw the weight to Rome, but left with it the discontent that was long to haunt British Christianity. But the decision was a boon to political Britons who had in the Roman church a model government they needed to rise from tribal chaos. To achieve the development of both England was blessed with the great Theodore of Tarsus, Archbishop from 669 to 690. The dark ages of cultural life were still ahead, but under Theodore British Christianity began to develop a taste for order and administration which would help it weather many a later political crisis.

Christian missions to the north were not a one-way street; the islands did not receive without giving. They were later to serve as the impulse for conversion of the north of the continent. By this time missionaries had learned much that was new: like Martin of Tours (Bishop from 375–397), who shaped the millennium's missionary tradition in this sense, they now knew that the future lay not simply with urban centers but with the Christianization of the rural folk of the countrysides. With Gregory they came to recognize the value of monasticism as an organizing and energizing center of advance. With the Celts they developed a seemingly paradoxical ability to be withdrawn in monasteries, only to foray forth as *peregrini* to extend the Christian borders: this was the stamp of Patrick and Columba and Aidan, of the men of Iona and Lindisfarne. With this equipment, the religion of the south was prepared to undertake the conversion of the north from the north.

Two names may symbolize the work in the lowlands and the north of "Germany": Willibrord and Boniface. Willibrord (—739) had been trained by monks and became a priest in Ireland, whence he invaded Frisia in 690. He combined his obsession for preaching to the heathen with the good sense to go to Rome to be endowed with sanctions for his mission. Utrecht became his episcopal center, and the famed Echternach the monastic community from which later missions would emerge. He was handicapped at first by Frisian mistrust of his credentials from Pepin; his later successes had to await certain political settlements. Biding his time, he worked among the Danes, also with little immediate success. Constantly hampered by Frisian military endeavor and by the antagonism of Duke Radbod, Willibrord saw time beginning to run out on him. Doggedly refusing to give up, he looked to the future and began to train monks to extend his work.

These translated hopes for Germany's future were not misplaced, for among his proteges was one Winfrith or Boniface (—754), who is remembered as "the apostle of Germany." The key to his success was the wholehearted papal support that he was able to summon. Like Willibrord, he was caught in the frustrating net of Frisian and Frankish politics; this prompted him to spend some time in England and in Rome where he was given the broad commission to convert anyone anywhere. After Radbod died he was free to advance his chosen work, pushing beyond the established borders of Christendom into the Teutonic wilds. With a new sense of direction he cut himself off from Willibrord's scene of work and went to win the petty rulers and the people of Thuringia and Hessia. In Boniface there is fusion of many influences: he united the heritages of Celtic and Northumbrian with Roman British Christianity; he joined barbarian and semi-Christian in new churches; he Christianized the Germans and lifted the low estate of the Frankish church. He combined intellectual acumen with a dramatic flair: in the historical lore of many a schoolboy is the account of Boniface's bravado in chopping down the great oak dedicated to the god Woden. With the wood he built a chapel. Like most of his colleagues, he left a monastery (at Fulda) as a monument, and died a martyr's death in 754.

LATER WORK IN THE NORTH

The first phases of medieval missions to the northwest began with Martin of Tours in the fourth century's late years and ended with the death of Boniface in the middle of the eighth. The next phase to follow the barbarian invasion and consequent Christian counterthrust differed in two respects: only in Scandinavia did it continue to encounter peoples who had no prior contact with the faith, and the Empire now was unified under the Carolingians and missions were connected with that act of unification. We need devote here but little attention to the winning of the extreme north. The sweep of Sweden was not complete until the twelfth century; Norway's fruition came in the eleventh. But with Ansgar (—865), the "apostle of the north," the work in Denmark was consolidated. Coming from Flanders, his heart was in the northland; when he approached the Danes he found that their King was already converted. He built the first Christian church in Sweden, returned to convert the king of Jutland—but all to but partial avail. The Scandinavians resented his Carolingian ties (a sign of the new age) and were of no mind to be converted in masses. The work was premature and the consolidated gains eventually disappeared in a relapse to paganism.

When mass conversions did come, a millennium after the death of Christ, they followed a consistent pattern: people adopted the ways of kings. Often, as in Norway, the conversion of the king was patently a strategy on his part to subject lesser nobles. His royal power and political methods became a handicap to the spread of true Christianity. Denmark was, as may be expected, the first, being contiguous to previously Christianized lands and retaining some traces of Ansgar's work. Under King Canute this process of Christianization bore a markedly English color, as he held power in both realms and there was considerable communication between the two. After several abortive royal attempts, Norway followed under Olaf Tryggvessön (—1000) and St. Olaf Haraldsson (—1030). Olaf also drew upon

English custom and initiative; the nobles resisted his regularization of laws and severe methods and there was temporary setback for the faith. Sweden trailed both; Iceland, Greenland, and the islands off Scotland were Christianized in the path of later conquest.

To the east conversion also reflected the coextension of Christendom and expanding Europe. Under Stephen (—1038) the Magyars were forced to accept the faith, not without resistance and reaction. Before this Poland had its bishopric at Posen (968) and under Boleslaw Chrobry (—1025) knew significant Christian expansion. German impulse moved Bohemia under Wenceslas (—929), and later under Boleslaw II, who founded monasteries and built churches throughout his lands.

The massive and pressured realmwide conversion of the ninth and tenth centuries differs so markedly from the methods of Augustine, Patrick, and Willibrord that one is tempted to identify it simply with national aspirations on the frontiers of Europe. But the less dramatic yet far-reaching missionary activity associated with imperial fortunes under Carolingian auspices was similar. We saw a foretaste of this in the reluctance of Germanic peoples to accept Boniface because of imperial sanctions. The technique was most clear in the record of Charlemagne himself who, though he left a legacy of strengthened catholicism, related missionary activity to conquest. Take Saxony: from 772 to 776 he raided Saxon lands and consolidated his own strength to their borders. Smashing pagan shrines, he built fortresses, and kidnapped the Saxon youth to make them missionaries. Only the softening character of the monastics who followed his storm troops removed some of the sting from this forced propagation.

THE CRUSADES

This introduction of the element of force on a wide scale characterizes another stage in the medieval missionary development. In this case the spread of Christianity was a secondary feature and often a by-product of the original intent: to crusade against the violation of holy places in the east of the Mediterranean. In the course of this book we shall have few occasions to deal with a movement which occurred under the Christian aegis whose motives and goals were so confused, complex, and contradictory as were those associated with the crusades. They can be seen as examples of high idealism, misguided fervor, military pragmatism, mass hysteria, or simple plunder. They were all of this, yet never simply any of this. The inheritance of tensions between Christianity and Islam were perhaps destined to erupt one day in this fashion. Coexistence of two half-worlds, one under the cross and one under the crescent, was a permanent source of frustration to the champions of each and to the universal claims of each. As systems of communication and transportation grew, East and West drew closer together in every respect except ideology. Interests would clash between Mohammedan raiders and Italian traders. The advance of the Seljuk Turks in the eleventh century brought conditions to their worst stage, for they closed the Holy Land, long in Arab hands, to Christian pilgrims. When Pope Urban II at the Council of Clermont in 1095 called for a crusade, Europe was prepared.

This preparation was in part a product of the papacy. "The attempt would hardly have succeeded had not the church been fired with a flaming zeal to Christianize the very fabric of society and to accomplish this end first of all by emancipating and purifying herself." [2] This was the process described in the last chapter, as the Church asserted its holiness both in extrication from the secular order and in monastic purification. Each attempt had heightened the power and prestige of the papacy and had unified Europe. Discontents in the West left people seeking a cause; their energies pointed to a crusade. Nobles were trained to fight; they looked for new worlds to conquer. Religion was the fuse or the catalyst. The powder was the popular faith in the power of pilgrimage, the orientation of otherworldliness. "God wills it!" was the logical response to Urban II as Europe marched off to wars.

It is not necessary to detail here the path past Constantinople to Jerusalem, the short-lived success after 1099 of the First Crusade and its capture of Jerusalem, the political bungling which followed in later less glorious crusades. By the fourth major effort plunder had become the motif, disgrace the outcome. Yet out of this shoddiness, out of this long diminuendo some positive changes enhanced the Christian mission. Some were external: the interchange of ideas among peoples, the promotion of acquaintance among nationalities, heightened intellectual response and scientific interests in the meeting of West and East. Internal and more direct was the enhancement of Christian witness as it had been fostered by the *esprit* of the earlier crusades. Men had gathered around banners displaying the cross. They became conscious of their separation from each other and conscious of the gulf between Christian and non- or semi-Christian. Second, there emerged monastic orders of a military cast which provided "troops for the Lord"— Templars, Hospitallers, Teutonic Knights. These were the guardians of pilgrims, builders of hospitals, architects of new outposts for the propagation of the faith. Finally, churches of East and West came into more direct contact after their nearly fatal schism.

But the most important lesson of the crusades was this: a Patrick or a Martin, a Boniface or an Ansgar could accomplish more for the Christian mission as such than could conquest by the sword. As a means of expansion the Church could well have learned to drop the crusading ideal. Such learning, however, comes hard, and this form of misguided zeal was to appear again and again. The record from the fourth to the early twelfth century suggests a progressive involvement of sword with cross, and with it a blurring of Christian perspective as the faith enlarged the borders of its adherence.

ANOTHER DIMENSION OF CATHOLICITY

If we leave this story of the attempt at universalizing the Christian faith somewhere in the eleventh and twelfth centuries we shall have done with but one of the dimensions of the Church's catholicity. The other, which we have marked as a quest for wholeness, an all-embracing intent, finds depth at precisely this period in education, in the universities, in cathedrals, in literature. The "dark" ages had passed and Europe was ready for the new dawn, the Christian share in cultural life and the making of a new world.

The recall of institutions and achievements cited in the previous paragraph prompts any reviewer of the Middle Ages to puzzle over how their triumphs could ever have been obscured by an "enlightened" age. For if one is to list the cultural climaxes of the West he need not blush to include authentic medieval creations: the Gothic cathedrals, *The Divine Comedy,* Gregorian chant. Institutionally, the university and parliament and canon law belong with the crowning glories of the west of Europe. And in each there is a suggestion of an interpermeation of sacred and secular with a fusing spirit, in each there is a hint of the grasp within Christianity that, in its wholeness, warrants the term "catholic."

THE UNIVERSITY

Perhaps the university will serve best to suggest the medieval ideal at its height, for in it we have a heritage, not from the Graeco-Roman world, but from the twelfth and thirteenth centuries at Salerno and Bologna and Paris. The name implied a gathering of teachers and students who shared, intellectually, a common life. Stirrings in the recovery of education begin with the court of Charlemagne and scholars like Alcuin who served that court from 781 to 796. Alcuin stood in the northern tradition of the Irish monastics and the Venerable Bede (—735), a bright moment from the dark ages. From the south Charlemagne drew on Paul the Deacon and Peter of Pisa. In the eleventh century cathedral schools nourished the traditions of monasticism and the courts. Gradually, at no one's behest and to no one's blueprint, there grew "universities," first at Salerno and more significantly at Bologna where Roman law was restudied, or in the north at Paris in the cathedral schools of Notre-Dame. Paris' prominence was due to its concentration on the queen of medieval sciences, theology: for this it became the ideal of the universities. From this line came Cambridge and Oxford. Including the ephemeral institutions (even in this we moderns copy that age), over eighty universities were founded in the Middle Ages.

Rowdy and reckless young men, immature scholars, fledgling masters joined the more serious theologues and venerated scribes of the disciplines of medicine or law; informally they clustered as colleges. "Campuses" as such would not have been known, but the embryos of modern curricula were there. And, yes, professors (only rarely of the caliber of Abelard) and final examinations also went into the making of student life at the time. Combining zeal for God with thirst for knowledge, seriousness of purpose with pursuit of *eros* and thirst for wine, these universities, growing in the shadows of the cathedrals, begin one of the longest institutional traditions still alive.

THE CATHEDRALS

"In the shadows of the cathedrals"—this implies that the cathedrals had already towered above plain, village, court, and school. Further, while human pride and aspiration had contributions to make to their development, the total triumph was more single-mindedly religious. Unfortunately, the overwhelming character of the cathedrals has cast a nimbus of holy ignorance around them. The symbolism that accompanied their rise was not, as fancy would have it, a triumph of cleverness:

> Medieval symbolism . . . was less the child of science than of ignorance; it was born and bred less in reflection than in imaginative impulse. [It was] a People's Art . . . it sometimes shocked the best and most learned men.[3]

The romantics of the nineteenth century would name this a humble, anonymous, monastic achievement: yet the marks of secular designers and craftsmen are everywhere. The intellectual tradition has attempted to see in the cathedrals the perfect intellectual synthesis in stone comparable to scholasticism in philosophy. Yet almost every development is demonstrably a practical solution to a structural problem: this is not theology but engineering. And if the crudeness of symbolism was truly a "people's art," the refinement of the masonry was not:

> We are too apt to believe that the great art of the Middle Ages was a collective work. The idea does contain a certain element of truth, inasmuch as that art reflected the thought of the Church. But the thought itself found its initial expression through a few superior men. It is not the multitude that creates, but individuals. Let us leave to the romantically minded the mystical notion of a people building cathedrals by instinct—an instinct less fallible than science or reason. [Abbott Suger, the genius who rebuilt the abbey church of Saint-Denis near Paris] was one of those men who set art in new ways. Thanks to him Saint-Denis was, from 1145 on, the hearth from which a rejuvenated art illumined France and Europe.[4]

But the removal of the halo of ignorance or romance does not detract from, but enhances the Gothic glory. For now, in the soaring arches and graceful buttresses, the tracery settings of stained glass and the luminous, numinous interior arena for the sacrifice of the Mass, the supremely catholic achievement emerges: all is process and development and movement, there is translation and transition "from the Kingdom of God to Nature, from the last things to the immediate environment, from tremendous eschatological mysteries to the more harmless secrets of the creaturely world . . . There is no better illustration of this development than the words of St. Thomas: 'God enjoys all things, for each accords with His essence.' "[5]

From the creche to the catacomb to the cathedral there is a long march of centuries, a radical transformation of values, but not a deviation from intent: to house the mystery, to draw men to the worship of God. From the ribbed vaults of eleventh century Lombardy to the arches and buttresses of twelfth century French and English Gothic building this awe and this love were to be reflected in glass and stone. Chartres, Amiens, Cologne; Reims, Durham, Salisbury—not monuments to a past age but enduring and useful creations. Malê has said it best:

Words, music, living drama of the mysteries, immobile drama of the statues—all arts were fused within the cathedral. And something more than mere art: pure light, light before it is broken into multiple rays by the prism. Man, confined within his social class, within a trade, his forces dispersed and frittered away in the work and life of every day, recovered here a sense of unity, and regained equilibrium and harmony. The crowd, assembled on great feast days, felt itself an organic whole, the mystical body of Christ, Whose soul mingled with its soul. The faithful were humanity, the cathedral was the world, and the spirit of God simultaneously filled man and all creation.[6]

Are we again verging on the romantic? Somehow the cathedrals awe their observers and chroniclers to the point of poesy.

The catholic spirit was not confined to these creations, however. Their obviousness overshadows the endurance of medieval hymnody. Not only are the liturgical hymns in large measure the growth of these times; individual poets —usually theologians or mystics—left a legacy: Thomas Aquinas, Bonaventure, Peter Abelard, Bernard of Cluny, Adam of St. Victor crowned what five and more centuries earlier Venantius Fortunatus, Gregory the Great, and Prudentius had begun. The mystery- and miracle-plays, the moralities that were presented in courtyard and market on festive days, seemed crude to later dramatists. But again, we are recovering from their naive expression their grasp of cosmic realities. Nor need the Church surrender to the secular literary tradition that critic of the Church he loved, Dante Alighieri, whose "lofty fancy pass'd as low as Hell, as high as Heaven, secure and unconfined." Dante died in 1321, still rightfully timed with these Middle Ages—as was his contemporary, the painter Giotto, also a harbinger of another renaissance.

THE LITURGY AND THE MASS

It is possible, of course, to look at the spires and the scores and fail to see that the more significant aspect of the catholicity of this "golden age" of Christian penetration lay in the absorption of most of life in the rhythms of the liturgy and the Mass. In the spread of parishes across the English terrain, in the chapels of feudal lords where peasants were often—and only there—seen to be equals before God, and in the spread of the secular clergy who went about doing good, gladly ministering to the people, we see not only the breadth but the depth of churchly influence. Unfortunately the general illiteracy of the times and the enduring edge of barbarism and violence made the people sometimes superstitiously dependent upon the sacraments and sacramental objects and upon the parish priests who seldom measured up to their calling. Illiterate themselves, products of inadequate training and often warped cloistered environments, grasping and greedy, many used the Church and the fear of the masses to advance their own interests. But these generalizations have never done justice to the countless examples of parish priests who quietly went about their business gaining the respect of their flocks and serving them with the sacraments and with Christian counsel. The conservative Reformation never wanted to repudiate this continuity of evangelical counsel in the centuries that preceded it.

In such an age the formal development of the seven sacraments seems logical and to be expected. In their tangible and visual appeal, a vivid objectiveness that transcended the personal weakness of those who administered them gave security to the anxious. On the other hand, superstitious regard for their powers gave rise to their misuse as political instruments and magical cure-alls. The Eucharist or Lord's Supper seemed most potent and most vulnerable; many excesses in relation to this sacrament grew out of official changes in the doctrines which pertain to it. An illustration of this is the feast of Corpus Christi, which encouraged the worship of the reserved host and which met official sanction by the papacy in the thirteenth century as the logical outgrowth of the twelfth-century doctrine of transubstantiation.

These holy days of the Church were observed both with sobriety before the altars and with revelling in the streets. Out of these observances there grew innovations in the concept and in the objects of Christian worship, as with the veneration of the Blessed Virgin and the saints, many of whom were accredited with contrivedly miraculous acts. But if in this the "catholic" spirit interpenetrated too easily the fallen structures of the created order, there were internal checks and safeguards in the prophetic lineage and in the evangelical preaching associated with the late medieval mystics and preachers.

This complex can only begin to outline the ways in which Christianity informed most cultural expression in the Middle Ages. When, in this long span of church history, we encounter an exception, as in the openly sensual court lyrics of the troubadours, we are shocked into the necessity —perhaps justifiable—of finding sources beyond Western Christendom. The tensions between church and world described in our discussion of the holiness of the Church and the limitations of the mission of the evangel in the same centuries have served to remind the overenthusiastic that much of the tarnish does belong on the gold of the "golden age" in the West.

7

SCHISM

But can we have forgotten that half of Christendom which grew where the faith was cradled? In all these pages of discussion of a millennium of the Church's life, was there deliberate distortion or neglect in this absence of the Eastern development? The answer to these questions is obvious, and in the obviousness of the answer is the theme of this chapter. The story of the Eastern church has not been postponed because it is insignificant. There Christianity can point to the longest continuous development; there perhaps, in its consciousness of tradition and its theurgic grasp, it has been most nearly catholic. Postponement may be partially due to unfamiliarity, to an inescapable Western provincialism. But most of all, during the long span of Christian history from the time of the ecumenical councils to the Reformation, two separate stories begin to develop. Only confusion can result from the attempt to create the illusion of a continuing unity in Christendom. Two stories, two histories, two traditions in the one Church: this is the problem that cuts through medieval history.

Twice in its long history the Christian Church after its severance from Judaism has been torn to its vitals by schisms which seemed to detract from the ideal of a united Body, which belie the united character of Christian truth and witness to one Lord. The second of these occurred rather abruptly (after a century of stirrings) in the Reformation of the sixteenth century. Its breach became "final" in the two or three decades following 1517. The first and at least equally agonizing schism was much longer in the making, occupying the time from Chalcedon down to 1054, the symbolic date of separation. In the magnificent clash of two opinionated men, Michael Cerularius in the East and Pope Leo IX in the West, all the quiescent issues of centuries bubbled to the surface. In 1054 the legates of the Pope excommunicated Cerularius with these words: "In prejudging the highest See, the see on which no judgment may be passed by any man, you have received the anathema from all the Fathers of all the venerable Councils."

That sentence comprehends the heart of the medieval development in the West: no man could judge Rome. It holds the point of offense for the East: you have received the anathema.

> *a-nath'-e-ma:* a ban or curse pronounced with religious solemnity by ecclesiastical authority, and accompanied by excommunication. An imprecation; curse; malediction.

There is no fuzziness or elusiveness of definition: one part of one church curses another. The schism is accomplished.

If we are to explore what is behind this anathema we are struck by the curious point of analogy with the Protestant breach so much later. Both revolved around Rome, that see which considered itself the unitive center of the Church on earth. A point of difference is here, too: in the sundering of West and East each continued to claim that it was *the* true Church in an exclusive sense. In the later division within the West a new critical principle had entered. Normative, critical Protestantism would not have existed had it not been principled, contending for the truth. But it bore within itself a prophetic seed which judged the contenders, leaving itself no temporal point of absolutistic reference. Despite this (or because of it?) the breakdown of communication, of basic discourse after 1054, seems more complete than that which follows 1517. Different authorities, civilizations, and languages competed: we draw a veil to a mystery when from the West we begin to discuss the East. In so many ways, it does not seem to the Christian of the Western heritage to be *his* story . . . all is so remote, so unfamiliar . . .

From the complicated welter of paths that led to the schism we must select several and follow them. One involves a different view of the relation of the holy Church to the world. Another trails the remains of Christological controversy. Still another charts the nearness of that mortal foe of the faith, the infidel Moslem. Controversy within the Eastern church, "iconoclasm," will next attract, and controversy leading to schism is the final path.

CHURCH AND "STATE"

While this story begins, as did the Western, with the account of relations between church and society, we are handicapped by the absence of a hinge figure to summarize the development: in short, we lack a St. Augustine. The transition to the medieval East is unmarked and smoothbreathed; little theory existed to justify changes. But the ellision is seen in the "actual pressure of events" by the relationship described institutionally as Caesaropapism. The term implies monarchical control over ecclesiastical affairs; particularly, it connotes the intrusion of civil officer in sanctuary, the crossing of line from the imperial to the priestly.

In the East this meant that the church was in some senses "a department of state organization":

> There was no possibility of an independent evolution, because the organs of the state interfered everywhere and there was no room for ecclesiastical autonomy. Those secular functions, which elsewhere were taken over by the church, had in Byzantium retained the character of public services.[1]

Constantine's General Council, the institutional center of Caesaropapism, was, according to Adolf Harnack: "a political institution, invented by the greatest of politicians, a two-edged sword which protected the endangered unity of the church at the price of its independence." Clearly, the Church was paying for its protection and buying trouble in the system that was too attractive to forego, too powerful to escape. After Constantine the Eastern ruler assumed episcopal functions; he was often the only person with the power and prestige capable of executing them on the highest levels.

Constantine shaped this tradition as he drew the center of imperial interest to the East and by his conversion established the new constellations of religious-political life in the Empire. The glory of the new capital, Constantinople, added glitter to his claims. It is futile to attempt to assess the Emperor's personal faith, but it is not difficult to discern that he saw the wisdom of recognizing that the prosperity of the state was bound up with the unity of the church. The emperors sought in the Church "a unifying force among their heterogeneous subjects." [2]

The historian French argued that the dealings of emperor with church and his intervention in its inner life are to be explained "not merely by zeal for abstract truth and theological principles" but by a more down-to-earth and laudable desire to maintain law and order, peace and unity. Yet the Church fell short of its potential, failing the throne because it had not yet developed an intellectual expression of the faith and because, while the Empire was one, the Church was torn between Constantinople and Rome.

An illustration of the difference in development between West and East appears in the arguments for the authority of these cities. In the West the decisive issue was the question of the apostolic origin of sees; the primacy of Rome was argued on an apostolic basis. In the East a more arbitrary claim on the basis of territorialism and geography prevailed. Constantinople claimed to be the "next after [meta] Rome" because it was the New Rome of the Emperor. As early as the Council of Antioch (341) this position was outlined; as early as this was the wedding of imperial-territorial and ecclesiastical fortunes prefigured. The Bishop of Constantinople became a sort of court

preacher and kept theologian, the "emperor's own bishop."
Necessarily, he had to rely upon imperial favor for his own
plans for self-advancement. This interplay on different
ground rules contributed greatly to rivalry with Rome,
which was insecurely basking in the setting sun of a setting
Empire.

Not everyone of Byzantium accepted the Caesaropapist
coddling. St. John Chrysostom (—407) took courage to
prophesy and judge at the time when Emperor Theodosius
engaged in a bloody massacre. A John the Baptist born
anew to preach against the Empress Eudoxia, he gave his
enemies occasion to bring about his death. But after
Chrysostom the critics are less identifiable. More typical of
the growing imperial power of the East, a power that not
only transcended personal criticism but even outdistanced
Roman might, was Marcian's (—457) success in holding the great ecumenical council at Chalcedon against the
wishes of Pope Leo, who had desired Rome. Incidentally,
the same occasion also reveals the limits of the imperial-
ecclesiastical tie. Marcian's resort to force to uphold the
council's decisions failed to "convert" the opposing parties.
A church dependent upon imperium became too dependent
upon the whims and heartbeats of emperors and upon
dynastic intrigues. The situation was similar to that more
familiar to most of us in England's history when the pope
conspired with the later Plantagenets. When these kings
deserted the Church, it had no further recourse, no further appeal or defense. In this respect the Western church
ordinarily held an advantage. Whatever its momentary
relation to the sword, its primary dependence remained on
the power and prestige of the Petrine "keys."

No moment provides richer opportunity to observe this
"Erastianism" than the reign of Emperor Justinian (after
527). This great monarch, whose power was nearly coextensive with his dreams, wanted to reunite the separating
churches of East and West as he would rebuild the unity
of the Empire. When he appeared on the scene he could
claim to be the viceregent of Christ on earth, as the pope
claimed to be in the West. The whole earth would be his
sphere of dominion. The Church would support him.

So the builder of St. Sophia and the protector of the dogma-builders involved doctrine with dynasty. His Empress, Theodora (—547), occupied center stage in much of the post-Chalcedonian drama. Her choice was the Monophysite party which contended against Chalcedon's settlement that in the incarnate Christ there was only a divine nature. *Vice versa,* the doctrinal situation might affect the political. Thus the second council at Constantinople (553), with its partial reaction to Chalcedon and its trend toward Monophysitism, tells us more concerning the growing consolidation of the church of the East and the emperor's authority over it (in opposition to the pope) than it does about the inner life of the church and its teaching. After Theodora's death Justinian was increasingly cool toward the Monophysites. His statement on the incorruptibility of the body of Christ was an "imperial creed" that towered over papal pretensions because it was able, with its imperial sanction, to bypass conciliar decisions on the subject.

It is fair to say that more of Justinian's theological effort was Caesaropapist statecraft than bad theology. The instance of this Emperor has inspired in men of later centuries in the West a sense of gratitude for the greater popes, Leo and Gregory among them, who kept alive within a theocratic ideal a measure of tension between the spheres of the temporal and the spiritual. In the East what tension there was existed between two "spirituals" in quest of imperial favor. Thus in the Monothelite controversy in the seventh century, Sophronius, the Patriarch of Jerusalem, had to attack both the heresy and the emperor because of the semi-heretical alliances of the time.

In later periods Caesaropapism was to play an unfortunate part in dividing the Church. In the Iconoclastic controversy the emperor initiated reform with little support from church or people. Germanus the Patriarch (—733) at best acquiesced and reluctantly followed in reform. The strength of Western reform had inhered in its "popular" character. In Eastern iconoclasm or iconodulism the church was secondary and often defensive.

Few single dates meant so much to the widening schism

as the crowning of Charlemagne by the Pope in 800—
henceforth two branches of the church were to regard competing emperors as rightful rulers. After the Photian schism
of 867 the Western church suffered with weak popes who
spoke loudly against the emperor but wielded little real
power. A pope could argue, "No apostle founded the
Church of Constantinople." Popes could criticize the idea
of a "new Rome" in the East. But they could in no way
enforce their judgments of their claims.

Almost every succeeding stage of the East-West schism
can be related to the fortunes of the two empires. In the
reign of Michael Paleologus the Patriarch Arsenius and his
successor Joseph (1267) brought the Emperor to his
knees, but this was a "moral protest, not an assertion of
ecclesiastical arrogance," [3] and is not comparable to the
reduction of temporal leaders as in the instance at Canossa.
Later centuries may prefer the concept of moral protest to
that of ecclesiastical arrogance, and here the East deserves
congratulations; but in the context of possibilities in medieval times the way of the West was more effective. Given
the choice of religious servility to civil caprice or continuing shifts of power and tensions, the West was bound
to the latter.

CHRISTOLOGICAL CONTROVERSY

More wedges than one were driven between churches of
East and West. The division of empire and alternative responses to imperial relations may have represented the foremost institutional difference. But theology also separated
the two. Different answers were given to different questions
in different theological languages. The change dates from
the period of the councils and takes decisive form in the
time of Justinian. Ironically, this capable and deeply religious ruler who shared so much in the division of Christendom had set out to reunite it despite a dividing Empire.
In his hands the faith of Chalcedonian orthodoxy seemed
an adequate instrument to achieve this. We have already

seen how Theodora was to complicate his purpose by her preoccupation with heresy; she distracted him by her taste for pride and pomp in the court.

Justinian's unitive goal was frustrated also by the rise of the papacy at Rome. Fortunately for his purpose his contemporary, Pope Vigilius (—555) was a vacillating pontiff who alternated between favoring and rejecting the Emperor in the latter's theological involvements. It demanded real finesse for him to do this without lending credence to the Emperor's quasi-papal pretensions. When Justinian summoned the fifth ecumenical council at Constantinople Vigilius refused to participate. Fury met with fury. When Vigilius conceded, this achieved little in the way of reunion: most Western bishops dragged their feet as far as acceptance of conciliar achievements was concerned.

If churchly intrigue of this sort failed Justinian, he could resort to force to establish universal orthodoxy. With law and with sword he attempted to abolish the remains of paganism. Despite his cultural interests, he had to appear anti-cultural in his suppression of the philosophical schools. This resort to force was most painful in its application to heterodox teaching within the Eastern church, as we find it in the two lagging Christological controversies which marred Justinian's reign: Monophysitism and Monotheletism. Both grew out of dissatisfactions with Chalcedon's solution. The first preserved the heresies of Apollinarius (—c. 392) and Eutyches (—454), even though Chalcedon had condemned their viewpoints. With its Alexandrian ring, this characteristically Eastern emphasis stressed Christ's divinity at the expense of his humanity. Few controversies have attracted men of such interesting names (Timothy the Cat, Peter the Fuller) or parties so complex (Corrupticolae *versus* Aphthartodocetae!); none could claim so much support from secular church leaders of imperial status.

In Justinian's time the storm broke out anew when the Monophysites of Alexandria rebelled against Chalcedon. Egypt was rocked; to this day the Coptic church there has adhered to this view of the exalted but not fully human Christ. Palestine shared the tumult—whence today's Ar-

menian and Jacobite churches, whose first master was
Cyril (—444). The allies of all these dissidents were
strategically placed. One of them was in the court; her
name was Theodora and she had the ear of her husband,
the Emperor. Justinian had originally used force to persecute the Monophysites, but they had entrenched themselves. When force failed he tried to find points of agreement with Chalcedon in the Monophysite view. He permitted the party to propagandize; he wooed it by favoring
one Anthimus, who held its view, for the patriarchate of
Constantinople. But the popes had learned to resist imperial pressures. One had rejected Emperor Zeno's *Henoti-
kon,* a conciliatory document of 482: now another deposed Anthimus. As Monophysitism hardened into sects
Justinian ceased conciliation and resumed force.

Some people cannot be forced. One of these was Theodora. She finagled the deposition of Pope Silverius to
have her lackey Vigilius elected: the Monophysite hour
seemed to be at hand. Justinian again wooed; by attacking
the "Three Chapters," documents of three Nestorian theologians, he hoped to attract the Monophysites. The role
of Pope Vigilius in ensuing intrigues is a singularly unattractive moment in the history of the Holy See. And Justinian, despite his amazing display of virtuosity at courtship
of heretics, failed to win them. The Empire was split by
his theologizing and the Church was less united than before.

We need devote little space to the subsequent distortion
of Chalcedon, Monotheletism, which pulled further at the
widening wounds. The bungling creedal position is unique
in that it was evoked by political necessity: invaders
threatened the Empire and the Church; it also involved the
papacy in heretical statement. We can date this controversy
from the years of Emperor Heraclius (—641); it erupted in
the 630's and died with the Council of Constantinople in
680. This council removed the sting from the hitherto
potent Christological issue and found the East guarding
orthodoxy while Rome erred. The "mono—" heresies, of
course, have lived on into modern times in every stress
which neglects the humanity of Christ and the finitude of

God's instruments among men. They are more important here for the ways in which they tore old Rome from new.

ISLAM

New Rome had concerns more pressing than theological statement to face at the time of these fracases: the Moslem was at the door of empire, ready to profane the holy places. The Western church, less affected, never fully shared the agony of empire and East in their struggle to survive and expand. How sudden, either to imagine that moment or to examine with the telescope of history, was the charge! Islam, a reflection of Arab monotheism in the dramatic career of the prophet Mohammed after his migration to Mecca in 622, burst upon the world in belligerence and aggression. Its goal was world-wide conversion. Under Abu Bakr a military organization was formed to cut through the East like a scythe of terror. It ruined the Sassanid Empire and weakened the walls of the Roman Empire. Within two decades Egypt, Syria, Palestine, and several Mediterranean islands were overrun. And the Eastern church was on the front line while the Roman church was relatively secure in its illusions of distance. The illusion gave birth to the nightmare as Mohammedans swept North Africa, ruining Carthage, to master the Mediterranean and dissipate the Roman civilization of the area. The arc moved across Spain, which had been weakened by the Visigoths. Charles Martel's victory at Tours in 732—the kind of victory whose possible alternative staggers the imagination —ended the threat to the West. But the East lived on in agony. Its responses, in the jaws of death, puzzled the unsympathetic West. Another wedge severed the two.

ICONOCLASM

As the seventh century heightened the threat from without, the eighth is concerned with an internal struggle which drove still another wedge. The issue was iconoclasm: the shattering of images, so vital in the glorious worship of the East. The controversy over images contributed to the divisions between two branches of Christendom in the formal authoritarian and theological sense—the popes and their rights were repeatedly called into question. More profound, however, was its reflection of an ethos that was to prevail and which remains characteristic of the church of the East. This "feel" is less preoccupied with distinctions between an image and a reality. Much of Christendom has always kept a conscience which recalls Yahweh's strictures against representation of the deity in the Old Testament; it is haunted by Christ's disregard of the arrangement of the stones of the holy temple. Its catholic strain is checked by Savonarola, its protesting Reformation prophesied against confusion of image and reality to the point of radical rejection of images. Not so in the East.

There the patinas of gold leaf and the weight of color and jewel carry a splendor and attraction that is overpowering. Two-dimensional representation of Christ, his mother, or the saints, in the constellation of worship has permitted depth participation in the mysteries. The eighth and ninth centuries with their controversy imply a prophetic and political protest against this participation—but the final effect of the argument was to strengthen the status of icons, to prop and undergird the iconostasis.

What brought on the famed fracas is difficult to determine. Perhaps the Islamic anti-image influence played a part, as did some of the Eastern heresies which rebelled against the idea of human representations of the deity since human artifacts—with the rest of ":matter"—were evil. The Emperor Leo III (the Isaurian, —741) had been educated by the Paulician sect, which held such views. Motivated by political hopes of making the Church more manageable in empire and, he said, by concerns for missionary activity among Moslems and Jews, he stormed against the images in 726. They were idolatrous; they must be destroyed. Churchmen like the Patriarch Germanus who resisted must be deposed. It would be as easy as that.

It was not. Leo found the iconostasis buttressed by almost the entire monastic movement. He met massive resistance among the people. He had completely miscalculated the hold of this form of veneration on the Eastern mind. And he had to face the most comprehensive and gifted systematic theologian the East had produced since Origen in John of Damascus (—c. 749). In three treatises on the subject John was able to show that faulty Christology was at play in opposition to images: a full doctrine of Christ would encourage portrayal of the divine Son in earthly form. Behind this Christology, he would continue, a false philosophical notion is implied, something which reflects ancient Gnosticism which also underplayed the role of the material. And he made a point of iconoclastic inconsistency: books, too, are images—are they to be destroyed?

> When we set up an image of Christ in any place, we appeal to the senses; and indeed we sanctify the sense of sight, which is the highest among the perceptive senses, just as by sacred speech we sanctify the sense of hearing. An image is, after all, a reminder; it is to the illiterate what a book is to the literate, and what the word is to the hearing, the image is to the sight. . . . The hill, Calvary, the tomb, the stone, the very source of the Resurrection—all are material; the ink and the pages of the Gospels, the table from which we take of our salvation and all its furniture, the very body and blood of the Lord—all are material. You must either forbid all respect to these things, or you must allow with it respect to the images consecrated to the name of Christ and to his friends, the saints, as being overshadowed by the grace of the Holy Spirit.[4]

Leo was unmoved by theology or eloquence; he saw the superstition which escaped John of Damascus and resented the pull this superstition had on the progress of empire. Nor would he lose love on the monks, whose immunity to taxation was a constant irritant. Monks and icons—subtract their power, and Leo thought, the formula for empire was there.

While Rome was moderately critical of the use of images, the East-West tug of war found Pope Gregory III aligning himself with the anti-Leonine forces. Leo's retaliatory confiscation of papal properties helped force the issue. Leo's son, Constantine V, was more oppressive, more stormy. Flushed with victory over the Arabs, he pushed reform on the anti-monk and -icon platform that he had inherited. After the Synod of Hieria in 753 radicalism had its day, accompanied by persecution. Monks died clutching images. "All beauty disappeared from the churches." Hammer and hatchet and sword—these were the weapons that were intended to divert the classically Eastern pattern of worship. Some of the people followed, and mob activity was common. But when the emperor's grandson assumed rule and was too young to execute it, the Empress-mother Irene assumed power.

With this, an about-face. Irene could throw off the wraps from her secret iconodulism; as fanatically as Leo III, but from the other side, did she consider herself God's instrument. The iconoclasm of the army and of much of the royal family was small deterrent to her cunning. She called an irenic General Council at Nicaea in 787. Hieria's decrees were negated, and monks were permitted to work for separation of church and state against the Caesaropapist tradition of centuries' standing. As the son of the Empress grew (Constantine VI) the issue was again complicated, for he was an iconoclast. Irene settled this family tussle in a quiet way: she had her son blinded and deposed. The monks rejoiced. Her hour had ended; and in the years when Charlemagne was resurrecting the Empire of the West, the East was again declining because of her extremism. Until that time a moderate reform was promised. Monks included moral guidance along with veneration of images in their routines; encouragement of secular arts by iconoclasts bore cultural fruit. But this was to be aborted in the final triumph of images after the second controversy under Leo V the Armenian (an iconoclast) and his successors *versus* iconodules like another Empress-regent, Theodora, who ultimately restored them.

The Western church was hardly involved directly in the later stages of the controversy and most of its involvements were accidental because of confused communications and misunderstandings. But later historians have always seen in iconoclastic controversy the storm before the lull which anticlimactically severed churches of East and West. For, as might be expected, so tense an issue as that of images showed to the church of the West the binding character of the Caesaropapism of the East. Rome was declaring its independence of the Holy Roman Empire in the same years in which Eastern patriarchs were increasingly dependent upon imperial whims. The strain was almost too great.

SCHISM

While the final severance is usually dated in 1054, the parting is customarily identified with the Photian schism, named after Photius (—895), Patriarch of Constantinople. He emerged against a re-emergent Caesaropapist issue and took turns being appointed to ecclesiastical office and then being deposed by the favorite of the Roman pontiff, one Ignatius. Intervention of the Pope in the Eastern issue sparked new fires between the competing authorities. Photius seems to have been an ambitious and scheming churchman who added what fuel he could, charmed by the prospect of new glories in Byzantium. Before his final deposition the lines and issues were clear. The Eastern conception of five reasonably equal patriarchates was coming into constant clash with the Roman claim to uniqueness and centrality. Along the way, Photius had further aggravated the differences on dogmatic lines by pointing the finger at Rome, accusing it of innovating with the introduction of the *filioque* clause into the creed (the Holy Spirit proceeded from the Father *and* the Son). And the ethos and expression which play a larger part than any documentable dogma clashed whenever East met West. The Latins chanted the *filioque,* they were celibate, only the bishop could confirm. The priests of the East abhorred the *filioque,* most were permitted to marry, they could confirm.

The end of all pretense came during the century in which Rome and Constantinople, unable to take decisive action, had stood each other off and glared. Caesaropapism, iconoclasm, Photianism, the *filioque* were the decisive issues, long waiting for the spark which came with two uncompromising personalities, Michael Cerularius (—1058), an eastern patriarch, and Leo IX. Michael, rising from laity through monastery to patriarchal chair in 1043, aspired to quasi-papal authority. Leo IX was a reformer in the West, and like his colleagues made a high view of his office a part of reform. Michael was "picking for a fight" in the issues he created—take that of unleavened bread in the Eucharist as an example. Mediation was attempted between Leonine legates and non-mediative Michael. The conclusion? The sting of the day almost nine hundred years ago still hurts the one Church of Christ: on the altar of St. Sophia the papal legates lay the letter of excommunication: "You have received the anathema." The Emperor preferred to side with the legates, but the people preferred the Patriarch. After July 1054 there were no more illusions and few more hopes of the one Church's retaining a semblance of unity.

THE GLORY OF THE EAST

With the next chapter the weight of this account will again fall Westward, but we shall not fail to balance this in the account of succeeding centuries with occasional Eastern prospects. The East was at the moment of breach rising to new heights that were not to be toppled until the fall of Constantinople in the crusades. Church life did not die with separation from the West; in many cases the East had better warrants for its own pointing to continuity and tradition; in many ways it was more catholic, more apostolic. Its lay theological tradition and its married clergy are marks of this positive approach to culture. But the Eastern direction and cultures have made it mysterious to the Western church and world; its history does not seem to be *our* history after the breach.

The West is poorer for this. We need not with the men of progress and enlightenment see the Eastern church entering a permanent dark age. We need not follow Brooks Adams and the larger fellowship which would, with him, term Justinian Christendom "hardly Christian," tending toward "paganism and scepticism." We must see it in its own guise, in the context of its own possibilities, in compatibility with its own ideal. And that ideal in the theological sense has been ennobling, a countervailing power and glory against modern matter-of-factness in the West. If it leans repeatedly to the incarnation and resurrection of Christ more than on his life and suffering death, if it counts splendor more than sacrifice, gold of crown more than wood of cross, empty tomb more than filled crucifix—for Origen, Alexandria, and John of Damascus are its fathers —the Antiochene lineage in Christendom has always felt its excesses checked by re-orienting itself in the etymological sense of that term. In words of Stephen Zankow, familiar through frequent quotation, the resurrectionist stress is clear:

> For the Orthodox Church, as well for its theology as for its popular conceptions, salvation is only finally complete in the Resurrection. Sin and death are conquered, and life is bestowed upon men. Only the Resurrection is the real earnest of salvation and of eternal life.[5]

The divine liturgy of St. John Chrysostom calls the whole Church to the numinous. All but iconoclasts in every age can respond to the elongated and mysterious inhabitants of the world of iconography. The hymns to the cherubim exalt Westerners from their prosody. The Eastern saints appeal to all. One need not be a gentle soul like Roman Catholic Karl Adam to respond with him to the character and career of "a Dmitri, an Innocent, a Tikhon, a Theodosius." Riches are there, to be discovered by the un-Orthodox world; the embarrassment of these riches is a mark of the depth of tragedy in separation of East and West, in the schism that marked an age.

8

THE CHURCH HAS NEVER ERRED

Threading its way through the millennium of events in the church of the West, as a parallel to the concern of the East, is a tradition of theological life that differs markedly from its Eastern parallel. The characteristic doctrinal development of the church of Byzantine lineage grew out of explicitly *theo*logical concerns. Monophysitism, Monotheletism, the *filioque* controversy, even the crucial question in iconoclasm—all revolved around questions of the nature of the Godhead and the revelation of God in Christ. In the Western development many of these concerns find reflection and at certain moments there is dialogue. But here ecclesiological questions, churchly questions predominate.

Some of these deal with the nature of the men who make up the Christian Church and human society (thus Pelagianism and semi-Pelagianism); others explicate the faith nourished in the life of the Church by specific reference to its rites and sacraments (thus Donatism, the Lord's Supper controversy, the issue of the power and primacy of the Roman pope, the later discussions of the place of councils). One of the few exceptions was the dispute over the nature of God's atonement in Christ, which attracted Abelard and Anselm. But even this raised the question of man's relation to God rather than of God's attitude to man. Not only were the doctrinal questions of the Church

155

"churchly": the corollary concern with Christian thought in its larger context against the background of philosophical reference also appears for the most part within the ecclesiastical framework. Seldom in Christian history has a philosophical line been so congenial to the needs of the Church as was scholasticism. The threat in the nominalist stream that appeared in late scholasticism inhered in its weakening of churchly status and authority.

Throughout the period from Augustine beyond Aquinas to Occam, from the Pelagian controversy of the fifth century to the conciliar discussion into the fifteenth, one question appeared in continuity with that which motivated the early Church: was the teaching or the thought apostolic? Yet in its temporal and spatial reference the question was strangely transformed. And in this transformation is a key to the entire medieval development and to the enduring Roman Catholic heritage into twentieth century times. It comes subtly, hardly noticeably, yet its final effect is almost overpowering.

First, in time. Perhaps it is partly illusion, but there seems to be a change of pace between the response to the apostolic and traditional questions in earlier and later times. In the earliest decades after the death of Jesus Christ an excitement and an urgency seem to spark everything: the missionary impulse, the quest for unity and holiness, the articulation of intellectual response. The Lord will come again soon! Earthly institutions are temporary and almost irrelevant in the time of proclamation of the Kingdom of God. In the question of apostolicity there was at first little organized pattern of historic reference to the time when Jesus had taught and sent out the apostles: the shaping of the canons of Scripture, of worship, and of doctrine and the development of the episcopate in the second and third centuries prefigure the medieval turn. The community of the Holy Spirit which encountered the world was to be transformed into an institution more content to live in the world. The cities may not be continuing, yet the City of God did coexist with a city of man—the terms are institutional. The very term "apostolic," which originated in the act of "sending out" the disciples, later implies little of this missionary and proclamatory appeal and refers largely to the historic doctrinal issue.

So, too, with space: the apostolic impulse "beginning at Jerusalem" and issuing into all the world seemed fluid both in source and in goal. Successively or simultaneously Jerusalem, Antioch, Ephesus, and Rome could be the centers from which the mission spread and at which the teaching was scrutinized and confirmed. This dynamic and critical relativism, with its attempt to "continue in the apostles' doctrine," changes to a more static and absolutistic claim to possess and guard the deposit of doctrine at a specific locus, namely Rome.

TRADITION

Yet we must only say that this was *"more* static," *"less* dynamic," for it did not totally petrify or stagnate. With this change of pace and reference to space in deciding the questions of Christian truth there was development; but the key word "tradition" suggests a more gradual turn and movement. In the New Testament, "tradition" meant the act of God's "handing over" of Jesus Christ to the human existence and experience (Rom. 8:31–32), a rather sudden and abrupt action at a definable moment in a specific place. Jesus, according to the witness of the Fourth Gospel, reshapes "tradition" by handing over the Holy Spirit to the apostles in his last moments (John 13:30). The Holy Spirit takes this rather sudden and isolatable historic act and constantly recreates the original "tradition" in the life of the ongoing apostolic community: here the Church begins to prepare for the long pull of historical development.[1]

This apostolic tradition of "handing over" becomes an ecclesiastical tradition of "handing down" in the papal line after those early centuries. Its content was assumedly defined, and those who "handed down" were seen as stewards or elaborators of the definition detailed in early creed and council, the original witness being the word of Jesus in the canonical Scripture. This assumption came to a climax which Protestants have found so abhorrent in the counter-reformatory Council of Trent (1546, Session IV), where Scripture and the ecclesiastical tradition were proclaimed to share equal authority (*pari pietatis affectu ac reverentia*). In the Middle Ages we are still some distance from Pius IX's nineteenth-century dictum "I am tradition," but this is implied in the classic statement of the *Dictatus Papae* of the eleventh century, which institutionalizes an impulse and then absolutizes it: the "Church has never erred and will never err to all eternity." Here not simply the community of Christ under the Holy Spirit is implied, but specifically the church under Roman dominance and development. A parallel and often differing source and norm had appeared alongside the scriptural reference to apostolicity.

Seen in certain lights the entire question of apostolicity and tradition throughout Christian history has been a question of authority: of God in Christ, the scriptural witness to this event, of the apostles and creeds, of the Church, or the pope and councils, of human reason. While some popes would have stated it more crassly, and while some irritating persons like Abelard would question the authority by pointing to contradictions within and between the authorities (he found 158 such contradictions), most of the churchmen of medieval times would have found acceptable the Aquinian outline. Divine revelation was handed over or handed down by authorities (*auctoritates*). Foremost were the canonical Scriptures, whose arguments were "intrinsically and of necessity correct" (*proprie et ex necessitate*). Secondly, the fathers of the Church argued also intrinsically but the truth was only "probable." Third, the philosophers argued (*extranea*) not intrinsically and therefore also only probably.[2] What was missing from this list of authorities was the one most concrete or most graphic to the men of the Middle Ages: papal authority in the church which could never err.

AUGUSTINE AND THREE HERESIES

Whenever we wish to pick up the strand of Western medieval thought, as we did in the earlier questions of church and society, it seems necessary to focus on St. Augustine. He illustrates perfectly what we have described as characteristic of the West in his times: the change from theological concerns to ecclesiological ones. He was preeminently a churchly theologian, a man who, having found the answer to his heart's restlessness in God, found in the Church the path to rest while he walked in the City of Man. As Bishop of Hippo from *c.* 386 to his death in 430 he was obliged to involve himself with three heresies, and out of such practical churchly concerns he forged the bulk of his theological thought. One of these heresies, Manichaeism, need hardly divert us here, for its often weird excesses recall in caricature earlier heresies typified by Gnosticism or by the dualistic aberrations. Were we to detail scholastic thought, his reply would assume greater importance here. It suggested the movement of scholasticism as it refused to follow the Manichaeans. They placed an eternal evil agency in opposition to the will of a good God. Evil for Augustine in a universe ruled by a good God represented an unfulfilled grasp of what ought to be held as good. Thus man's free-will, which is good, can also be diverted toward evil in the moral realm, while in the physical realm mere creaturehood implies distance from the Creator and thus imperfection.

But it is the other two heresies which better illustrate the churchly development. The first of these, Donatism, involved Augustine centrally in questions of authority, tradition, apostolicity, and the sacraments and discipline in the life of the Church. To trace the background of Donatism would carry us too far back into the times of the persecutions and the martyrs, when the consecrator of a Bishop of Carthage had been a surrenderer to the Romans in a moment of pressure. The Donatists were an ascetic and rigorous group who allowed for little frailty or foolishness, insisting on the complete holiness of the saints and disallowing validity to the sacraments when administered by the unholy surrenderers. Economic, cultural, and racial differences complicated the theological dispute. In their extremism the Donatists argued that all who received such sacraments were polluted and finally, as perfect schismatics and sectarians, argued that only Donatists were pure, were

Christian. The Donatists, in arguing that the holiness of the ministrant bishop was essential, fell one step short of Augustine's view.

Augustine, as a "doctor of the Church," was involved in the later stages of the conflict which tore the African church in the fifth century. Here his position toward churchly authority becomes clear and nearly normative for the West. His pastoral heart refused to accept the absolutistic sectarianism of the Donatists, who gave scant security to a sinner. Certainly there must be something of a more reliable and objective basis to the Church's unity and holiness as witnessed also in its rites and life! Indeed there was, argued Augustine. The sacraments were valid not because of the holiness of the administrant—for no man would be holy enough in that case—but because of the perfection of Christ who is the authentic minister of the sacrament. The Church is holy not because of the perfection of its members but objectively, because of its origin and intent in the plan of God through Christ and under the Holy Spirit. Meanwhile, good and evil men coexist without full marks of external identification until the day of judgment at the end of time.

Even this brief reference to the Donatist struggle and Augustine's view of it shows clearly the degree to which a doctrine of man in imperfection and in holiness is at the basis of every concept of the Church. This doctrine of man illustrates another aspect of the Western development to which we have referred: from the almost ethereally abstract discussions of remote deity in the past and in the East to the very empirically concrete discussions of man in the West. Augustine's view of the objective character of the Church and the dispensation of grace within it is a clue to the stand he would take when confronted with a doctrine of man which argued that initiative in the divine-human encounter lay with man, who was capable of climbing many rungs of the ladder to heaven with only certain modified forms of assistance from God. This was the teaching, crudely stated, of a British or Irish monk named Pelagius, who arrived in Rome at the turn of the century when Augustine was much in repute as a teacher in the Church.

Pelagius reacted negatively when he heard someone quote Augustine's word: "Grant what Thou dost command and command what Thou wilt." Would not this jeopardize the entire structure of morality and responsibility? What would keep man from gross sin in such an irresponsible view? Before long the monk was lining up impressive opposition to Augustine, especially after the latter went to Africa. Condemned within a decade by virtually everyone in the Church that was involved, the Pelagian teaching persisted in modified form or in isolated places until the Second Council of Orange in 529. Augustine picked up a view of his predecessor St. Ambrose, who had stressed the grace of God; this was the decisive critical principle against the Pelagian high view of human potential. To Pelagius, a personally irreproachable man according to what little view of him emerges from the shadows of personal obscurity, "sin" was not a basic mistwist in the human character. It represented momentary, isolated, individual acts of willful evil. If sin seemed to be quite in vogue across the world and in the long record of human experience, this was largely because man had had enough practice at it to become almost perfect in his habitual sinfulness. So man was a sinner. He did need help, he was not completely the master of his fate. Grace was needed daily and for every act—but grace was merely the catalyst or the enabler.

Augustine saw instantly that this view tended to identify grace with the exemplary life and moral teaching of Christ more than with his atoning death. He saw in this a perversion of the Christian gospel into a new legalism, and a detraction from the crucial character of the work of Christ or the transmission of grace in the Church. In combatting the view he outlined a theory of grace that guided, but did not control, the movement of the West for many centuries. Augustine listened to Paul's complaint about his own character in the letter to the Romans: "O wretched man that I am." He was sufficiently the empiricist to analyze his own most obvious sensual bent (tending to overidentify sin with the senses and the flesh in the neo-Platonic fashion he found congenial). As his thought pushed beyond the borders of Ambrosian teaching, he contended that while God had indeed created man good and just, as Pelagius taught, Adam obliterated this goodness in what the Bible describes as the Fall of Man. Then following Paul in Romans 5, he urged that all men shared this guilt for the historical reason. Yet his observations about himself and others showed that it was also possible, perhaps only fleetingly, for man to live a just and righteous life. Something had happened to bring about this new possibility.

The something was grace, which enters history and frees men; this happened in Christ. Grace operated in this way; it infused a new being, new will, new love into man by the working of the Holy Spirit. While Augustine did not separate the strands as radically as Paul had, yet he stands in the same line for his stress on the uniqueness of grace in Christ. His sticking-point in all Pelagian debate was the glory and grace of God and the grandeur and misery of man as just and as sinful. Many of the later debates over providence and predestination, selection and election, grace and responsibility were outgrowths of this controversy; one of the first was the "Semi-Pelagian" (more properly "Semi-Augustinian") controversy. There were those who had not accepted the idea of man's total inability, the idea of predestination and complete dependency upon grace. After Augustine's death they forayed with new boldness to modify his position. With them the discussion moved from Africa and Italy into Gaul, where anti-Augustinians had been safely more belligerent in their argument that Augustine was too dualistic, almost Manichean and fatalist.

Sometimes the followers of Augustine gave their opponents good cause for attack as they carried the master's views to logical conclusion through extreme statements. Bishop Faustus (—c. 495) was champion of a mediating view which attracted a substantial party to a position known as Traducianism (the human soul is traduced from parent to child, not created new and *ex nihlio*); the whole range of Pelagian tendencies was condemned at Orange and the Augustinian teaching was orthodox in the apostolic line.

A reference to these early controversies over holiness of

life and churchly rites, over the status of man in the situations of sin and grace, is important as the backward glance that reveals the change in direction from ecumenical or Eastern concerns. For in these same years (between Augustine and Orange) the Council of Chalcedon defined Christ's divine and human natures, and the Monophysite and Monothelite struggles enlarged upon it. The institutional feel and organizational grandeur of ancient Rome were being inherited by the adminstrators of the spiritual life in the down-to-earth West, to usher in an age of ecclesiastical development conscious of authority and tradition. The spokesmen for this development were the popes.

THE PAPACY

How suddenly and dramatically the papacy emerged as the new force in doctrinal controversy is clear if we skip two centuries beyond Orange to see the Western side of the iconoclastic controversy which rocked the East. In the East the Caesaropapist issue was entangled with the image-question, while the prestige theologian of the millennium in the East, John of Damascus, apologized with intellectual sophistication for the use of icons. But in the West no extensive body of theory was developed to encounter iconodulist claims; the popes spoke out of whatever authority their office then held. This authority did not always mean much in Byzantine realms: Patriarch Germanus made his appeal to it in 730 and was deposed. Gregory III summoned two synods at Rome in 731 to condemn Leo the Isaurian and the image-worshippers, but this did not terminate the issue. When the East took initiative as in the Synod of Hieria in 753, the Pope refused to attend; but this policy was fruitful, for in the Seventh General Council at Nicaea in 787 Pope Hadrian I's legates were listened to. This glimpse should suffice to show how strategy and prestige more than theological acumen were coming to guide the West; few intellects (Hincmar of Reims was one of them) were attracted to the mysteries involved with icons—most were content to defer to ecclesiastical authority.

This is not to suggest that there was no creative theological effort in the Roman church; there was, but it was directed to a different type of object, a defense of enlarging ecclesiastical claims.

This defense took three forms in the three Western dogmatic developments which Troeltsch and others have seen to be the new contributions of the Middle Ages (and which were to be at the center of attack in the Reformation and modern era). The first of these was the issue of the primacy and universality of the Roman bishop. The second, which was discussed in an earlier chapter, argued the supremacy of the spiritual power over the temporal. The third turned on the question of transmission of grace through the sacraments which we have seen to be prefigured in Augustine. The first and third of these need further exposition.

The magnetism of Rome and the steely defense it attracted are best seen in the Pseudo-Isidorean decretals and in Gregorian theology, but the Church did not need to wait for the ninth and eleventh centuries to see the beginning of this pull. As early a witness as Irenaeus could write of the Roman church:

> By its tradition and by its faith announced to men, which has been transmitted to us by the succession of bishops, we confound all those who in any way by caprice or vainglory or by blindness and perversity of will gather where they ought not. For to this Church, on account of its higher origin, it is necessary that every Church, that is, the faithful from all sides, should resort, in which the tradition from the Apostles has always been preserved by those that are from all parts (*Against Heresies, III,* III).

In 341 Julius, Bishop of Rome, could write the council of Antioch: "I am informing you of the tradition *handed down* [emphasis mine] from the blessed Apostle Peter," who was seen to be the head of the Roman see. St. Jerome could write to Pope Damasus in 376: "As I follow no leader save Christ, so I communicate with none save your Beatitude, that is, with the chair of Peter. For this, I know, is the Rock on which the Church is built." But the strength of papal authority was in its pragmatic appeal: it worked, it had power in dealing with emperor and king, it became a center of religious life. When the artificial and even false defenses of the papacy come, they seem hardly necessary. The most famous of these was that series of false decretals, now known as Pseudo-Isidorean, classed with the decrees of ancient councils. The decretals were intended to demonstrate early Roman and papal authority and supremacy, among other matters.

The Roman claim did not have to depend upon such illegitimacy; churchmen of the stature of Gregory VII (Pope from 1073–85) immeasurably enhanced the office by their pastoral care, administrative ability, and argumentative skill. Gregory came to office in one of those hours which leave room for greatness and he provided it; he pulled together the loose ends of the Western line and tied them into a bundle eminently usable by the Church. Not that Gregory was a pure type, a model of the Christian theologian; mingled with his Augustinian strains were strange superstitions and crude theological views. He could incorporate pagan mythology into Christian witness. But he had behind him the experience of Cluniac reform and the fortunate asset of a theology which centered in Christ—a check on much of the superstition that had found its way into the Church. While struggling with William the Conquerer, Henry IV, and Philip I he developed a religious authority which makes him the model of medieval churchmanship.

The bitter controversy between Gregory and Henry VII provides the best illustration of tensions between papacy and national rulers and the bishops loyal to those rulers. Gregory had suspended some German bishops and was countered by an angry Henry who nominated some bishops on his own. When the Pope announced his intention to use the ultimate weapon of excommunication, Henry and the bishops loyal to him at Worms, in January of 1076, wrote to the Pope: "We renounce, now and for the future, all obedience unto thee—which indeed we never promised to thee." [3]

In February Gregory deposed Henry, absolving "all Christians from the bond of the oath which they have made to him or shall make." Matters got worse before they got better for Gregory and the papacy, but in the end they did get better and after some papal compromises had been made, the papacy essentially was able to assert its rights and prerogatives at the expense of the emperors.[4]

Gregory made the most astounding claims for his office before Innocent III or Boniface VIII and backed the claims with political power. In his theories the Church, as Augustine said it, had foundations in the City of God, while the secular order was grounded on sinful conditions. The pope heads the universal apostolic Church, carrying on the Petrine tradition; bishops, responsible to him, also represent him. Princes must bow to him, emperors receive their power from him as the moon draws light from the sun. What gave charismatic force to Gregory's claims as opposed to Boniface's in a later day was this fact: they were not mere political tools—he honestly believed these sanctions to be laid upon him and the office by God. In the stormy waters of the day the Church was the ark and the pope the pilot. In the terrors of medieval life that Church was the center of solace—designedly attracting people to the comforts of the sacraments. In ministering to fear and to hope the Church fulfilled itself; but the admixture of superstition obscured the simpler evangelical brightness and detracted somewhat from the pastoral dispensation of counsel and Good News along with the sacraments.

The papacy was to know other types of growth apart from the dialogue with the emperor. Canon law as detailed by the great jurist Ivo of Chartres (—1116) served this growth well, and the new universities concentrated on legal undergirding of ecclesiastical life. Notable among these was Bologna, which elevated canon law to disciplinary status; there Gratian (—1140) penned his *Decretal* which brought this body of literature up to date. The collection includes decrees of councils, papal proclamations, sayings of the fathers, all in a systematic corpus. This was to grow in the late medieval times to a positive place in the papal claim.

THE SACRAMENTAL SYSTEM

Here we must turn from the institutional sanction to an understanding of Troeltsch's "third dogma," the impartation of grace through the seven sacraments. This is closely related to the papal and hierarchical system. If it is true that

> the Pope sums up in himself the whole conception of miracle and becomes the central miracle of Christendom; his miraculous power then radiates forth from him again in a precise and regular way through the different degrees of the hierarchy down to the most obscure village *curé*,[5]

so also is the corollary true: the sacraments are the mysterious means of nurturing the Christian life through miracle; their power is radiated from Christ through the apostles and the later Church to the bishops, the priests, the beneficiaries of the sacrament who are dependent upon the churchly system. Or, viewed from the other direction: "The priest alone, by the appointment of Christ, has in his hands the power of the sacramental impartation of grace, and thus of the redemptive miraculous element of the Church, without which there is no deliverance from original sin or from purgatory." [6]

The sacramental development is also characteristically medieval. While the New Testament contains descriptions of baptism and the Lord's Supper, with the part which outward signs divinely fused with spiritual realities should play in the Church; and while in the *Didache*, in Justin Martyr, and in the fathers a formalization of sacramental life begins to appear; this reaches institutional climax in the complex network of means of grace in the Middle Ages. The number has varied widely, from the two just listed to the thirty cited by Hugh of St. Victor (—1141); the number depends upon the definition. Peter Lombard's seven have proven most durable: Baptism, Confirmation, the Eucharist, Penance, Extreme Unction, Orders, and Matrimony. The Council of Florence in 1439 regularized this list, which was ratified again at Trent in the sixteenth century.

Of all seven sacraments, the one which lay closest to ecclesiastical development and which was most involved in theological thought in this period was the Eucharist. This elaborate rite (or system) grew out of the meal of the Lord with his disciples the night before he died. The tendency of the medieval development was largely external. It laid more weight progressively on the act of celebrating the Eucharist, on the powers that came with this re-enactment of the sacrifice of Christ, than on the spiritual reality to which it pointed. Popes found denial of the sacrament (and thus of heaven) a potent political force to use against obstinate rulers; priests saw it useful in encouraging penance and throwing the fear of God into the wayward or the recalcitrant. People came to attach magical significance to the reserved Host, or bread. The holy communion became the Mass; its sacrifice benefited even those who did not receive the bread. All in all, no single element of the worship life of the Church contributed so much to the weight of Roman authority and the complexity of Western tradition. Inevitably so valued an entity would come under much discussion, and theological controversy in several periods revolved around it.

A first instance of this appeared in the dispute between two monks, Ratramnus and Radbertus, in the middle of the ninth century. Until then Augustine, Ambrose, and Gregory had articulated views of the Eucharist largely apart from controversy. Popular expectations raised the sacrament beyond what was biblically claimed for it to the view that Calvary was being re-enacted before the eyes of the faithful. When this occurred theological justification had to be found, and this was provided by Radbertus, a Benedictine (—860). His "On the Body and Blood of the Lord" seems to have been the *first* doctrinal treatise on the subject, and its complex presentation was to lead to the official Roman Catholic view of transubstantiation. Christ is really present in the sacrament; the "flesh" in the sacrament is not bread but the flesh born of the Virgin, crucified, risen, miraculously reproduced. Men who eat this flesh participate in the life of the mystical Body of Christ in the Church. This mysterious view (not yet termed transubstantiation) has often and easily been caricatured most crudely, but the seeds of the crudeness are in Radbertus' presentation. This is obvious from the immediate reaction from Ratramnus and Hrabanus Maurus. The latter, with Augustinian warrant, argued that the Eucharist effected a spiritual union between the person and the mystical Body of Christ; bread and wine received in the sacrament are symbols (in the high sense of the term) for that body. When Charles the Bald asked Ratramnus' opinion he wrote a treatise aping Radbertus' title from the opposite viewpoint: the elements are a symbol, the presence of Christ is spiritual, the result is a communion. But Radbertus had the needs of the Church and the desires of the people behind him; his realism was overpowering in the medieval context, and later development was able to begin where his view left off.

Augustinian spiritualism was left far behind during the time between this eruption and the controversy involving Berengar of Tours (—1088) and Lanfranc (—1089). Berengar touched new fire to the ashes in renewed attack on Radbertus' theory by arguing that in it only "pieces of Christ's flesh" were received, whereas in the biblical view the entire Christ was a gift to the participant. This was a challenge to the Roman view, which prevailed again when a confession was forced from Berengar. Such confession was not good for the soul, however, and Berengar was soon again in trouble for new writing. An avalanche of defense of transubstantiation fell on him. Its massive impact embarrassed protectors of Berengar, who was forced to about-face once more. Rome was well on the way to the official definition of transubstantiation at the Fourth Lateran Council in 1215:

> The Body and Blood are truly contained in the Sacrament of the Altar under the appearance of bread and wine, after the bread has been changed into the Body, and the wine into the Blood, through the power of God. Only the rightly ordained priest can perform this sacrament.

This official viewpoint received ultimate support from the high medieval theological tradition of scholasticism, which was notably conservative in its support of papal tradition as it fused Gregorian pastoral concerns with classic hierarchical tendencies. In this definition the sacraments receive their power from God and are valid *ex opere operato,* by the very act of administering them. All are at the center of the Church's life.

It is no longer necessary to regale the reader with elaborate accounts of the excesses to which this piety and authority were lending themselves: the men of the times lived close to nature, close to life and death, in the face of drama and violence. Their spiritual nourishment was often too realistic, too concrete, too little symbolic. But despite the papal misuse and the unevangelical character of much of the development, later centuries have learned something from the theology and practice of the times:

> What the medieval Mass always maintained was its objectivity. This has been something lacking in much Protestant worship. The Mass was an *actio,* a living drama constantly reenacted for the salvation of men. The very realism of the medieval mind helped to keep this important point central. Worship was not "having a religious experience," it was traffic and communion with the Living God. It was the recognition of His condescension to man in Jesus Christ and at its best it was an act of offering in which Christians gave themselves to God and received the divine Life through the continued presentation, by the priest, of the sacrifice of Calvary.[7]

If ecclesiology prevailed over Christology in these centuries; if anthropology was more weighted than theology, or concrete thought more than abstract; and if the discussion of the papacy and tradition or the Lord's Supper is a perfect illustration of this, so too is the discussion of the atonement—though at first glance it appears to be an exception to the Western trend.

CHRISTOLOGY AND ATONEMENT

Curiously, despite the Christological concerns of the creedal period, the central issue of how God saves man in Christ was seldom elaborated. While it is somewhat summary to overleap the centuries from St. Paul to Anselm in 1098, efforts to rewrite the Greek fathers to suggest that this is the heart of their concern have never been very convincing. In the creedal definitions much of this was implied. Athanasius detailed a view in which Christ is the bearer of incorruption; Irenaeus and Origen—in the contention of Gustav Aulén—saw the meaning of the atonement in Christ's victory over hostile powers. But the reconciling circle from God's initiative to Christ's activity to God's ongoing response and activity is not systematically broken until the concerns for men and the Church emerge in medieval times.

The very title of the seminal work of the time, *Cur Deus Homo,* why did God become *man?,* is a clue to the emphasis that places it in context. Its author, Anselm, Archbishop of Canterbury (—1109), pulled the earlier abstract discussion into the obviously Western concern in a distinctively "Roman" manner, and his theories are often described as the "Latin" view. That Anselm's view is open to slightly divergent responses is clear from a juxtaposition of comments in a recent study by William J. Wolf: "Denney praises Anselm's writing as 'the truest and greatest book on the Atonement that has ever been written.' At the opposite pole Harnack complains that 'no theory so bad had ever before his day been given out as ecclesiastical.' " [8]

Wolf suggests that Anselm's view has as its vital center "the institution of penance in the Latin Church"—and this is its proper context for the way it brings together man and sacrament through institution under God. The stress lay on "satisfaction"—God's holiness was profaned by man's sin. Some satisfaction or restitution must be made. Only the God-Man could make it: hence, the Christ. In Christ's voluntary sacrificial death God saw something he could reward. The God-Man needed no reward. He had done this for man, to whom he gives the fruits. This legalistic view of a juridical transaction did not hold the field all by itself: as usual the myth of medieval monolithicism is shattered, here by Abelard, who was almost "modern" (mark the word!) in his more relativistic approach.

Abelard's view detracts from the horrendous weight given to sin in most Christian orthodoxy; his view of the atonement had to be compatible with his anthropology. Would God kill His Son and thus be more guilty than man? No: in the Christ-event God's love was shown to man in an infinite degree and man responds with love and thankfulness. Answer followed answer: Bernard of Clairvaux entered the ranks with a critique of Abelard's evasion of the necessity of Christ's cross, his suffering and bloody death. Examples (Adam's sin and Christ's teaching) effect little in the presence of real sin and real human need. The vicarious death of Christ was the only event of both personal and cosmic significance that could alter the human situation. Curiously, this crucial doctrine was never forced to the point where papal or conciliar settlement seemed necessary, and various views have always coexisted. But it is fair to say that Anselm's view of "satisfaction" was most congenial both to the current views of man and to the hierarchical and sacramental Church.

SCHOLASTICISM

A review such as this of highlights of substantive theology must neglect the refined expressions of piety that appeared as seldom before or since in church history, a devotional theology associated with names like Bernard of Clairvaux, Hugo and Richard of St. Victor, Bonaventure; or St. Francis of Assisi and his school of "holy poverty" and humility; or the school of the imitation of Christ. It remains only to follow briefly the course of high medieval thought which would synthesize philosophy and theology in the services of the Church: scholasticism. It gladly lent itself to the custodians of the apostolic tradition until, later, a group of schoolmen known as nominalists began to tear at the roots of the system. Seldom has Christianity found intellects as useful to ecclesiastical purpose as did the medieval Church in Anselm, Albertus Magnus, and Thomas Aquinas.

Scholasticism, the medieval attempt to systematize and explicate revealed truth in correlation with a philosophical system, long was considered uncongenial to the modern temper. More recently Christian and non-Christian alike have been called to examine the system which climaxed the Middle Ages and helped form modern Europe, a medieval achievement as monumental and impressive as the cathe-

drals. Here as elsewhere it would be possible to begin with
Augustine and his quest: "Understand so that you may
believe; believe so that you may understand." An oasis in
a barren stretch of history, Boethius (—524) extolled the
consolations of philosophy and translated or edited Aristotle and other Greeks. In Carolingian times the interest
received an academic assist from the cathedral schools
which preserved ancient learning.

These represent spurts and stops; continuity in the line
of the schoolmen begins with John Scotus Erigena (—877),
who recalls in his work the old attempts to fuse neo-Plato-
nism with Christianity, to echo the Gnostics who would
blend emanations with creation. A lonely scholar and
faithful son of the Church, Erigena was probably not so
orthodox as he appeared in his own time. Holy Scripture
was the source of apostolic reference, but reason must
elucidate and elaborate upon this authority. "Authority is
the source of knowledge, but our own reason remains the
norm by which all authority must be judged." Faith has
limits, it is "a certain beginning by which knowledge of
the Creator begins to be produced in the rational nature"
—faith and reason could never appear in opposition to
each other. Erigena's sweet reasonableness led him to
theological positions which now often appear to approach
pantheism.

But sweet reasonableness did not always prevail. Erigena
is a watershed figure; scholasticism would flow from him,
but he also stood at the end of an age; his work "synthesizes
the philosophical accomplishments of fifteen centuries, and
appears as the final achievement of ancient philosophy." 9
For after him followed the stormy period of controversy,
with Berengar and St. Peter Damian at loggerheads,
Berengar and Lanfranc in dispute, Berengar and the Pope
arguing over the papal relation to true Christian dogma
and tradition. In this time of dispute, dialectic (the method
of the "yes" and the "no" in confrontation as a way toward
truth) emerged as a new tool for the schoolmen, and
scholasticism was in position again to serve the orthodox
cause.

Then came Anselm, a second Augustine and a precursor of Aquinas, the thinker who provided scholasticism with an outline and a goal. "I do not seek to understand that I may believe, but I believe in order to understand. For this also I believe, that unless I believed, I should not understand." In his *Proslogion* the great eleventh-century thinker presented the classic "ontological proof" for the existence of God by "proving" to his contemporaries the inconceivability of God's non-existence; his practical churchmanship and his renewed statement of relations between reason and faith came to be of great use by the Church in a time of the reawakening of philosophical interest as a means of correlating this knowledge with what had come to be assumed as a deposit of apostolic faith in the Church.

After certain twelfth-century innovations in technique, particularly the introduction of a catechismal question-and-refutation method, we note next an antagonist of Anselm, Abelard, whose *Sic et Non* was a sophisticated dialectic. Abelard's ability to reach the root of philosophical problems —"He sees," complained Bernard, "nothing through a glass darkly but stares at everything face to face"—anticipates the difficulties certain scholastics were to have in their application of the canons of reason to the apostolic tradition. Abelard burned his fingers on the questions of atonement and the divine Trinity. In this time Peter Lombard proved himself servant of the Church in his preparation of the *Sentences,* which would serve as theological textbook for centuries.

When in the thirteenth century the introduction of Arab thought, the Avicennan and Averroean commentaries on Aristotle, made their impact, scholastic patterns were skewed. Some Averroists were not averse to following Aristotle and the Arabs right out of the catholic church; the Augustinians appropriated only what was "safe" in Averroism. A great third force, the Dominican synthesizers, capped the effort: here was the climax in Albertus Magnus and Thomas Aquinas.

Thomas (—1274) appeared in the great century of Francis of Assisi and Innocent III and of Emperor

Frederick II, the wonder of the world, and with them reached the kind of greatness that has made later centuries measure stature in relation to their achievement. An Aristotelian who found other philosophical influences also capable of incorporation in his synthesis of revealed and rational truth, his sometimes suspect teachings later were regarded as orthodox in an official sense. He dedicated his entire life to the "intellectual apostolate," serving the tradition with all his mind. At Paris after 1245 Albertus Magnus introduced him to Aristotle; he spent much of his life there, in Cologne, and in Naples. Out of an immense body of literature the *Summa Theologica* stands as summit.

It is not possible to do justice to a thinker like Aquinas by brief reference to his thought; we can do nothing more here than to place it in context. Heightening distinctions between reason and faith and allowing high status to reason, he removed many areas of thought from its realm. Yet these mysteries, unattainable by reason, are neither irrational nor beyond rational explication and illumination. Such areas: the incarnation, the resurrection, or the Trinity, are vastly different from the rationally accessible ones: the existence of God and many of His attributes. These distinctions suggest two lines of Aquinian thought, the philosophical and the theological, where he devoted himself to discussion of the sacraments and to biblical exegesis. The Eucharist was the great sacrament among the seven instituted by Christ. As thinker, hymnist, devotionalist, disputant, he well deserved the title "Doctor of the Church" granted him by Pius V in 1567.

When in doubt, Aquinas bowed to churchly authority: "The weightiest authority is the Church's custom. It should be constantly and punctiliously observed. Ecclesiastical writings draw their warrant from the Church's authority. We should take our stand on the Church's traditional teaching, rather than on the pronouncements of Augustine or Jerome or any other doctor" (*II Quodlibets,* iv. 7). His faithfulness to the medieval ideal is consistent and obvious: reason has its place but the apostolic tradition is in no danger. It is inviolable and it has its custodian.

To the Supreme Pontiff, who has this authority, major difficulties are submitted . . . One faith should be held by the whole Church, *that ye all speak the same thing, and that there be no divisions among you,* cannot be ensured unless doubts about the faith be decided by him who presides over the whole Church, and whose decision will be accepted by all. The publication of articles of belief is like the convocation of a General Council or any other commitment affecting the Universal Church: no other power is competent but that of the Pope (*Summa Theologica,* i. 10, 2a-2ae).

Once burlesqued by his fellow students as a "dumb ox," Aquinas lived to see his teacher Albert's prophecy fulfilled: "This dumb ox will fill the world with his bellowing."

But even while the Doctor of the Church was bellowing, there was distant bleating rising in chorus to challenge his synthesis; opposing his realism were nominalists who would not allow for reality in universal concepts, and thus they subtracted the essentials of the faith from the provinces of reason—to foredoom scholasticism. Some of the earlier clashes with Aquinian thought came out of the work of Duns Scotus (—1308), "Doctor Subtilis," a Franciscan rival of the Dominicans whose sun rose during the early eclipse of Thomas. With William of Occam (—1349) came the real nominalist breakthrough or breakdown—depending upon the point of view. "Doctor Invincibilis" belonged to a new day; if there were men to throw stones at cathedral glass, Occam threw rocks at the synthetic glass house. In denying the possibility of proving God's existence or uncovering His attributes by reason, he espoused an empiricism that was embarrassing to the Thomists and to the Roman church as a whole. Soon he was extolling faith, laying bare the Scriptures as single source and norm of churchly teaching, attacking transubstantiation, in conflict with the Pope. Nor was he alone: a whole school of Franciscans were to join him or find parallel courses. Still a healthy mile from the impetus that brought on the Reformation within two centuries, Occam and the other walkers of the modern way were spelling the end of the great synthesis of philosophical thought with apostolic teaching in the stewardship of the Church.

THE WANING OF THE MIDDLE AGES

To walk further down this *via moderna* would lead us to the disintegration of medieval life, which it was signalling, but which becomes part of a later story. The drama of the crisis to come is clear when we see the challenge of Occam's words to counter those of the *Dictatus Papae:* "Holy Scriptures cannot err . . . but the pope . . . can err." Ideas have consequences; an idea like this could lead to the widespread skepticism that soon appeared to challenge the temporal claims of the Church. It could unnerve the culture-informing Church. It could encourage the sects and heretics who had made their pilgrimages from Rome. It could mean the end of a chapter in the Church's history and the beginning of a new one. It could and it did.

Despite the obvious disparities in medieval times between the Church's ideal and its action, one glances wistfully back after such a survey. The Church affirmed its unity and divided into East and West. It affirmed its holiness and produced conniving popes and corrupt bishops. It confessed its catholicity yet never extended its horizons to the limit. It assumed its apostolicity yet arrogated to itself new views of tradition and an absolutist claim, "the church can never err," even though here "the church" is institutionalized and thus partakes of historical relativities. All this is true in the Middle Ages, and who is to say it is more true or less true than at any other time?

A survey of that long span of Christian history from the fifth to the sixteenth century balances fear with hope. One would fear for a church that had to make its way in the violent tenor of feudal life and in corruption of court and bishopric—honest research finds tarnish on the Golden Age. But the other extreme is equally inaccurate: one dare not overextend the Dark Ages in time or space. The ages that produced universities and cathedrals and pastoral theology, that created synthetic systems and sacramental hymnody, that saw the conversion of the barbarian and the turning back of the Crescent's tide, that saw

reform from within and expansion beyond the Church—
the age of St. Francis and Thomas Aquinas—and the in-
spirer of Gothic architecture Abbot Suger, such an age and
such a span cannot be written off as a dead loss.

PART III: *The Pivot*

9

NIGHT FELL

Suddenly, after the long span of Christian history in its
medieval development, everything is changed. No longer
is it practicable to speak in terms of increase and decrease,
decline and rise, growth and disintegration; now the Christian movement experiences reformation or revolution. Having gone as far as it could go in one direction, it engages in
an about-face, it pivots. There is a basic change in direction
for a large segment that would not repudiate its recent
past. But behind the word "suddenly" there is the usual
tangle, the usual complication. Everything seems so easy to
the reader after the historian tidies it up. The birth of
Jesus can be seen as occurring at the least likely time and
place in history—this is part of the offense of the faith. But
the story-teller, cued by St. Paul's reference to its occurrence
in "the fullness of time," can reframe the picture. A great
language and a great Empire were nearly universal; when
would be a better moment for the divine interruption of
human history?

So it has been with the writing of Reformation history
by Protestants. Manipulating the concept of Providence,
they are tempted to adjust God's purpose to the time-
tables of German politics, Italian art, and English statecraft. Then everything falls into neat patterns. In this picture the entire fifteenth century is seen a-tiptoe, peering to-

ward the sixteenth. The achievements of the Middle Ages are behind; the breakthrough of the Reformation is ahead; and the century after the Council of Constance marks time merely as a parable of disintegration. One can almost picture the citizenry opening a newspaper awaiting the announcement: "The time is here. The Reformation will now begin."

Of course, it is never so tidy. Let Henri Pirenne serve as witness. After his review of the corruption within the Roman church at the time, he wrote:

> However, the faith was still intact. Since the twelfth century, it would really seem that there had never been so few heretics as during the fifty years that preceded the outbreak of Protestantism. Wycliffism in England and Hussitism in Bohemia were almost extinct. And this in itself is a proof of the religious lukewarmness of the age. No one deserted the Church, or dreamed of doing so; but religion had become little more than a habit, a rule of life for those who observed the letter rather than the spirit. . . . There was nothing, indeed, that could have enabled anyone to foresee the sudden explosion of Lutheranism.[1]

But if we have this firmly in mind we can enjoy the luxury which the perspective of our own times places on those which just preceded the Reformation. And such a view does, indeed, illustrate the ways in which the medieval development had gone about as far as it could go: a new direction was needed.

"Night fell on the German Church, a night that grew ever deeper and darker . . ." This judgment by the kindly and perceptive Roman Catholic theologian Karl Adam can be spread across the face of Christendom: night fell.

> It was night indeed in a great part of Christendom. Such is the conclusion of our survey of the end of the fifteenth century: amongst the common people, a fearful decline of true piety into religious materialism and morbid hysteria; amongst the clergy, both lower and higher, widespread worldliness and neglect of duty; and amongst the very Shepherds of the Church, demonic ambition and sacrilegious perversion of holy things. Both clergy and people must cry *mea culpa, mea maxima culpa!* [2]

It was not all night, only night—never is the pattern that simple. We cannot share the old Protestant view that from the time of Augustine to the sixteenth century European Christians walked through the gloomy corridors of the Dark Ages of fear, frustration, and despair, heaven-bent on breaking through to new light at the signal of Reform. Our review of the long span of centuries has revealed too many splendrous glimpses of Gothic architectural and scholastic philosophical achievements, too many encouraging asides to the warm pieties of the parishes. The conservative Reformation also affirmed this: God had not left Himself without witnesses. There had always been a faithful flock, there had been good doctors of the Church in every century. But this affirmation was not sentimental. Reform was needed.

THE FIFTEENTH CENTURY

These pages will sketch the developments from the Council of Constance in 1414 until the time of the sale of indulgences, an event which triggered reform activities. They will deal with ways in which the Church of Christ attempted to assert its objective holiness in the life of the people, in creative movements, in the creativeness of individuals. They will face the matter of the visible unholiness so patent in the years after "night fell." They will delineate the issue as it emerged: where was the seat of unholiness? After a review of the various national situations and the beginnings of the stir that heralds a new day, they will summarize several abortive pre-Reformation attempts at reassertion of the holiness of the Church.

PARISH LIFE

Night fell. Did it fall on the front line of the Church, where God wrestled with Satan (and the Middle Ages saw the match in a vivid way!) in the parishes of Europe? The same Reformers who made much of the breakdown of piety in the late medieval Church found it necessary to berate their own flocks and to judge themselves for their own ethical and spiritual failings. Parish life was more often a reflection of a too simple adaption to a bad environment than it was a result of official hierarchical conniving and corrupting. Of course, common Christians were illiterate and superstitious—most common people were. Learning had been neglected, education had been devalued. This inevitably reflected itself in ecclesiastical life. In the violent tenor of life, in man's closeness to nature and terror of his fellow, was a clue to the ignorance and fear that marked religious rites. What had earlier flowered as a vivid appropriation of the faith now hardened into gross idolization of images and relics; fluid forms froze, creative imagination atrophied, and grotesque acceptance of the fabulous was common. The Lord's Supper had become the sacrifice of the Mass, and the sacramental fusion of divine word with visible sign was all too often part of a magical picture. All these are commonplaces.

But such commonplaces and stereotypes obscure the survival of parishes as cells, in some sense or other, of the Body of Christ, according to Christian affirmation. There were literally thousands of such cells in western Europe; in them works of mercy, worship, and instruction survived. The re-enactment of Calvary in churches in every town and at every crossroads before the eyes of simple folk must have had telling effect on them, must have led to some sort of renewed confrontation of a deeper meaning in the events. The church tower, standing in overpowering relationship to its environs, beckoned. Certain monastic orders had begun to stress preaching, and the sermon was finding new place. Baptism was taken seriously. Marriage was a sacrament consecrated at the high altar. Innumerable holy days, days of rest and festivity, marked the year. The calendar controlled the months as the bell-tower controlled the hours. If bodily preparation for the Eucharist was often reduced to caricature by the gloom of its atmosphere, religion had its brighter side in the gaiety associated with some feasts, in the comic versions of moral and religious themes that found their way into primitive drama. However much it is necessary to describe the inefficiency, the arbitrariness, the laxity and injustice of parish life under the fattened and sluggish clericalism of the time, it is necessary again and again to stress that the holiness of the Church still found a front against the world in the common life of people too easily blamed for following a weak leadership and for accommodating themselves to an overpowering environment.

THE NEW COMMUNITIES

Nor is this all. "Night fell," but there were still bright comets that sped across the sky. There was still holiness in the lives of men and women who rose above the limits of their times and singly or in movements demonstrated that unselfish motivation persisted in a corrupt church. The Reformers found points of contact with this portion of the past in many aspects of monastic life, in the new brotherhoods with their evangelical discipline, in communities of scholars and saints.

Few better examples of this residue of holiness survive in Christian memory than that of the Brotherhood of the Common Life, which flourished in the Low Countries in late medieval times. Founded in the fourteenth century for the encouragement of learning and the development of piety, the Brotherhood was under a freer discipline than were monastic orders. But in this freedom was a new spirit which encouraged scholarship, self-giving in teaching, and a re-exploration of the achievements of the past. The Brethren could at the same time distinguish themselves for research and routine copying of ancient manuscripts, and for, cultivating a language of devotion with a simple if mystical bent that survives to our day. Under men of great piety and administrative skill—de Groote (—1384), Florentius (—1400) and their successors—and attracting saints like the obscure Thomas a Kempis (—1471), the Brotherhood provides welcome contrast to its century. Thomas was probably the author of the famed *Imitation of Christ*. Educated by the Brethren, he entered a daughter house of the mother at Windesheim and in 1406 adopted the rule. He was soon famed beyond his modest vocation's ordinary possibilities: beyond the copying of manuscripts, laborious writing and instruction, and preaching, he was honored for the depth of his spiritual counsel and the scope of his devotional penetration in whatever he touched with hand or pen. His meditations called all to serious pursuit of the path Christ had walked in marked contradiction of their times. While the Brotherhood was to harden and lose its creative flow later in the century, and while it may be so well known partly because it was so exceptional, yet it cannot be discounted as a spiritual and ethical force in northwest Europe.

MYSTICISM

Mysticism, too, flowered. It can take forms of holy asceticism or of sensual attachment, and in this century it assumed both. In its more evangelical cast it was to be appreciated by the Reformers of the next century. Martin Luther frequently quoted from some of the manuals and sermons of the period, notably those of Johannes Tauler, who flourished in fourteenth-century Germany, and from the famed *Theologica Germanica,* an anonymous work from the end of that century. This latter work urged desertion of worldly attachments and passionate avowal of the divine intent for man through devotion and works of love. Three great Catherines stand out above their century. Catherine of Bologna (—1463), Catherine of Siena (—1380), and Catherine of Genoa (—1510) span one hundred and fifty years, but are as one in their mystic devotion and records of holiness. The youngest of the three, Catherine of Genoa, turned her back on the patrician comforts to which she was born and fastened her interests on service to the sick and the dying. To read her records of mystic involvement is an almost embarrassing experience at times, for the pathological fascination they hold; but to read the record of her ministry to the needy in a time of plague and mass disease, poverty and ignorance is a heartening experience.

Neither Italy nor Catherinedom had a corner on sanctity and fanciful expression. At the beginning of this period England produced Lady Julian of Norwich (—1413), another somewhat obscure mystic, an anchoress who claimed experience of ecstatic visions of divine love. She picked up, perhaps unconsciously through reading earlier English mystics, a neo-Platonic strain that is again evident in Margery Kempe (—1373), who combined mystical experience with the example of intercessory prayer and religious pilgrimages. In the succession of Vincent Ferrer (—1419) the Spanish Dominicans urged the power of preaching, wrote manuals of devotion, and developed new paths of piety through concentration on the way of the cross and the art of dying.

MONASTICISM

Piety did not limit itself, then, to the non-monastic line; that not all was corrupt with monachism is clear from the ready identification of conservative Reformers with this form of religious life in their earlier quest for personal holiness. When Martin Luther could discover no other outlet he tried Augustinian asceticism and found in some of his counsellors, particularly in one Staupitz, evangelical example. Some validity must have remained; for souls somewhat less tortured than Luther's, satisfactions remained.

Unfortunately, there was a double-sidedness to the enduring validity or the renewal and reform of monastic orders, as in the example of Spain. Purification of corrupt movements curiously resulted in their perversion as instruments of power. In Spain the remarkable Francisco Ximenes de Cisneros (—1517) rose to the cardinalate at Toledo. He lived to the very year which serves as the symbolic date for the beginning of the Reformation in northern Europe, and has served conveniently as a last-minute entry into the ledger by Catholic historians who try to balance the books on pre-Reform times. He is frequently cited as the example of what could have developed had the Reformation not interrupted the continuity of the Western church. Ximenes found himself the prime religious figure in a nation that was rising to new prominence with the union of the houses of Castile-Leon and Aragon in the marriage of Isabella and Ferdinand.

The career of Ximenes began with a dispute with the Archbishop of Toledo over a papal appointment; Ximenes was imprisoned. Chosen by Isabella as a confessor in 1492 (mark the year!) he rose to ecclesiastical prominence in the court and three years later, to his own great dismay, was appointed to the Archbishopric of Toledo. Turning his back on the conventional privilege and pomp associated with that office, he set an example of asceticism and devotion. Involved against his will in the dynastic intrigues of the day, Ximenes yet found time to devote himself to education, founding the university of Alcala in 1500, and attracting to it learned teachers from the older Spanish academic tradition as well as from Bologna and Paris. His *Complutensian Polyglot* (achieved as a tribute to the birth of Charles V of Spain) was witness to his biblical scholarship. It brought together Greek and Latin with the Hebrew Old Testament and Latin with the Greek New Testament in parallel columns. Ximenes used his power and prestige for purification of clerical orders and for reformation of the hierarchy.

Among the lands of Western Christianity at that time, Spain alone had many non-Christians in organized factions: Moslems and Jews. Ximenes undertook to convert them. His methods of conversion illustrate the other side of the reformative movements within Catholicism: he seized upon the Inquisition to force baptisms. Mention of the Inquisition calls to mind an institution that was in theory planned for churchly reform; but it lives in modern memory as an instrument of terror unparalleled in cruelty in its day. The Inquisition was a formalization of the church's long temptation to enforce its claims for truth with the sword; it was not an invention of this period, for it had been called into being in 1232 by Emperor Frederick II as a weapon against heretics; Gregory IX rescued it from imperial use and made it a weapon of the church. The monastic orders entrusted with the task of heresy-hunting would prescribe penance or lead the victims to imprisonment for denial of the "catholic faith." Torture was permitted by papal decree. A final punishment could mean death by burning. It was this institution which was seized and transformed as the "Spanish Inquisition" toward the end of the fifteenth century. Ferdinand and Isabella sanctioned it against the Moriscos and Marranos, who were converts from Mohammedanism and Judaism. A Grand Inquisitor and a High Council tightly administered its affairs.

To mention Ximenes' employment of this torture is to detract from the glamour of his career of reform, for it calls to mind the career of his contemporary, Tomas de Torquemada (—1498), Grand Inquisitor after 1483. In the past the number of burnings for heresy under Torquemada was greatly exaggerated: now it is believed that a mere two thousand suffered this fate at the hands of the followers of a gentle Galilean in the time of Spanish reform. Instead of the dawn promised by Ximenes, Spain fell into a period of early, new nightfall.

A final example of the double-sidedness of most examples of persistent calls to holiness appears in the career of Jeanne d'Arc, the Maid of Orleans (—1431), who distinguished herself by strength of purpose during the Hundred Years' War's rough-and-tumble political life. On the one hand she remains a symbol to all ages of courage in danger, of conviction and commitment to truth, of seriousness of intent to fulfill holy vows, of achievement. But these are knotted with a strange pattern of obsessions and supernaturalistic experiences which always bordered on the superstitious. Seeing a light, hearing a voice, she responded to the epiphanies of Sts. Michael, Margaret, and others: she was to lead France. When some of her prophecies were fulfilled, military and royal leaders began to listen to her. Her end came after her capture, in a trial for witchcraft and heretical teaching. She died a heretic. In 1920 she was canonized a saint. Her heresy: I am directly responsible to God and not to the Church, sounds strangely "Protestant." Her warrant: I am receiving direct revelation, sounds uncontainable by any normal measure. Through the confusion, however, there remains a glow of holiness in an example of steadfastness the world cannot lightly forget.

Still, night fell, beyond the parishes, the brotherhoods, the imitators of Christ and the mystics drawn to God, beyond the educators and reformers, the saints and the scholars. It fell because of the nature of the consolidation of power in the Roman See, which was unable by itself to extricate itself from its own pretensions and corruptions, its own involvement in the alien moral standards which properly belonged to "the world." The hated Inquisition was but one example of this power in operation.

In this review the church of the East need play no major part because it did not undergo a parallel upheaval in sixteenth-century reform. It passes into relative obscurity for a time. With the fall of Constantinople in 1453 the might of the Empire of the East came to an end, and with it the Byzantine consolidation of ecclesiastical power tumbled. Turkish conquest had lessened the effectiveness of Eastern Christianity. A new star was rising in the East in the form of Russian Christianity, which was experiencing geographical spread and ecclesiastical embodiment in Moscow as the "third Rome." But maturation of this development comes somewhat later. There was little contact. Western popes undertook occasional endeavors toward reunion through wooing the East, particularly in the ecumenical councils at Ferrara and Florence in 1438 and 1439. But when it comes to the question of papal authority, a compromising statement did not serve well for enduring understanding. When the legates of the East returned home their agreements were repudiated. These councils merely served to exaggerate the schism of four centuries past. The Christianity of Greece, the Balkans, and Russia was little disturbed by the Reformation.

THE PAPACY

This dismissal of the East leaves us free to isolate the institution most involved in the decline of Western solidar-

ity: the papacy. Previous chapters have detailed its rise
to the peak of absurd claims after the achievements of
Gregory VII, Innocent III, and the disproportionate claims
of Boniface VIII. The West was still living under the description in *Unam Sanctam:* there is but one Holy Catholic
and Apostolic Church, and outside this Church there is no
salvation. There is one head, Christ. His vicar "is Peter
and Peter's successor." "Therefore, if the Greeks or others
say that they were not committed to Peter and his successors, they necessarily confess that they are not of Christ's
sheep."

The papacy had claimed the fullness of power, *plenitudo
potestatis,* which it enforced whenever it could and with
which it bartered or begged when necessary. The constant dialogue in emergent European structures of power weakened
the spiritual vitality and potential for holiness in the institution. Whenever the pope picked up his "second sword"
of temporal authority there would be conflict with temporal
rulers. Papal criticism and intrigue, temporal monarchical
power and the rise of national states, the conciliar movement for reform, inner corruption—all this had weakened
the papacy until it found itself in "Babylonian Captivity"
at Avignon in France from 1309 to 1377. Worst of all, with
this exile and the sense of discontinuity and disruption it
engendered went a schism caused in part by claims of
rival popes to be the one successor necessary to the stewardship of salvation. There was little prestige left.

Meanwhile the spiritual authority, the "first sword" of
the pope, was stained by his abuse of power in the weapons
of excommunication and the interdict. The power was there
because men believed that this sword could cut them off
from heaven. The power was perverted because under this
sword revenues could fatten Roman coffers—revenues from
the collection of the tithe from the clergy, from the census
of the rulers, from annates (the "first year" tax of the
clergy), from income out of vacant benefices, from padded
"expense accounts" for the entertainment of visiting papal
legates. The financial grip of the papacy on Europe was
still tight, but now it had been reduced to collection from
"spiritual" sources.

Perverted power repeatedly led to scandal and fall in the papacy. The combination of extravagant claims and extravagant incomes with extravagant papal personalities fattened the office for scandal. The new hope which the schism-ending Council of Constance (1414–18) had engendered lived on for a time. The papacy was out of captivity; there was, again, one pope. The conciliar movement had much of its sting removed. Power was again centralized; it was massive and could overrule councils. For its place in this momentary redirection the Council of Constance bears a moment's examination. It was convoked by one of the master statesmen of the period, Emperor Sigismund, who worked through John XXIII, one of three contenders for the papacy. Several of the great nominalists were there, especially Gerson and d'Ailly. All the three men who then claimed the papacy finally abdicated or else were deposed. The emergent pope was Martin V.

The Council of Constance is remembered as the greatest hope for reform in the fifteenth century and for the greatest breach of faith of the times. The hope arose after Jean Gerson had detailed in a sermon the ways in which the Council in its "popeless" moment actually represented the whole Church. Out of this fact grew the "Articles of Constance," from which later Catholic but anti-papal movements would draw sustenance. The Articles argued that as a general council, the assembly drew on divine authority; its resolutions bound all men of God, including the pope. But the success of Constance in healing schism and reconsolidating power cut off this potential of greater success for it. It is remembered equally for its manner of dealing with heresy. The famed Bohemian reformer John Hus was summoned under the promise of protection, only to be burned at the stake. This offensive example and the limitations of minor reforms were marks of the failure of the conciliar movement.

The beginnings made by Martin V and his successor Eugene IV (Pope —1447) were auspicious. Although they were men of high personal morals and considerable ability, they prevented reform by continued discouragement of conciliarism. Eugene did find it necessary to make temporary and temporizing concessions at the Council of Basel in 1431, but a new schism created by the Council further dimmed the luster of the movement. But at this time a new brand of papal critics was coming to prominence, men like Nicholas of Cusa and Laurentius Valla; their participation in philosophical attack and in historical criticism of papal claims indirectly led to later extremism and warrant for reform. Seven years later a new development was clear: the King of France through the Pragmatic Sanction of Bourges claimed new powers that countered Rome's temporal claims and began the long tradition of Gallic independence within the Western church. None of these attacks was sufficient to bring on an age of reform. Conciliarism met its virtual end in the councils of Ferrara and Florence, and the papacy was free to fall into further corruption. Morality ebbed. The secularism of the Renaissance intruded. The Holy Father represented much of what was unholy in Christendom.

Not that the papacy was without achievements in the Renaissance period. Nicholas V (Pope from 1447 to 1455) blended personal piety with the new humanistic ideal, and is fondly remembered for his interest in creating the storehouse of the Christian past in the Vatican Library. The first Renaissance Pope was clearly the best. But his positive attitude toward the new learning and the new arts opened the door for less religious pontiffs to walk through toward open acceptance of a pagan ideal. Examples: Callistus III (—1458) reintroduced nepotic practices on a grand scale, granting favors to his relatives the Borgias. Pope Pius II (—1464) was a humanist among humanists, proud father of an illegitimate heir, and a man widely held in ill repute for his amoral writing and immoral diplomacy. When he was professedly "converted" from this, damage had been done. Paul II (—1471) shared the pomp but not the learning of the Renaissance. Then came a reaction in Sixtus IV (—1484), learned and more devout, a man frustrated by his failure to form new crusades against the Turk. His monument is the Sistine Chapel. But Sixtus was also lax in his understanding of the moral commitments associated with the pontifical power and was not above doling out offices to relatives.

After him there are for some time no more swings of the pendulum, only more falls into the pit. The man who, ironically, bore the title Innocent VIII had fathered illegitimate children before he mended his ways as the Vicar of Christ; when he ran into financial difficulties he went into the business of creating and selling new offices. The Medici of Florence found their way into papal councils. The papal court, duly Borgiaed and Medicied, came to be known for its intrigue and immorality; the mistress came to be established with the institution. Out of this circle came one Rodrigo Borgia (—1503). His promise as an able administrator and a powerful personality was frustrated by his political involvement and his nepotism. Congenitally unsuited for clerical office, he remains the mark of the abyss of misfortune to Catholic historians describing the papal landscape of the day.

Not slow to recognize the vulnerable position of the unholy popes were the temporal rulers who resented the papacy's temporal claims over their areas of rule. They blew bellows of publicity to exaggerate the tales of papal immorality and encouraged the growing resentment against papal extravagance. They learned to deal on the local level with the underlings of the Holy Father in the cardinalate, then a pompous and artificial institution, and in the episcopacy under *them*. The cardinals had come to power with the decree of Nicholas II in 1059 that they were to be the electors of new popes. When kibitzers and eavesdroppers were barred from elections after 1274, intrigue was inevitable. Today it is hardly possible to picture the power of this office before the Reformation. Its holders enjoyed generous revenues and exacted from the popes grants known as "capitulations." The popes used these men as legates and lackeys and saw to it that they were generously provided for in return. Under the cardinals were some seven hundred bishops whose jurisdictions varied greatly. These represented even more the front line of churchly authority and were even more exposed to the public eye. The episcopal office was often "for sale," to its great detriment. No wonder that in this chain of command the parish priest was often faithless and ignorant. Finances for support of the vast system were always a problem, always pulling it toward corruption.

None of this is new exposure, of course. The revelation of fifteenth-century corruption in the papal system belongs to the public domain, and serious papal historians make little effort to conceal it or explain it. What is most remarkable is this: to post-Puritan sensitivities the stench of this record is so strong that it would seem to moderns that moral unholiness in religious circles could have set off the movement for reform. Indeed it played its part. But the reviewer of the documents of that happily forgotten age is impressed again and again by the clear fact that immorality and depravity merely supplied fire for the rhetoric of the reformers. What concerned them much more was the unholiness of the *teaching* of the papal church. The reformers believed that the Roman re-direction of God's channels of grace through a priestly system had gone too far. It prevented the free flow of God's righteousness among men and thus dammed or diverted the stream of churchly holiness. The pictures of corruption were but illustrations of this more profound theme. The absence of creative theology in the period was merely one more aspect of life in the Christian movement which seemed to be spending itself entirely.

NATIONAL SELF-CONSCIOUSNESS

To prepare the stage for the onrush of reform, a view of church and world in the nations rising to self-consciousness will be profitable. It will suggest the reasons for the church's political weaknesses and institutional insecurities. The old dialogue between pope and emperor now was transformed to a more complex haggling and barter between the papacy and a welter of secular authorities, each thirsty for power and seeing Rome as a pawn in its own aggrandizement. The Roman church found its fortunes subject to the rise and fall of these European monarchs and princes. The day of feudalism and petty lordship over small regions had passed; in its place a realignment and consolidation of authority took prominence. The development of "modern," more effective and more expensive weapons changed the rules of warfare and rendered feudal-type rulers impotent. Seapower entered the reckoning; this required coalitions and alliances among nations.

ENGLAND, FRANCE, AND SPAIN

A survey such as this could center in England, where the shock of theological reformation was perceived less than was the drama of dynastic interplay which led eventually to the Puritan revolt. The growth of the central monarchical authority in England had been long and gradual and the growth of law and constitutional life had served to make the development seem relatively undramatic. The Parliament, a distinctively medieval achievement, had grown to limit by constitutional power some of the aspirations of the king. It had considerable control of the pursestrings and a certain say in the selection of the king out of the list of royal possibilities. Despite various checks such as these, it was under the Tudors that British monarchical power was consolidated.

Under Henry VII (—1509) the Wars of the Roses came to conclusion. Henry's ruthless Star Chamber court made it possible for him to gain power over late feudal rulers. He involved England in the political fortunes of other European states. Treaties with France led to recognition of his throne by that power; the marriage of his daughter Margaret to James IV of Scotland in 1502 and of his son Arthur to Catherine of Aragon in the same year webbed the fortunes of those three nations. Henry VIII, monarch in the time of the Reformation, was handed a strong empire and a reasonably prosperous land. The middle classes and the great cities had grown; textile manufacture occupied the towns; prestige had come with victories in the long war; the printing press fostered education; contacts with the continent opened the Renaissance to England. Interest in the Roman church was low and dissatisfaction with it ran high.

In France, matters were seemingly worse for Rome. After the Pragmatic Sanction of Bourges the Gallic empire was to become and to remain a maverick within Catholicism— massively Catholic, yet never fully worthy of Rome's trust. France had advantages of definition in its rise to modern nationhood: its possibilities for growth were largely co-existent with the territories where the French language was spoken. One royal family had ruled from 987 to 1328; parallel lines would hold power for two more centuries. With boundaries and successions clearly delineated, a certain order accompanied the total development. By the time of the Reformation the king was master of what he surveyed. Charles VII was granted new taxing powers to raise an army; Charles VIII was enabled to dream great dreams and to see them fulfilled, even to the point of intrusions in Italy, until he met frustration by Ferdinand of Spain in 1494.

And Spain? The century saw its dramatic rise to a world prominence it would never again know, particularly after the marriage which united Aragon and Castile. The climate of consolidation which spread through Europe was congenial to Ferdinand and Isabella, "Catholic" rulers who used religious uniformity as a step in their climb to power. They extinguished heresy through their encouragement of the Inquisition against those Moors and those Jews who had become Christians through coercion. Through marriages as a diplomatic tool they made possible the involvement of Spain in the affairs of the Holy Roman Empire and most of the western European states. Duplicity was also part of their arsenal, as witness Ferdinand's turning against Charles VIII in Italy. It was the marriage of their daughter Catherine to Arthur, Prince of Wales, and later to his brother who became Henry VIII, that tangled Spanish affairs with those of England. Ferdinand became the sole ruler of Spain because of the derangement of Joanna, decreed successor to Isabella who died in 1504. His successor in 1516 was Charles V of imperial fame during the Reformation. Spain ruled the seas in the years when mastery there mattered: these were the days of Diaz, Vasco da Gama, and Columbus.

Nearer the Vatican matters were different. Italy remained but a collection of late feudal states in which five duchies were particularly prominent: Venice, Florence, Milan, Naples, and the Papal States. Much of the intrigue that characterized the period in the time of the Medici and Borgia popes is traceable to the desire of the Papal States to join the general European pattern of consolidation of temporal powers.

NIGHT IN GERMANY AND BOHEMIA

And Germany—there the initial and more and more dramatic aspects of the pivot of reformation were to be concentrated. Germany was in ferment, limited as Italy was in its attempt to find a national expression because of the persistence of several still potent feudal states. While night fell on the German church, the Holy Empire was shrinking and growing weaker. As yet no purely Germanic sovereignty was in a position to take its place. The involvements of churchly hierarchs complicated the efforts of those who aspired politically. Three of the seven German electors were the archbishops of Treves, Cologne, and Mainz. The electors saw to it that a weak and controllable man who would not interfere with the sovereignty of individual rulers would be elected. As the office rotated its various holders would attempt to improve the fortunes of their own territory at the expense of national unity.

One attempt to bring Germany out of chaos was the development of a three-house Diet. The electors we have met; the princes are familiar. The Free Cities represent the new age. The Emperor who ruled during much of the century, Frederick III, a Hapsburg (—1493), serves as an example of persistent particularism for the way in which he used the imperium to advance Austrian claims. *Gravamina*, serious attacks on this policy, forced him toward retirement and placed Maximilian I (—1519) into the succession. This diplomatic dreamer, like Charles VIII of

France, learned many of the diplomatic arts, particularly demonstrated by the way he married his children to royal persons who enhanced his Hapsburg line. He inspired political reforms and participated in others. Diets held at Worms, Augsburg, and Cologne in 1495, 1500, and 1512 strove to end feuding and to define the lines of imperial command. But these measures failed to prevent the decline of empire. Perhaps this decline and this particularism were the greatest non-religious boon to the Reformation, for they permitted a greater variety of religious emphases and creative new institutions.

For the rest, Bohemia's nationalism was apparent in its support of John Hus, condemned and burned as a heretic at Constance in 1415. Like Germany, Bohemia found it difficult to unite despite this nationalism. Scandinavia lived a life apart from the Empire, though it was coming under cultural and religious influences from Germany. This made possible the push of reform to the north. Whether in the shape of the monarchies of Charles VIII or Henry VIII or Ferdinand and Isabella, or in the territorial sovereignties of Italy, Germany, and Bohemia, the rulers conceived of themselves more and more as autonomous powers who could take or leave the papacy along the way.

NEW FORCES IN THE RENAISSANCE

Nationalism in every land was not all that served to prepare for reform. Capitalism was a new force: in Italy the Medici had power, in Augsburg the Fuggers became a great banking interest. Where advisable, they played along with the Roman hierarchy; where possible, they came to virtual independence and saw themselves as competitors of the revenue-seeking church. Guilds of merchants and craftsmen provided new centers of life away from the provinces of ecclesiastics and became organizing focuses for the new Europe which found more and more of the old Europe irrelevant. Towns and cities grew, population spiraled after the Great Plague. New vocations found new prestige, and the pattern of peasant life so profitable to the medieval

Church was disrupted. The rise of educated classes detracted from the uniqueness of the clergy. The Church was still growing in wealth but its financial power induced a feeling of disfavor; its days as Europe's banking institution were numbered. Reckless aggression by Renaissance popes was sorely mistimed. The free passage of wealth across the Alps to Italy for the building of cathedrals and chapels was resented. For this reason the sale of indulgences was an explosive innovation to the north.

New intellectual forces in Renaissance humanism pulled the exclusive intellectual charter out from under Roman ecclesiastical dominance. Even though the intellectual ferment bubbled from churchly sources and often flowed in churchly streams, its overall effect was to erode the church's claims. Much of the initiative for the movement was drawn from classic Greek and Roman sources which carried with them paganizing and secularizing tendencies. The church was no longer the cultural depository of Europe, nor could it maintain its isolation from the worldly thrust. Thus when Leo X was elevated to the papal chair the Eucharist was accompanied by the pagan gods bearing the inscription, "First Venus reigned [the age of Alexander VI,] then Mars [Julius II,] and now [under Leo X] Pallas Athene holds the scepter."

As an Italian expression and a Mediterranean sunbath, this further served to blind the more somber northlands to the enduring potential for holiness in the visible center of the Church. Cicero, Virgil, Horace, and the pagan poets displaced Augustine or Aquinas. Humanist scholars went out of their way to deride scholasticism. The new Italian art, often dedicated to religion, breathed a new spirit that overpoweringly suggested that the medieval monopoly of religious themes was passing. Political philosophy in the age of Machiavelli (—1527) may have elevated the papal practice of expediency to political principle, but it was ultimately detrimental to ecclesiastical assumptions. The Platonic Academy may have intended to be faithful to theology, but its philosophical assumptions could not square with this.

Humanism did have a "right wing" of learned men dedicated to exploration of the Church's antiquity and illumination of the Church's present. Grammar, logic, and rhetoric could serve church as they did world. Recovery of ancient languages would aid in understanding the Bible afresh. Textual criticism in its primitive forms was recognized, though in its discovery of forgeries to support papal claims it worked against the institution's interests. Humanism helped usher in the Reformation, even if its forms were seldom acceptable to the Reformers.

Night fell also across the face of a Europe that early in the fifteenth century still saw the outbursts of freedom in the Wycliffite and Lollard movements in England and the Hussite heresy in Bohemia. The Lollards were critics of the church who stressed the authority of the Bible and attacked the unholiness of Rome. Most of the medieval abuses were held up for public abhorrence by the sects that broke out across England after the impulse of John Wycliffe. In the fifteenth century the more educational phase of the movement gave way to a popularistic and often rash outbreak, a social force that encouraged actual revolt. After the middle of the century the force was largely spent. Hus was killed at Constance, but the followers of the preacher at Prague's Bethlehem Chapel and rector of its university lived on. Their attack centered on the institutional unholiness of Rome. Called Utraquists and Bohemian Brethren, these parties persisted through the century in their consistent calls for holiness and for free preaching of God's word. But never after Hus did a new leader rise.

The less familiar reformers of the later half of the century were pygmies by comparison, but they did succeed in pulling away, prop by prop, at the massive structure of Romanism. John of Wesel (—1481) at Erfurt pressed for the primacy of the Bible, as had Wycliffe, Occam, and Hus before him. He criticized indulgences, as did all the other Reformers, particularly because they implied that the pope had power to "sell" absolution. Tried by the Inquisition, he was condemned and imprisoned and his books were burned, despite his recantation. Similarly John Pupper of

Goch (—1475) and Wessel Gansfort (—1489) held the biblical mirror to the unholiness of the latter-day Roman church.

SAVONAROLA

Only one figure stands out in the last half of the century to compare with Hus in the first half. This was Girolamo Savonarola (—1498) who symbolizes the most rigorous attempt to purify the church. Those who enjoy historical drama will never tire of the suspenseful tale of the latter-day prophet who laid his ax at the root of the hierarchical tree. Savonarola versus Alexander VI: here were foils fit for each other. Savonarola, of course, failed. He was premature in his reforming attempts (fortunately the Savonarolas do not know when their services are going to be effective but only when they are needed!). The residue of papal power limited him. But before he was killed he had lit up the sky with a bright view of what was expected of a holy church in the century which found his type unlovable.

A Dominican, Savonarola led a severe monastic existence and was capable of the rigors he detailed as an ideal to others. Like Jeanne d'Arc he considered himself set aside in a special way by God, particularly inspired to preach and denounce. Ferraran Renaissance life repelled him with its neo-paganism. His later years were spent at Florence, where he met sudden acceptance as a preacher against Rome. When his following grew large and his measures had a telling effect, he became the first citizen of the great city—in a very difficult public position. Forsake the images of evil! he cried. So Florentines rose up to destroy works of art and the artifacts of frivolity. Men denied themselves to follow Christ and his newest messenger; extravagances were repudiated, works of mercy found new favor. But Savonarola's enemies roused Alexander VI to opposition. When the monk refused to come to Rome he was commanded to desist from preaching. But he could not restrain himself—in some men the fires burn so hot! No longer able to content himself with quiet work against carnivality and for moral purity, he began to criticize church and pope publicly in Lent of 1497. Excommunication followed. He had power enough to preach against the carnivals of 1498, but he had gone too far. Humankind had borne with too much reality; commercial interests rallied; the Pope threatened an interdict. Savonarola's plea to national sovereigns was pathetically unanswered, was indeed unanswerable; and after he and two disciples were hanged and burned few lived on with the courage of the ecstatic fire to continue. Once again, few seemed to care. Night has its comforts, and Savonarolan fires only blind the eyes.

As Pirenne observed, there was little to anticipate the Reformation when it finally came. But the century of falling night had in many ways omened the dawn. The conciliar movement, the shattering philosophy of nominalism, the power-play of princes, the experience of vital "heresies" and reforms lay behind. The Renaissance and the humanist ideal could serve ultimately to undercut Rome. Most of all, when they focused on the unholiness of the teaching of the church the Reformers found response among all who were confronted, as they described it, by a divine call which served as a contrast to what they saw around them. The disparity between the ideal and the reality was seldom before or since so gross. Perhaps in no other respect was this unholiness so obvious as in the fact—contrary to all higher Christian callings—that when night fell, few cared

10

THE TRUE TREASURE
OF THE CHURCH

In a fortunate historical coincidence, the dynastic lines of
Europe experience a change of pace on the eve of the
Reformation, permitting a slow-motion view of the religious
issues involved. It is almost as if the characters of the political drama sensed that they must remain on stage long
enough so that everyone might become acquainted with
them, not worrying about who should soon replace them.
Thus the audience is left free to follow the central dramatic
themes. Just before the Reformation broke, Henry VIII
became King of England in 1509; when he disappeared
from the scene in 1547 his realm had undergone a spiritual
change which carried with it seeds of future turmoil. But
England could not "go home again" to Rome. In 1515
France saw the crowning of Francis I, who remained in
power also until 1547, allowing the slow-motion camera
of Reformation historians to view his reign familiarly.
Charles V followed in 1516 in Spain, to become Emperor
in 1519, surviving even longer, until 1556. German electors
and Roman popes may come and go against this relatively
stable monarchical background. Little else in Europe was
stable in that century.

Instability, flux, and change occurred mainly within the
souls of the several men who guided the Church in its pivot

from dependence on tradition to confrontation with apostolicity, from its dependence on a churchly system to encounter with the law of God and the gospel of grace. At
the base of the movement which began as a challenge to
the holiness of the Church was the enduring question of
apostolicity. Moderns find it difficult to fit themselves into
this lost background. For all the plausibility of their elabora-
tions, historians who have traced the crucial questions of
reform to economic, social, or political stances are guilty
also of asking of those times a question which was then
secondary. The deep stamping of conscience on the consciousness of the sons of the Hebrew-Christian tradition
was revealed. The effects of a millennium's emphasis on
penance and the need for justification prompted the Reformers' question, "How can I find a gracious God?" Final
dissatisfaction with the Church's provided answers, undergirded by the Church's developing tradition, led men to
new satisfaction with the Church's original authority, the
apostolic witness.

The argument, when it erupted, countered treasure with
treasure, "the treasure of indulgences" (*versus* in the
language of Luther's original theses) "the true treasure of
the Church [which is] the holy Gospel of the glory and grace
of God." We shall not be likely to discover what the stir
was all about if we deviate from the weight of this question as it was accepted by both sides in the Reformation
struggle. Concerns over the unity of the Church were
prominent when the Reformation threatened schism and
division. Concerns over its catholicity were understandable
in the face of the Protestant principle. Concerns about the
holiness of the Church triggered the action and remained
a major sub-theme. Deviations in ethical life by men of the
Church were understandable, and whatever else the Reformation was it was not a guarantee that in the future the
Church would be in the hands of the perfect. But concern
over the apostolicity of the Church's teaching motivated the
Reformers and replies to them demanded the energies of
the papal system's defenders. And the apostolic question
has its reference in that profound personal issue: the Reformers had found in their own lives, they had uncovered in

the recesses of their own souls, that the custodianship of the tradition by the fathers of the Church was no substitute for the apostolic witness to God's direct activity in Jesus Christ.

Perhaps the Reformers were somewhat naive in the way they isolated the apostolic witness, in their belief that they could determine this by simple reference to the Scriptures. They did not always realize how bound they were by their own past, their outlook on life, their schooling in philosophy, their personal predilections. They were somewhat unrealistic about the ease with which one could slice through the complications of centuries to an original witness. "The Reformation principle of *Sola Scriptura* [Scripture alone] is fraught with the difficulty that the *Scriptura* has never been *sola!* [1]" We can still observe this: "Give a basic New Testament passage to an Orthodox, a Lutheran, a Calvinist, an Anglican, and a Congregationalist to interpret—and the discrepancies in their interpretations will correlate much too closely with the various historically conditioned traditions in which they stand to justify any claim that they did no more than reproduce the original meaning." [2] History, liturgy, tradition, psychic make-up, the experiences of life color the interpretation of the *Scriptura.* Reformers who may have minimized this complexity would never have let it detract from the central position this question must assume in understanding the turmoil of their day.

The crucible was personal experience of dissatisfaction with what was offered by the Roman church. This throws the story into an area we have seldom had time to explore in this account. Here a different pace is demanded. While the monarchs of Europe stand still to pose we shall examine the birth of modern Christianity in the souls or experiences of men, much as we have had to pause with St. Paul or St. Augustine on the threshold of new ages before this. Such exploration is not intended as a contribution to the heroic view of the Reformers and the movement. It merely affirms that the ideas of the Reformation belonged to men who had bodies and souls, who were living on earth, whose every decision arose out of the dark and labyrinthine passages of their own minds and forced fresh encounter with God.

THE EXAMPLE OF LUTHER

The classic example, of course, is Luther, whose prominence in the account needs no explanation or defense. Now as then his life and teachings are seen as pivotal. What occasioned his experience, what the experience was, and by what authority it was to be tested—these were the issues. The solitariness of Luther's soul, whose thought was nothing if it was not—pardon us, please—"existential," is what occasioned the issue for him. That experience began in his youth (1483—) as a member of a lower-middle-class miner's family in Germany. His parents were able to provide him with a reasonable elementary education; he was influenced and befriended by devout families while he was at school at Magdeburg and Eisenach. But there is little in his early career to suggest any profound awareness of what would later test his soul. By the time he enrolled at the University at Erfurt (1501) to pursue the legal career which pleased his father, he seems to have been quite serious in his religious faith—a living example that the flicker of concern before God had not wholly died, that in the church in his day there was the ability to make some young men, at least, care. His schooling in the *via moderna* (the nominalist philosophy of Occam and Biel) and in the classics (Virgil and Cicero) was to help him cast his later thought.

But the direction of his life was to change suddenly on July 2, 1505, when the wind and lightning of a thundering day drove him to face the storm of soul within him. He knelt before St. Anne and promised to enter a monastery. It would be difficult to envision Luther—living close to nature and life as a young man of his time and place would have lived—trembling simply because of a storm. He was later to say that the sound of a trembling leaf could cast him into fear, the numinous in nature finding response in heavy heart and frightened soul. In the face of his father's anger he entered the monastery of a rather strict Observant order of Augustinian Eremites at Erfurt.

> When I was a monk I was wont to shrive myself with great devotion, and to reckon up all of my sins (yet being always very contrite before); and I returned to confession very often, and thoroughly performed the penance that was enjoined unto me: yet for all this my conscience could never be fully certified, but was always in doubt, and said: this or that hast thou not done rightly: thou wast not contrite and sorrowful enough; this sin thou didst omit in thy confession, etc.[3]

The authority of the Roman system was small comfort to a man so beset by fear and doubts. While the monastery provided a climate for serious pursuit of the path to heaven, it did not seem to Luther to provide a road map. The Mass represented not so much a loving gift of God as a terror-inspiring enactment of Calvary which threw him into a traumatic condition (1507). "How can I find a righteous God?" "Am I among the elect of God?"

An evangelical counsellor, the Vicar General Staupitz, was of some help. Luther reported Staupitz' counsel:

> In the wounds of Christ is predestination understood and found, and nowhere else; for it is written: Him shall he hear (MATTHEW 17:5). The Father is too high, therefore He says: I will give a way by which men may come to Me . . . in Christ you shall find what and who I am, and what I will; otherwise you will not find it either in heaven or on earth.[4]

Staupitz did more: he urged Luther to study the Bible and to teach at the new university at Wittenberg, that poor dungheap of a town which the elector sought to make great. When Luther returned to Erfurt he again undertook serious study and began his first lectures on that well-worn textbook of the Middle Ages, Peter Lombard's *Sentences*.

A trip to Rome, the city the apostles themselves had known, was of no help. In the year of Our Lord 1510 the apostolic imprint on this earthly city was obscured by the Renaissance papacy. Luther tried everything there from sightseeing to pilgrimage, without solace. He would have agreed with a late-date convert to Catholicism, Ronald Knox, after his visit to Rome: it is better for the inexperi-

enced seaman to avoid the boiler room. The counsel of
Staupitz had done more to help Luther, for it opened
the question of apostolic authority in Scripture. From
1513 to 1517, the years of Luther's pivoting, the
young monk was drawn to the Bible and profited by his
exposition of the Psalms, Genesis, Galatians, and Romans
in the classroom. In the famed "tower experience" at the
monastery he felt he came face to face with the living God
—and he was not annihilated. The saving word, in the
rush of revelation, was Paul's in Romans 1:17: "The
righteous shall live by faith." This righteousness had to be
a gift of God in the Gospel, not a demand of God in the
Law—this was the good news, the turning-point. In this
truth was the true treasure of the Church, now obscured
and tarnished. Grace was not infused into the soul as
a supernatural quality, with its admixture of works and
merits, as Rome taught. Rather it was a revelation of a
miracle accomplished in himself which made possible
trust in and communion with a forgiving God. This good
news must be preached.

Luther did not at the outset see the need for repudiation
of the past. More than he knew, his thought was pre-formed
by the *via moderna* of the late Middle Ages. In the piety
of Bernard of Clairvaux he was to find evangelical witness
to the wounds of Christ; in the sermons of John Tauler he
saw a pastoral meaning which would remain a treasure.
But his vision of the church that surrounded him raised the
question: Why could this not be the main stream of the
Church's life instead of a minor expression? Why did it
need to obscure the apostolic clarity of the original witness?
Clearly, if the tree bore only a little fruit on a few green
boughs there was something wrong with the tree, something wrong at the roots. Luther was soon to strike a blow
at the roots of the entire medieval ecclesiastical and sacramental system.

THE BEGINNING OF REFORM

The axe was poised; the heart of Luther and a sudden concatenation of events made it fall. The time: October 1517; the place: Wittenberg; the event: the sale of indulgences. An indulgence is the remission granted by the church of the temporal punishment due to sins already forgiven. It is dependent on the merits of Jesus Christ and the saints. It implies a "treasury of merits" piled up by Christ, the Blessed Virgin, and the saints of which the head of the church on earth is custodian and in some sense dispenser. In the late Middle Ages the granting of indulgences was vulgarized and commercialized by mountebanks and professional pardon-peddlers. Specifically Julius II, then Pope, had established a Jubilee Indulgence to gain funds for St. Peter's in Rome. This would offend German national sensitivities; and the way the scheme was carried out violated the idea of free grace in apostolic witness.

A complicated rearrangement of ecclesiastical benefices had resulted in the dual titling of Albert, Archbishop of Magdeburg (1513) and of Mainz (1514); the Pope could wink at this duality only after a generous financial settlement. Germany had to pay ten thousand ducats for the dispensation. Half would go to St. Peter's and half would be retained by Albert and the Fuggers' banking house. A Dominican agent, Johannes Tetzel, was the huckster of indulgences in regions familiar to Luther. The activity of Tetzel provoked Luther to rage. He would not accept Tetzel's proffer: upon payment for a certificate of indulgence the buyer would know full remission of penalty in purgatory and would have purchased a share in the merits of the saints—even without a confession. The method of counterattack seems mild indeed. In the customs of the day and almost down to the present in German universities one might, with the approval of the dean of a theological faculty, propose theses for debate and defense. Luther proposed ninety-five such theses on October 31, using the door of the Castle Church as bulletin board. One question obsessed him: the matter of indulgences. A crowd gathered to view the latest batch of saintly relics on All Saints' Day might, he thought, respond. The attack was not planned as a massive revolt against Rome. Luther still saw validity in God's "vicar, the priest." Purgatory after life and the pope during life loomed large. He was not opposed to indulgences yet, but to their misuse: "Whoever speaks against the truth of apostolic indulgence, let him be accursed and damned" (Thesis 71).

Perhaps because he intended no revolution, Luther started one. He poured new wine into old bottles and the bottles were to burst. The medieval sacramental system which undergirded all of the spiritual life was being threatened, as was the institution related to it. The confessional system was at stake, and the indulgence abuse was simply the part of the iceberg that showed above water. Heinrich Bornkamm, recent student of the Theses, claims that the first four alone "introduce a world-historical revolution." [5]

> Our Lord and Master Jesus Christ, in saying; Repent ye! intended that the whole life of believers should be penitence. This word cannot be understood of sacramental penance, that is, of the confession and satisfaction which are performed under the ministry of priests. It does not, however, refer solely to inward penitence; nay, such inward penitence is naught unless it outwardly produces various mortifications of the flesh. The penalty thus continues as long as the hatred of self, that is, true inward penitence, continues, namely, until our entrance into the kingdom of heaven.

These words of Luther's, writes Bornkamm, "rend the tie between the Catholic sacrament of penance and Christ's words on penitence." In place of the system Luther offers "the true treasure of the church," "the holy Gospel of the glory and grace of God." Perhaps Bornkamm overloads the significance of these words in partisan fashion, but the stress of succeeding centuries suggests a certain plausibility for his contention that they are of world-historical significance. "The two greatest revolutionary changes of human history" emerged from Jesus' proclamation of repentance and Luther's recall of the drastic simplicity of that call:

> No ruler, statesman, general, philosopher, or minister of culture has influenced the course of history as much as these two Christian proclamations. Not only the inner life of Christians but also the political and cultural structure of the West have been more profoundly changed by these proclamations than by any other historical happening.[6]

LUTHER VERSUS ROME

Rome reacted at first with semi-detachment. Leo X could not fancy that a theological dispute between monks could have significant consequence. But Luther was soon involved in defense of his theses in the Heidelberg Disputation, where he outlined his theology of the cross, and in encounters again with Tetzel and then with papal emissary Cajetan at Augsburg. In John Eck, who was among the first to label him a heretic publicly, he found a foil. Reform proceeded apace as Luther, with a combination of political naivete, good luck, and evangelical insight, pushed forward, finding all sorts of supporters among the clergy, the faculties, the humanists—and the people. By the time papal legate Miltitz confronted him, Luther had pivoted too far to return to his former stance.

In the Leipzig debate of 1519, Luther was seen to be moving to the logical conclusion of his indulgence theses: to the attack on the medieval sacramental system with its emphasis on works and merits, even to the possibility that the pope could err. And then, to the horror of the moderates, he pushed still further: in his role as obstructor of the free flow of grace the pope was the anti-Christ prefigured in certain New Testament writings. Monasticism, the Mass, penance, and merits—these were not paths to a better life but perversions of the free grace of God in Christ; they tarnished the treasure. In a holy rage and with the brusqueness and even uncouthness typical of him, Luther swept his fist across the tables of debate and compromise, clearing them for new debates, new documents.

Rome countered by placing on those tables open denunciations. These called on God to rise and purge his vineyard of the rude German wild boar. In a grave miscalculation of his power in Germany and his popularity elsewhere, the Pope issued the bull *Exsurge Domine,* which Luther and his colleagues disposed of in a bonfire outside a gate at Wittenberg on December 10, 1520. More significantly, they burned a copy of the canon law. The breach was final, and all the world could see it. In controversial tracts during 1520 Luther issued rhetorical Magna Chartas. He defended them and all his writings at the Imperial Diet of Worms, where he pushed aside the last opportunity to recant by reference to his reliance on the apostolic witness and adherence to the voice of his conscience. There he stood. Out of the tower, out of his soul, had come an experience which would remold Christendom. When his followers whisked him off to protective custody at Wartburg Castle, he would turn to study to consolidate his view of the Scriptures. He would live on for more than a score of years, preaching, teaching, writing, administering, always escaping repression by the political and popular support he could summon in the unrest of Germany. But those later years belong to a biography of the man and not, like the crucial early years, to a church history discussing the argument about apostolicity.

FOUR THEOLOGICAL QUESTIONS

A certain economy has been involved in this expansion on Luther's experience, for it has anticipated and outlined the realms of concern and the points of controversy for other reformers. We can view each in four aspects. The central question was the matter of God's grace and man's faith over against law and works. This led to the contextual question of institutions which were to have been stewards of the mysteries of grace. Third, Luther could seldom deviate from the sacramental question and its obstruction of grace. Finally, there came the question of authority and apostolicity in tradition and in the Scriptures.

First things first. Einar Billing of Sweden has argued:

> Whoever knows Luther, even but partially, knows that his various thoughts do not lie alongside each other, like pearls on a string, held together only by common authority or perchance by a line of logical argument, but that they all, as tightly as the petals of a rosebud, adhere to a common center, and radiate out like the rays of the sun from *one* glowing core, namely, the gospel of the forgiveness of sins.[7]

Everything that is complex in Luther can be reduced "to a simple corollary of the thought of the forgiveness of sins." This was, for Luther, the point of apostolic doctrine. The Scriptures were important because they were the cradle which carried Christ. Christ was important because in him the fullness of the Godhead was pleased to dwell and in his death reconciliation was effected and the sinner—who remained a sinner all his life—was saved. This was the treasure. Monasticism had failed in the pivotal experience at just this point. Luther would do "what in him lay," and it was never enough. Then he recognized what God had done for him.

An intensely human man, Luther was too conscious of the persistence of self-love to fail to see that this could interrupt the promise. For that reason, if the path to salvation depended in any real sense upon man, it was worthless. When Luther later said that he knew a man who had experienced the pains of hell he spoke of this last pre-pivotal point: if he did not experience grace as it was promised, was it true that he had not shown that he wanted it enough? Was he beyond the pale of God's ability to help him? Only constant reference to the Pauline writings—that help was a gift of God, that the righteousness was Christ's own offered to man—helped him. Luther was never able to provide a simply rational structure for the details of what happened in the gift of grace. God remained partly hidden even in His act of self-revelation. In Luther's theology of the cross man receives only a glimpse, a partial vision, a retrospect of "the hind parts of God." To probe more deeply into the divine majesty than was revealed in the wounds of Christ was a temptation not to "let God be God." Contentment with the mystery opened the way for distinctions between the Law, which demanded obedience and accused for failure, and the Gospel, which restored man to new relation to God. Nature, reason, intellect, works, all failed: they belonged to the anthropocentric orientation of medieval Christianity. Faith was what mattered. "Justification by faith," later a slogan and party word, was originally the vital center. Faith is not mere assent to true propositions about God. It means being grasped by the message of faith and the reality of God in Christ. It remains a gift of God, not an achievement of man.

This view countered that of the medieval church as typified in the writings of Thomas Aquinas. What is the final end of man? Thomas had asked. The vision of God. Man, a reasoning being with desire for this vision, strove for it. God had provided man with power to transcend his own nature and to share in the divine nature. For this, grace was the supernatural, divine, created agent: thus Thomas. But for Luther grace seemed, in the medieval system, to be so infused into man's capabilities that salvation was somehow credited to and contingent upon man's successes. Grace to Aquinas was a "sort of perfection which elevates the soul to some supernatural existence." This perfection is related to the glory and greatness of God revealed through Christ and then in the doctrine, the teaching, and the ministration of the holy Church. Faith assents to this teaching.

Difference over the point of the custodianship of the apostolic witness led to the controversy over the authority of the Roman church. By 1520 Luther had torn at authority from top to bottom. He attacked the pope at the head, the hierarchy and the priesthood, the sacramental system, the complex of monasticism and canon law. But the greatest offense was the papacy itself. In the Roman view the pope had come to be the one and supreme pastor of souls. After his election he occupies by divine right a seat of ultimate character and authority. The pope, basing his claim on Christ's words to Peter concerning the establishment of the Church, comes to the point where he can say, "I am the tradition." This trend was subjected to attack in Luther's

Babylonian Captivity of the Church. His own high and pervasive view of the Church is incompatible with the indi-
vidualistic rewriting of Reformation history of modern
times. The Reformers did not intend to repudiate the
communal and churchly character of God's redemptive
activity. They did not intend to invent autonomous man.
They merely wanted faith, and not the institutional church,
to be the rock: here man would stand before God in confession of Christ.

Nor was Luther anti-sacramental. He repudiated the
"captivity" of the sacrament in the denial of the chalice
to the laity, in the doctrine of transubstantiation (which
in the document of 1520 he explicitly repudiated) and in
the sacrifice of the Mass, which in its ritual formalism and
its part in the system of merits and works detracted from
the spirit of the sacramental gift. "The closer any mass approaches to the first of all masses, which Christ celebrated
at the supper, the more Christian it is." Sacraments are
visible physical signs in which Christ is really present, but
they are not effective apart from faith, merely by the act
of "going through them." The Reformers criticized the
magical view associated with the Mass, the reduction of the
divine mystery to the mechanics of institutionalism. A
check on this could come through the dramatic preaching
of the Word, continued proclamation of God's good news.
The number of sacraments was reduced to Baptism and
the Eucharist.

Finally, the bedrock question of apostolicity. Having
faced the issues of grace, the Church, the sacraments, each
time on "apostolic" grounds, Luther finally found himself
constrained to spell out his view of the authority which
countered that of Rome. Rome saw tradition and Scripture
not as either-or, but as both-and. Luther and the Reformers
stressed the contradictions between the purity of the witness
to the Word of God in Scripture and the traditions of men
in the Church. At Leipzig Luther argued with Eck that the
fathers, the councils, even the popes could err in ways in
which Scripture could not. In conflict, Scripture was decisive. Authority remained with Christ; the source and norm

of Christian teaching remained in the witness to that authority in Scripture. Luther thought of himself as being "under"
the Word—by which he meant subject not simply to Christ
the word, but also to the Scripture as a witness. While his
own rather free "divining" of Scripture implied an attitude
which would never have fit the reformed or seventeenth-
century Lutheran straitjacketing of the Bible in theories of
verbal inerrancy (Luther was not above correcting Paul
or John here and there, and his criticism of the Epistle of
James is well known), he had a reverent attitude to the
totality of the book, and has shared perhaps only with
Origen a reputation for familiarity with its contents.

Going to some length on these four points may seem
to have been a theological excursus, but it too provides some
economy for the telling of the rest of this story. For the
issue of the Reformation was religious, and these were the
points in question. Yet we have told only one part of the
narrative which must incorporate also the Reformed half
of Protestantism with its roots in Switzerland, Holland,
and Scotland; its spread in France and England and Germany; and its world-wide growth from origins in Zwingli,
Calvin, and others.

Unlike the schism of 1054, the Reformation did not
leave the Church with but one new faction. In place of
churches of East and West, there would be a new complication among churches of the West. This occurred because
the original groping for the apostolic reference in Christian
teaching followed various leaders on parallel lines, with
the result that early differences hardened. The best symbol
of developing non-Lutheranism in Protestantism contempo-
raneous with Luther was an amazing Swiss who has guaran-
teed himself last place on any alphabetical list of churchmen, but who has few peers among first places when
abilities are measured, Ulrich Zwingli (—1531). His concerns were to coincide with Luther's on the four points we
have studied, but his sacramental teaching placed him on
the more "radical" side of reform.

ZWINGLI

Four preliminary generalizations are in order when the name Zwingli appears in an account of reform. First, from the comparison with the Lutheran Reformation, it is clear that humanism now plays a much larger part. In a time of secular renaissance, the recovery of classical and Koine Greek, the thrill of reading the Bible in the vernacular, the philosophical orientation of a new day, the recovery of interest in law and jurisprudence, in ethics and morals, we can observe the field of interests which shaped Zwingli. Second, there seems in the career of the Swiss reformer to be much less stress on the shattering personal religious experience; he neither claims nor documents a psychological point of pivot in his own life. He seems to have glided into reform against a background of political abuse in the Switzerland of his day. Third, the political realm looms larger than it did in the case of Luther. Perhaps Zwingli's decisive emotional experience was reaction against the practice of employing Swiss mercenaries for alien military purposes. He served as chaplain to anti-Hapsburg armies and, characteristically, lost his life on the battlefield. In his political teaching he was nearer Calvin than Luther, holding to a quasi-theocratic view of the state. On the statue which is his monument he carries two "swords": one is the Bible, the other is a military weapon. Fourth, an iconoclastic tendency colors the Zwinglian reform; he and his followers shattered much of what the Germans wanted to preserve.

In many respects Zwingli was closer to the tradition of Savonarola than to Luther or Calvin. Influenced by the Wittenberger, he tried to cover his traces to the more rhetorical German. Less "logical" than Calvin, less "empirical" than Luther, he can best be described as the humanist-activist of the reform. In some respects the religious stress is less marked in Zwinglian Protestantism. Luther and Calvin still spoke of the Church as the mother of all Christians. Zwingli set out to build a people's church. His colleagues saw justification by faith to be a saving doctrine; Zwingli agreed—but he was more ready also to make it a weapon with which to fight Rome. But ultimately it was theology that carried Zwingli, too.

Born in Wildhaus in St. Gall, he was educated at Bern, Basel, and Vienna for a career as priest. He was ordained in 1506, after which he continued to pursue his studies of classicism and biblical language. After 1516 his impulse to reform abuses was quickened, and in 1518 he became minister in Zurich. Reform was a gradual development; it is difficult to date. His debate with Johann Faber in 1523 placed him clearly with Luther in defense of the Bible as the document of apostolic authority. Much of his career centered in the abolition of the Mass and formation of his teaching on the sacraments in opposition to Catholicism and Lutheranism. He interpreted the sacraments symbolically; bread, wine, and water were but signs of grace, representations.

As in Luther's view of grace, so with Zwingli Christology was central. He too chose to preserve the classic Chalcedonian view of Christ's divine-human person, but found himself in certain difficulties in this respect when he applied this concept to the sacrament. Like Calvin he stressed God's sovereign initiative in the activity of showing grace. God was absolute causality, the first moving cause. God is the occasion for election: "It is election which saves." We have referred to Zwingli's radical views of sacrament and church. On the other point, the authority of the Bible, he argued with other Protestants that this was the basis of reference to the apostolic character of the Church in every age. However, he was not concerned to divide Law and Gospel within the Scriptures as sharply as did Luther. The formal break between Swiss and German reform movements occurred in 1529 at Marburg in a controversy which can concern us later. Zwinglianism as a movement never gained normative status in Reformed Protestantism alongside Calvinism; it will be profitable to explore the eruption of this third force even though it occurred somewhat later.

CALVIN

It is most important to bear in mind that Calvin was a quarter of a century younger than the other two; he grew up in a world that was already becoming Protestant—deep conversion experiences were no longer so necessary in his generation, when men had the luxury of less painful choice. In many respects his teaching will parallel Luther's. Man is depraved, unable to help himself. It is impossible for him to fill the law. He is made righteous through faith alone in Christ. Good works are of no avail. Says Philip Hughes:

> The essence of Luther's message is the essence of Calvin's message too. And for both men, the one source of all our knowledge of God's mind and will is the test of the divinely inspired Scriptures; which all men have a right to read for themselves, which all have the duty to read. Calvin never indeed lays claim to such a specific inspiration on the part of God as the Tower incident brought forward by Luther. Nevertheless, he does not hesitate to proclaim his conviction that he is God's messenger and that he has the right to demand assent to the message he delivers.[8]

Roman Catholic historian Hughes, a referee in these comparisons, continues: Calvin is less afraid of "Law" than Luther; no one exceeds him in stress on God's holy law. Calvin is more like Zwingli in the radicalism of reform. Unlike Zwingli, Calvin admired Luther and did not despise having his own name associated with his predecessor's. "The true source of Calvin's teaching is the Bible—'the Word of God.' "

John Calvin was born on July 10, 1509, at Noyon in Picardy, the son of Gerard Calvin, a reasonably prestigious lawyer. At the age of fourteen he was enabled to enroll at the University of Paris, where he moved in the brightest intellectual orbit of the day, near the French throne and the cultural interests stimulated there. The scholarship of the University reflected the relative independence which had been developing in France after the Pragmatic Sanction of 1438. The moral life of the French church was poor, but reform was in the air. Jacques Lefevre of Etaples mastered the group under the influence of the Platonic Academy. No linguistic genius, he promoted the study of ancient languages for the purpose of reading the Scriptures in the original: this encouragement brought the French church into confluence with Protestant developments. Guillaume Briconnet, Abbot of St. Germain-des-Pres, fell under the Lefevreist spell; disciples carried on the teachings down to the period when Luther's teaching began to be published around Paris. Condemnation by the Sorbonne in 1521 did not stamp out the heresy. The noble Louis de Berquin went out of his way to publicize Luther's activity in France.

Through an uncle Calvin was drawn to the new learning but, interested in the priesthood, he transferred first to the once orthodox College de Montaigu. His austerity amazed pleasure-loving contemporaries. His personableness made him attractive to several fine Parisian families. His lessons under the Scot John Major, an Occamist, exposed him to the subtleties of dialectic and the modern philosophy which reform found congenial.

At the age of eighteen, in 1528, Calvin received the master's degree, and was all but forced to undertake legal studies which influenced his mind but did not redirect his career. Wherever he turned he seemed to face the influences for reform. After his father's death he felt free to pursue studies of his choice and, after some impressive humanistic work, he moved to the Scriptures with his fine logical mind and classical orientation. At about this time he underwent some sort of conversion, about which he is mysteriously abrupt:

When I was too firmly addicted to the papal super- stitions to be drawn easily out of such a deep mire, by a sudden conversion He brought my mind (already more rigid than suited my age) to submission [to Him]. I was so inspired by a taste of true religion and I burned with such a desire to carry my study further, that although I did not drop other subjects, I had no zeal for them. In less than a year, all who were looking for a purer doc- trine began to come to learn from me, although I was a novice and a beginner.[9]

There are no clues, chronological or psychological, to explain the conversion. Long before this time Calvin had inclined toward Protestantism, but by the early 1530's he had stepped to the point of no return.

To espouse such views was then still hazardous. De Berquin was put to death for heresy in 1529; he was not alone. In 1534, however, Calvin came out into the open in anti-Sorbonnist attack; anti-papalism would come later. Only as Lefevre, Cop, and his other masters met defeat from a repressive hierarchy did Calvin learn that humanist contentment, acquiescence, and anonymous pamphlet warfare were not enough. He surrendered his clerical benefices and showed that he had cut himself off from Rome.

He never returned; his conversion was profound and genuine. He made clear his abhorrence of the Roman confessional system, which he found not sufficiently radical to involve a true turning from sin to the sovereign saving activity of God. He felt himself to be a new man in ways that the sacramental life of the past had not achieved. He undertook new patterns of conduct and teaching, and by 1536 had shown his genius for theological system in the first edition of his *The Institutes of the Christian Religion*. His subsequent career falls into a later chapter: this is the point to explore his perception of the true and apostolic treasure of the Church in the gospel of the glory and grace of God.

A convenient distinction would be to take that phrase from Luther's theses and say that the two Reformers supplemented each other in the way Calvin stressed the glory, Luther the grace of God. But the distinction has limitations; neither would be content with it. Luther puts much more stress on God's monarchical sovereignty and Calvin on God's free grace in Christ than this distinction allows. From the earliest edition of the *Institutes* to the last Calvin's teaching was consistent. He chided the moderates who were ashamed of the gospel and averred that "our doctrine," the evangelical witness, could not be overthrown because it stood upon the Word of God. On this basis Calvin refused to regard the reform movement as a disruption of the continuity in the life of the true Church, but he attacked just as vehemently the heresies that had grown up in the Roman church of history.

THE THEOLOGICAL ISSUES

To follow the outline of recovery on four points, grace and faith come first. The chief end of man's life is not, as with Aquinas, to enjoy the vision of God, or as with Luther, to find a gracious God, but as with the later reformed tradition, to know God, to give Him glory—and to "enjoy Him forever." Knowledge of God is not mere speculation or intellectual achievement: it is response to God's revelation of Himself in worship and glory. Therefore God shows Himself as Creator in His work and in the Holy Scripture, where alone He is seen to be the savior of the world in Christ. In other words, God does not abandon man, despite His remoteness and majesty. He condescends to come in Jesus. But this revelation is apprehended only by the elect who are predestined in the will of God to be drawn to Him. God has mercy on whom He has mercy, and whom He will He hardens—this is the offensive word of Calvin and St. Paul. Calvin acknowledged that this word could not be defended before men, but this did not remove the responsibility for its assertion. And he softened the edge by placing the doctrine of predestination always in the constellation of Christian redemption. Thus Calvin-editor Joseph Haroutunian:

> As in Scripture, so in Calvin's mind it was no small comfort that the sufferings of the church were predestined according to the will and the purpose of God. Predestination meant to Calvin, as to Paul, that the sufferings of the Christians were no accident in the history of mankind. The unfolding of history was the realization of God's purpose which went back to the beginning. The doctrine of predestination for Calvin was bound up with the doctrine of history as the continued fulfillment of God's purpose. There had been, there was, and there was to be nothing fortuitous, nothing apart from God's intention, nothing that originates from man's will and caprice. Jesus Christ had been called and predestined by God for his mission, together with his

suffering and cross. His gospel, scoffed at and rejected by the world, was no novelty. It had been in God's purpose and was promised in prophecy through the ages. So as age followed age, fulfillment followed fulfillment, all according to God's own eternal purpose.[10]

In this context the Calvinist found exhilaration and freedom in the possibility of participating in God's saving plan in history; and the reformed Christian, more than the Lutheran, would be a political activist.

With Luther, Calvin attacked the idea, second, of Rome as the saving institution. He agreed that the Church was one, holy, catholic, and apostolic, and shared with the German the view that the whole body of the redeemed in all times was the Church universal which is invisible—God alone can recognize its borders. But a visible church can also be outlined; it is the visible company of those who profess the faith and enjoy the sacraments. It is *not* coexistent with the boundaries of Roman rule. The concept "communion of saints" appealed to him; he was no individualist in the Enlightenment tradition. But the Roman institution violated the commonness of the communion by its innovation of a priestly order and an exclusive sacramental system. Theologically Calvin may have held a less "high" view of the Church than Luther, but his fine feel for the power of institutions built into him a sense for the proportion and the greatness of the visible company of the elect. In it the minister was steward of the mysteries of God, responsible for the sacramental life of the Church.

The sacraments as administered in the tight Roman system had often become magical. Calvin insisted on evidence of faith. Infant baptism remained, but the parents must bring the child in awareness of what is happening; baptism is more the initiation into the Church than the effective agent of salvation. Similarly, the Lord's Supper must be purged of its centuries of false accretion. Christ is really present, he asserted with Luther against Zwingli. But he did not share Luther's view of the "ubiquity" of Christ's body. The Lord's Supper is an especially dramatic moment in man's communion with God in Christ.

Underlying Calvin's whole theological position was an extremely high view of the Scriptures as the deposit of the apostolic tradition. Second to Luther in his depth-perception of the book, he was superior in his systematization of its teachings. But in Calvin theories of inspiration of the documents began to appear which opened the door for static conceptions of God's revelation, and seventeenth-century scholastics could find in him a source book for their new doctrine of verbal-inspiration. His legal mind needed a codebook, a document, a reasonable address of God to man, and he found it in Scripture. The writers of Scripture were "amanuenses," "penmen," "clerks." "The Holy Spirit dictated to the prophets and the apostles," he wrote in his commentary on Jeremiah. In those days which preceded historical and literary analysis of the Scriptures reformers could make such assertions without complication; later generations have hardened these into dogmatic categories which do not do justice to the reformer's own witness to the human dimension of the revelation in the Bible. As in Luther, so in Calvin there is a responsible submission to the Scripture, accompanied by a freedom of interpretation which allowed him to see a superior value in the New Testament, where God's redeeming activity was more explicit in his once-and-for-all revelation in Jesus Christ. From the Old to the New Testament there was an increasingly explicit view of revelation, from the diffusion in the promise to Adam to the concentration at Calvary.

We have carried the development of Luther to 1522, of Zwingli to his death, of Calvin to 1536, and then summarized their pivotal change. The matrix of their ideas gave birth to the many variations of Protestantism; they began in united negation of what in Rome they saw to be contrary to the apostles' doctrine. They miscalculated in their assumed ease of united affirmation on the basis of New Testament authority. Protestantism was never to overcome its difficulties in this respect: it appealed to the Scriptures, but men of different birth and land and tradition and experience read them differently. This makes generalizations about Protestant teaching difficult. Yet a Copernican revolution had taken place in the stance of Western Christianity, a revolution to which the Roman church was to address itself later in the Council of Trent.

Trent would attack the doctrine of justification by faith; justification was the "translation from the standing in which man was born as a son of the First Adam into the standing of grace and adoption of the children of God." Faith? Man perceives God's call in the Word "to which he may assent and with which he may co-operate." This was asserted in rebuttal to the Protestant stress on the fully divine character of initiative in grace. Second, the Council would criticize the Protestant view of the priesthood of all believers as a detraction from the Roman view of the priestly office. On the Eucharist it reaffirmed transubstantiation and continued to deny the cup to the laity; the Mass was further elevated after the controversy. On the basic question of apostolicity, Trent made explicit what had long been implicit: Scriptures and Tradition are together the seat of Christian truth. Both are inspired. The church formed the canon and defined its extent. The church is the official interpreter of Scripture. Rome was the custodian of the mysteries.

After Wittenberg, after the double-fronted Swiss reform, after Trent the breach was clear, definite, and apparently final. A significant portion of the Western church had pivoted and found itself confronting anew in the gospel the true treasure of the Church.

11

THE VINEYARD, TORN

On the fifteenth day of June, 1520, Leo X issued the bull *Exsurge Domine,* intended to give Luther sixty days to submit to the Roman authority. In it the Pope chose to use somewhat less irenic terms than we did to describe the pivot of a churchman in quest of a gracious God:

> Arise, O Lord, and judge thy cause. A wild boar has invaded thy vineyard. Arise, O Peter, and consider the cause of the Holy Roman Church, the mother of all churches, consecrated by thy blood . . . Arise, all ye saints, and the whole universal Church, whose interpretation of Scripture has been assailed.

A wild boar had torn up the vineyard, the Holy Roman Church in its unity and catholicity, over the issue of apostolic teaching. "Arise . . .": the call had now an overtone of regret and an undertone of panic. It was too late. The visible unity of the church of the West that had endured the stresses of a millennium was torn by the "wild boar" of Germany.

Never again was it to be reunited. Luther must have foreseen the consequences of his action; and as he was joined by other reformers, they also must have recognized the high responsibility they held for supplanting it with an alternate and worthy growth.

The tender grapes of the old vineyard were being trampled. The torn vineyard would not provide for ter-

227

raced and disciplined growth. The very act of plowing the soil and planting new seed provided a rich and varied thicket of new life. Roman Catholics have never ceased to make much of what is an obvious fact about the churches of the Reformation: once the authoritarian control of Rome is shattered or disrespected, once its cultivation of the vineyard is hampered, everything seems to splinter or tangle. The Bishop of Meaux, Bossuet, in the seventeenth century placed this movement in the context of the Church's history. It was obvious that Protestantism had sown the wind in the vineyard and would reap the whirlwind.

If every man was to be his own judge, if every man was to be of the universal priesthood, standing before the Scriptures as his own pope—what would prevent the growth of as many churches as there are men or factions or parties? The experience of Europe in the half-century following 1517 certainly seemed to thunder corroboration. It is difficult to find many traces of a line of unity or a consciously developed attempt to preserve one. Repressed desires of decades, repressed scholarship of centuries, repressed nationalistic tendencies: all these broke and burst at once in an explosion of individuality and in a proliferation of new sects and churches. There were other wild boars.

If we were to pace off the vineyard of the West, we would do well to complement the German, Swiss, and French developments by a northwestward turn to Britain. Return to the continent profitably would direct itself to the free spirits' flowering in the sects and Anabaptist movements. Still other types of reform tore the church in the Romance lands and then in Scotland. The survey concludes with the revisiting of lands where Lutheranism and Calvinism were being consolidated. Then a final glance at Roman counter-reform.

THE BRITISH EXPERIENCE

England: everything seems different, so far different that the Reformation there is usually described with so much dependence on the bedroom life of Henry VIII that vital reform is neglected. But, in contrast to the continent, England seems to have elided doctrinally into the Reformation. It is not fair to prolong the familiar charges that England could produce no ideological justification for its religious change. To be sure, less change was needed there; true, the pressures of dynastic confusion detracted from the theological side of reform; but England should hardly be blamed for needing a different kind of justification and finding it. Instead of reform's being born in the dark night of men's souls or in their perusal of the Scriptures, it seems to have been born in the subtleties and vagaries of institutional revision. Nor is it correct to say that in a different kind of battle men showed no courage because they showed a different kind of courage.

One thinks almost instantly of Thomas Cranmer (—1556), so involved in English reform, so easily portrayed as weak and vacillating, a man of few ideas lightly held. What a contrast, at first glance, to the "wild boars" of the continent! He seems not to pivot but to spin in his adaptations to monarchical change from Henry VIII to Edward VI to Mary Tudor, under whom he met his death. When the smoke cleared, however, it was apparent that Cranmer had moved from a fixed point. His Erastianism was a profound theological principle. We might ponder with Trevelyan the mystery of this man:

> Cranmer [took] a line at last. He had honestly held that the Crown ought to decide on religion in England. Was he then to obey Mary or was he to stand up for his own convictions? It was a real dilemma for a convinced Erastian who had also become a convinced Protestant. Roman Catholics could only be in a like difficulty if the Pope were to turn heretic. There is no wonder that his timid nature hesitated and recanted in the presence of a terrible death. It is more wonderful that he saw his way so clearly in the end, and held the hand, which had signed the recantation, in the fire until it was consumed. Had the men of those days a less highly strung nervous system than ours, or can the power of a scholar's mind be so triumphant over physical pain? In that magnificent gesture the Church of England revived.[1]

A different taste goes with the Cranmerian reform. Many an Anglican feels to this day that all that was lost in the sixteenth century was the gain of the rejection of papacy. Jeremy Taylor (—1667) was later to detail the result:

> For to the Churches of the Roman Communion we can say that ours is reformed; to the reformed churches we can say that ours is orderly and decent; for we are freed from the impositions and lasting errors of a tyrannical spirit, and yet from the extravagancies of a popular spirit, too. We were zealous to cast away the old errors, but our zeal was balanced with consideration and the results of authority . . . we shaked off the coat indeed but not our garments . . .[2]

This "tame boar" theory of the torn vineyard finds substantiation in the later development of the Anglican church. Yet to have lived in those days would not have deprived one from drama of a high order.

England was conscious of its selfhood as a nation, in its historical sense recalling the long developments of personal liberties and its mistrust of the papacy. Papal taxation was resented; immorality of teaching and of life created a revulsion in many; the new learning opened new interest in reform. The Scriptures were accessible. All that was needed was an event. In a sense three clusters of events occurred. First was the aftermath of Henry VIII's struggle with the Pope, resulting in constitutional, chaos. Second was the pendulous movement from Edward VI's radically Protestant times to Mary's attempt to return the country to Catholicism. Third was the resolution in the Elizabethan settlement with its principle of comprehension.

For larger detail we must begin with larger-than-life Henry VIII (—1547). When he was crowned in 1509 England had broken with the Middle Ages in everything but religion. It was developing a capitalist economy; guilds, crafts, towns, new "industries" were characteristic. The new classes rebelled against the medieval church's landholding policies; one fifth of the nation's wealth was hierarchically controlled. Wycliffism and Lollardry had set schismatic precedents; the Bible was known in the vernacular. Occamism at Oxford, humanism at Cambridge and London prepared England for the change. Henry VIII was a man of this new day, educated, theologically alert. It seemed wise to him in his own providence to become recognized as Defender of the Faith in papal eyes by replying to Lutheran ideas. The flow from Wittenberg had brought these ideas to England particularly through the efforts of the Bible translator, William Tyndale (—1536), and through several other "Protestants" who were to die for their ideas.

The humanist Thomas More (—1535) had effectively quashed this unrest, teamed as he was with Cardinal Wolsey, efficient minister to the King. Henry's reply to Luther's *The Babylonian Captivity* in 1520–21 was informed by the school of More. It was this reply which merited the Pope's attention, and the title subsequently bestowed on the monarch must have flattered him into the desire for faithfulness to Rome. This desire was soon complicated, however, by Henry's personal desires in their clash with Catholic interests. He was not the kind of man to let principle violate his interests in succession or in choice of bed partner. Having grown arrogant on the field in foreign battle, Henry had overreached himself in France, to return with his head under his wing from his forays in 1512. His efforts to regain prestige at first failed.

At his ear was Cardinal Wolsey, who had the difficult task of advising Henry in his policy of self-enhancement *and* in his loyalty to Rome. By 1519–20 he was playing both ends of the Valois-Hapsburg rivalry against the middle, to Henry's gain. Thus when Wolsey was by-passed in the choice of the papal successor to Leo X, England moved further from support of Catholic France and from Rome. Experiencing difficulties in Parliament, Henry looked for new conquests. He had no need to look further than his chamber. Catherine of Aragon, who was palling on him, failed to produce a male heir. Appealing to the Pope, now Clement VII, for an annulment, Henry had every right to expect one. When Catherine resisted, the Pope became reluctant to be involved in an act which would anger Spain. Since the Pope had granted a dispensation to permit Henry to marry his brother's widow, it would be embarrassing now to about-face.

The year 1529 was crucial. Wolsey was falling from

favor; Thomas Cromwell and Thomas Cranmer were finding it. They gained Henry's desires before Parliament in an act that embarrassed Rome. The reform Parliament swung wildly at the immorality of the clergy, the fatness of the church's holdings, the malpractices of ecclesiastical courts. The Pope still refused to scurry into retreat; Henry rolled on. In 1532 he obtained the "Submission of the Clergy." The next year, in the Restraint of Appeals, all appeals to Rome were forbidden. The marriage of Henry to Anne Boleyn symbolized the completion of the uprooting of the vineyard. Cranmer was appointed to the archbishopric at Canterbury and to headship of the Church of England; Parliament ratified the breach with the Supremacy Act of 1534:

> . . . be it enacted by authority of this present Parliament, that the king our sovereign lord, his heirs and successors, kings of this realm, shall be taken, accepted and reputed the only supreme head in earth of the Church of England . . .

Thomas More and Bishop John Fisher (—1535), refusing to support the Act of Succession which favored Anne's offspring, paid for their refusal with their lives.

The juggernaut rolled on. Monasteries were dissolved and the properties tied up with them were released. While the monastic strongholds had become weak, Henry did considerable harm to the cause of scholarship and religion by this abrupt activity. Parliament went along. The poor of England suffered, many of them having been attached to the monasteries as laborers.

It does seem strange that one can discuss the story of English reform down to 1536 without theological reference beyond Henry's attack on Luther. But theological development of a minor character there had been, spurred by the Bible translations of Tyndale, Coverdale, and Rogers. The intellectual leader of the English development was Cranmer, who caused the spread of the translated Bible which gave the Anglican church one pillar, and who left the *Book of Common Prayer* as its other. The Prayer Book shaped Anglicanism the way the Augsburg and Heidelberg Confessions were to mold continental movements. This classic of worship and devotion grew out of the breviary of the Roman church and incorporated many elements from the Sarum tradition, from the writings of Chrysostom—even of Luther!

Henry seemed reluctant to fall headlong into reform, and kept the trend in control through the Ten Articles of 1536, which urged that little had happened doctrinally except the repudiation of Rome. In their condemnation of Roman transubstantiation and Lutheran justification doctrines they suggested that Anglicanism was finding the middle way it would treasure. Some reaction came when Henry saw to the passage of "the bloody whip with six strings," the Six Articles of 1539. These Articles blocked further theological reform during his life. They reaffirmed transubstantiation, for example; in their strictures against married priests they embarrassed Cranmer and created considerable discomfort for Mrs. Cranmer. The Six Articles were a setback for Protestants. Little more need be said of Henry except to recall that he married several more Catherines and Annes (and one exceptional Jane, Jane Seymour, who mothered Edward VI). Seldom has a marital career been so productive of ecclesiastical change.

Henry's ten-year-old successor Edward ruled from 1547 to 1553 under the dominance of Edward Seymour who, as Duke of Somerset, extended Protestant influence. By 1549 the Prayer Book was forced on the churches through the Act of Uniformity. When Somerset fell from favor in time of peasant revolt he was succeeded by John Dudley, Earl of Warwick. Dudley was more radically Protestant. He attracted high-caliber continental Reformers like Martin Bucer, Bernardino Ochino, and John à Lasco to prepare confessional statements. Bucer was to influence the second and more "Calvinistic" edition of the Prayer Book. Cranmer, a convinced Erastian who was able to adapt himself theologically to much of the change, did refuse to follow in the more extremely Genevan statements concerning the Lord's Supper.

In the reign of Mary Tudor, England was ready for reaction. Attempts to prevent her accession had soured English folk on Edward's Protestant advisers. Mary (who ruled 1553–58) reimposed Catholicism with the sword and earned the fond nickname "Bloody Mary." Tragedy and frustration marked her career. Her husband Philip, of the Spanish line, left her childless. She was a moderate Catholic with a moderate adviser, Reginald Pole, who had Parliament absolved for the part it had contributed to schism in recent years. When the new Pope Paul IV (—1559) miscalculated English trends and hurried matters he overplayed, and alienated England. After the death of Stephen Gardiner, another moderate adviser, Mary underwent the change of heart that issued in a flow of blood. Cranmer and others were martyred. "Marian exiles" drained fine intellectual resources from England as they escaped to the continent, where they became further involved in the Protestant movement and influence.

The pendulum had swung from the Catholicism of Henry VII through the Catholic-to-Protestant temper of Henry VIII to Edward VI's Protestantism back to the Catholicism of Mary; it resolved itself in the Protestant-Catholicity of the compromising and comprehending Elizabeth I (ruled 1558–1603), who succeeded in molding the enduring character of the Establishment. A daughter of Henry VIII and an extremely able person, she brought England from ruinous to stable foreign policy and domestic economic stability; she repealed Marian Catholic legislation. The monarch was again ahead of the church in England, though the terms in which this was stated were less offensive to Catholics. The revised second *Book of Common Prayer* became compulsory with the Act of Uniformity in 1559; this pleased the Reformed. Finally, the Thirty-nine Articles, an outgrowth of Cranmerism, became the formal and comprehensive statement that satisfied almost everyone. A popular document, it shared status with the English Bible and the Prayer Book.

Elizabeth's personal strength backed up her policies. There was no question as to who held authority; the evidence for this shines through any reading of the literature of her times. Her note to a bishop is typical:

Proud Prelate,

You know what you were before I made you what you are now. If you do not immediately comply with my request, I will unfrock you, by God.

ELIZABETH

Undoubtedly the bishop got the point. Elizabeth could balance this directness by a studied ambiguity in theological expression. She could phrase the controversial issues of the Lord's Supper in terms acceptable to everyone, though really acceptable to no one. She could draw direct fire from the papacy, as in the Bull of 1570 which sundered the churches:

> He that reigns in the highest, to whom has been given all power in heaven and earth, entrusted the government of the one Holy Catholic and Apostolic Church (outside which there is no salvation) to one man alone on the earth, namely to Peter, the chief of the Apostles, and to Peter's successor, the Roman pontiff, in fullness of power. This one man he set up as chief over all nations and all kingdoms, to pluck up, destroy, scatter, dispose, plant and build . . . Resting then upon the authority of him who has willed to place us . . . in this supreme throne of justice, we declare the aforesaid Elizabeth a heretic and an abettor of heretics, and those that cleave to her in the aforesaid matters to have incurred the sentence of anathema, and to be cut off from the unity of Christ's body.

And the cleavers did not care; the Elizabethan Settlement was satisfactory. All that remained was the consolidation of its comprehensive position in the writings of Richard Hooker (—1600): "as the main body of the sea being one, yet within divers precincts hath divers names, so the Catholic Church is in like sort divided into a number of distinct Societies, every of which is termed a Church within itself." And Parliament made it clear: the church *in* England was now the Church *of* England.

THE FREE SPIRITS

How different is all this from the next type of eruption in the formless movements of "the free spirits," the radicals who formed the left wing of the Reformation—the Mennonites, the Anabaptists, and later the Quakers and some Puritans. Most of them better conform (a word that is hard to use in connection with this ferment) to the picture of the Reformation often popularized by latter-day Lutherans and Calvinists. These, and not their more churchly contemporaries, were the real "Bible-believing" Christians, often literalistic in their interpretation—or "free" in their claim to the same direct inspiration from the Holy Spirit as the early Church had claimed. They lived in the consciousness that they were playing a dramatic part in the plan of God for the last days, to the embarrassment of conservative reform and to the harassment of conciliatory Romanism.

The sectarian impulse, with its rejection of churchliness, the formal priesthood and sacraments, and the use of art and the artifacts of culture, was partly a political and social thrust, though it was not the "Bolshevism of the Reformation" as it was pictured but a century ago. Its leaders were self-convinced men of God who set out to storm the fortresses of privilege in church and society, if necessary (as in the case of Thomas Münzer) with the sword.

The term Anabaptism, coined to refer to their repudiation of infant baptism and their insistence on rebaptism, applies to most of the rebels. Conrad Grebel (—1526) was the first to rebaptize a follower, Georg Blaurock (—1529), in Zurich in January 1525. This date reveals how soon after Luther began his work these radical forces were taking over. Grebel became the spiritual leader of the Swiss Brethren and the patron of Anabaptism. He had separated from the Zwinglian movement because it exuded to his nostrils too much of the scent of old Rome. A people's church based on voluntary profession and eventuating in holiness of life was his goal. Worship among Anabaptists was informal, in theory adding nothing to New Testament practice. Sacraments affirmed and strengthened fellowship in remembrance of Christ. An earthy, pragmatic group, the Movement reflected the aspirations of the disaffected in both its forms: the Grebelian wing was pacifist, the Münzer type bore arms.

Protestant joined Roman in attack. More reformers would have agreed with the Belgic Confession:

> We detest the Anabaptists and other seditious people, and in general all those who reject the higher powers and of magistrates and would subvert justice, introduce community of goods, and confound that decency and good order which God has established among men.

The Diets of Speyer and of Augsburg, 1529 and 1530, found Protestants and Catholics in rare agreement as they decided to persecute the "Baptists." Luther, who opposed anarchy as he opposed Satan and the pope, felt obliged to discourage the social unrest they bred. But the Baptists thrived. Repression began in Zurich in 1525 when Zwingli and the civil authorities exiled Grebel and others who would not desist from their teachings. Blaurock and others were later executed.

Forced exile encouraged the spread of their views to most of western Europe except France. In Austria the Hutterites formed communities in which spiritual and economic sharing took place. At Nürnberg Hans Denk (—1525), a humanist who pulled Platonism and mysticism into the Baptist orbit, propagated the movement until he tired of its excesses. In Moravia Balthasar Hubmaier (—1528) settled; he led many Lutherans to rebaptism and led himself to martyrdom. The apocalyptic views of his followers brought them into disfavor.

Two leaders stand out. Most important was Menno Simons (—1561), who made the movement more respectable and began to make the outburst more conservative. Influenced by Lutheran writings, he was inspired by the example of his brother's martyrdom to pursue the religious vocation. With publication of his views in 1539, they became normative for a "Mennonite" group: baptism does not produce grace or effect forgiveness or faith. It is the seal of spiritual rebirth. The Eucharist is a memorial. The church retains holiness through excommunication of the unholy. Christians must obey the government where it does not conflict with the Bible. But they must be nonresistant, must not fight wars. In many other of his seeming departures from historic Christianity, semantics more than substance was involved. From its origin in the Low Countries the Mennonite movement has persisted and grown to a world-wide fellowship of perhaps half a million Christians.

Spiritualism also veered toward mysticism, as in the case of Sebastian Franck (—1543), who rejected all organized forms of church life. No true church has existed since apostolic times; only an invisible fellowship of holy believers exists. Franck verged on rationalism, as skewed mysticism has done before and since. With Franck we may mention Kaspar von Schwenkfeld (—1561), whose followers endure to our day to correct Luther's stress on justification by a counterstress on sanctification, and to out-Zwingli Zwingli in a spiritualistic view of the Lord's Supper and the inner life. In its spiritualistic emphases the left wing of the Reformation left itself most open to schism and the formation of rival sects. It issued in individualism and sometimes veered toward pantheism. Its conservative forms remain to this day; its robust radicals were dissipated in the time of the Enlightenment.

REFORM IN THE SOUTH

Only a passing glance is necessary here at the fate of reform movements nearer the center of the vineyard, in the Romance lands where the papacy was to prevail. The thrust was largely aborted in Spain and Italy. France was divided between Lutheran influence and a more predominant Reformed Christianity with a mysterious name, that of Huguenot. The Gallican tradition of semi-independence from Rome removed some of the necessity for rebellion against the papacy. Social discontents did produce some dissatisfaction with all institutions, among them the church, and intellectual leaders (we have met Lefevre, Briconnet, and others) introduced Protestant sentiment and opinion. But Briconnet himself did not become Protestant. The Sorbonne in Paris was the center of Catholic resistance, and against this stronghold few prevailed. Suppression forced the more consistent French Protestants into asylum in Switzerland. Moderate toleration existed from 1529 to 1533, when Francis gained some papal favor for again suppressing Protestants. It was difficult for reform to take root in the times of rapid change between toleration and suppression.

When radical reformers pushed their luck in 1534 by carrying placards, most of them directed against the Mass, hundreds were imprisoned and some were put to death. Francis leaned toward toleration again in 1535, and toward repression in 1540 when many Waldensians met death. In 1546 fourteen reformers were martyred at Meaux in an action all too typical of inquisitorial authority in France.

Spain saw even less change from its Roman Catholic past, partly because reform within that church had begun under Ximenes before the time of Luther and partly because of the Inquisition's direct effectiveness. Some "Lutheran" sentiment appeared in isolated circles at rarefied levels, as among the family de Valdes, a circle of humanists and mystics who stressed the Bible, evangelical witness, and spiritualism. Evangelical groups gathered at Seville and Valladolid met suppression. The most famed of the Spanish reformers was the ill-fated Michael Servetus (—1553), a "Unitarian" and a medical scholar, who walked into a Calvinist trap and was martyred by the Protestant movement.

Italy showed little inclination to move toward massive reform. Protestants clung to toeholds in several cities, but most of them veered, as in Spain, toward anti-trinitarian radicalism, often on a humanist or Platonist base. Bernardino Ochino (—1564), Francis David (—1579) and most of all the somewhat younger Fausto Sozzini (—1604) were prominent there; Polish Unitarianism (Socinianism) was shaped by Sozzini. Their example seemed, in Italy, to prove Rome's point that peripheral reforms, when consistent, would conclude by attacking the heart of the Christian faith, belief in the divine Christ.

SCOTLAND

At the opposite extreme from these Protestant failures
was the complete reformation of Scottish Christianity under
the influence of Calvin through John Knox (—1572). Like
England, Scotland had been prepared for reform through
late-medieval Lollardry, humanism, and national consciousness which looked for faults in Rome. Under James V there
were signs of Scotland's going Lutheran. Patrick Hamilton
(—1528) brought ideas from Melanchthon and Luther
from Wittenberg, but was executed for them by Archbishop
Beaton. Beaton was the scourge of Protestantism. George
Wishart (—1546), a converted priest, was burned as an
example to other reformers. But Beaton was murdered by
colleagues of Wishart who had the encouragement of
Henry VIII; Beaton had flirted with the French against
the English. These colleagues called Knox to the court until
France came to the rescue of the Scottish regent and took
Knox and the Wishartians to the galleys. Parliament was
controlled by Catholics who worked through royal marriage
to bring France and Scotland into one political orbit. Knox
made his own way from England through Geneva back to
Scotland at a time when the nobles were gathering force
against French influence and for Calvinism.

From pulpit and platform Knox supported Calvinism
and Scottish nationalism against France and Catholicism.
He welcomed, not without distaste, the help of Elizabeth
(of "the Monstrous Regiment of Women") against Mary
Stuart of France. In 1560 the Parliament declared itself
to be Protestant and radically rejected papal practices. The
presbyterian order was established in the same year under
a "Book of Discipline" and a Scottish Confession of faith.
A rather austere and legalistic form of Calvinism was
nurtured under Knox and later under Andrew Melville
(—1622), who saw to it that Scotland should not deviate.
With Switzerland and the Low Countries, Scotland became
the most Calvinist of lands.

REFORM REVISITED

The examples of England, of Anabaptism, of Romance-land ferments, and of the capture of Scotland's head and heart suggest the ways in which to Roman eyes the vineyard of the Lord was being trampled and torn. Nor did this activity slow in the provinces of Zwingli, Luther, and Calvin: it is time to revisit each to see the ferments settle into forms as a backdrop for counter-Reform. Zwinglianism was soon to be dissolved into Calvinism in its one branch, into Anabaptism in its other; only one aspect of its ongoing life need detain us. This was its sacramental extremism. Zwingli had centered his attack on the Mass, replacing it with a simple supper around a simple table. As the movement spread from Zurich to Bern to Basel, under men like Oecolampadius (—1531), a humanist and linguist, some sort of showdown became necessary with German Protestantism, for different views on the Eucharist had become current. Zwingli and Luther differed in nationality, in temperament, by educational background, and theologically. The Supper was to Zwingli a symbol and sign; this view became sophisticated into the interpretation that the New Testament's "This is my body," meant "This signifies my body." Zwingli made his bid for attention with a mild polemic. Luther answered with a good measure of polemic, pressed down and running over. Bucer's attempt at compromise failed.

Enter the politician. Philip of Hesse saw great strategic advantage in fusion of the two parties; to settle the question of the Lord's Supper both were invited to Marburg in 1529. There was agreement in most respects, but Luther argued that a different spirit separated the parties. The point at issue was Christ's bodily presence. Zwingli's spiritualization of the sacrament was abhorrent to Luther's interest in Christology. Agreement failed to come; each went his own way. Luther would hereafter stress the more profoundly theological aspects of the rite; Zwingli and the Reformed retained the emphasis on communion-fellowship. "The Zwinglian view has no bold crags; everything is tidy and rationally ordered. But the idea of Fellowship stands on its highest point." [3]

Zwingli is soon to be removed from the scene by death in the second battle of Kappel; so too it is not necessary to detail the remaining years of Luther's life beyond the barest outline. After his defense at Worms he was confined by friends at the Wartburg in 1522; he left this hiding-place to break the iconoclastic reform at Wittenberg. His consciousness of the continuity of the Church was violated by the activity of his friends led by Carlstadt, and he hastened to dissociate himself with his usual vehemence. Despite his moderation in reform, Roman Catholic attacks increased. Cochlaeus, a humanist, has remained for later centuries the symbol of vulgar attack on Luther. Henry VIII and John Eck were more familiar antagonists.

LUTHERANISM

Despite attacks from right and left, Lutheranism advanced. From Wittenberg it spread through Thuringia and Saxony, then along the Rhine, and in the south around Augsburg and Nürnberg. Scholars aided the cause: the prodigious Philip Melanchthon, who produced Lutheranism's first systematic theology; Johannes Bugenhagen, Johannes Agricola, and Justus Jonas joined Luther's professorial contingent. Albrecht Dürer, Lucas Cranach, and the younger Hans Holbein aided the cause artistically. The chorale and other types of music made Luther's a "singing church" that has seen few parallels in Christian history.

There were defections. The theological emphasis offended many; the conservatism of worship forms repelled the rebels. Luther's liaison with the princes (who virtually assumed episcopal functions in the young churches) was abhorrent to those who preached that spiritual and temporal realms must be fully separate. Humanists like Reuchlin, congenial to Luther, remained aloof from partisan participation, and others like Pirkheimer shrugged off the Lutheranism which they had first embraced as being too belligerent. Towering above them all was Erasmus of Rotterdam, an irenic humanist who provided much ammunition for attack on the excesses of Rome but refused to man the cannon himself. By 1525 he had come to break with Luther over the question of the freedom (Erasmus) or the bondage (Luther) of the will. In 1519 Luther could speak of Erasmus as "our ornament and our hope," "an amiable man." Later he found a different set of terms useful to describe the gunshy scholar.

Perhaps more serious for the future shape of German Protestantism was Luther's alienation of the "peasants," the disaffected social classes who had seen in him the Lion of the North, a sort of secular Messiah. Luther was poorly cast in this role, obsessed as he was by religious concerns, politically naive as he seemed to be, ruthlessly empirical and pragmatic in his decisions on social matters as he was. Two years after Luther returned from the Wartburg the peasants revolted, particularly in the southern third of Germany. The disorganization, the immoderation of demands, the violent means, the mingled motives led Luther to discourage the revolt after his earliest signs of interest in it. In his horror of anarchy, he turned on the peasants in his familiar and unforgivable order to stab, smite, and slay them. Less familiar was his similar reproof of the princes in the mirror of the law of God. The masses lost interest and turned to radical and secular social movements for new hopes. Ever after, the Lutheran movement was to tend toward more comfortable relations with political conservatism.

Political developments in the face of the Turkish onrush and the lasting rivalry between the Valois and Hapsburg houses made moves toward political reunion necessary. The religious implications were obvious. Pope, emperor and princes welcomed any trends toward unity that were apparent. But each was selfish in his goal; reformers were disunited; little was achieved. A stalemate developed during which the principle of *cuius regio, eius religio* (the region adopts the religion of the ruler) was taking shape, to be formalized in the Peace of Augsburg in 1555. Protestants had tried to unite at many times. At Marburg they failed in 1529. The same year at the Diet of Speyer they were first denominated "Protestant," but they protested too much against each other. Zwinglians turned in a minority report in matters religious to political leaders, and the presentation of the Lutheran Confession at Augsburg in 1530 further blocked reunion.

After Augsburg the Lutherans entered into a fifty-year period of razor-sharp and hair-splitting theological definition which produced its confessions, pulled together in the *Book of Concord* of 1580. By the time of Luther's death the secular leaders were well poised to assume spiritual functions and make the church in many respects a lackey in their temporal pursuits. Parallel with its relative political impotence, Lutheranism developed a cultural strength in the universities and in the widespread educational system being developed under its auspices. Luther went on with his task of supervision, preaching, and writing; he died in 1546, towering above all the other early Protestants except, perhaps, John Calvin.

After his death new religious wars broke out. Charles V had taken the offensive when he noticed that the Reformation was threatening both the Empire and the church of the medieval lineage through its alliance with nationalism, territorialism, and social unrest in the provinces. He attacked the Schmalkaldic League, which had been organized in order to counter such aggression. He was successful in his attacks but was unable to carry out the implications of victory in religious war; he had to settle for compromise. The Peace of Augsburg was a sign of the stalemate; territorialism had triumphed. But Augsburg did provide Europe with a time of rest and peace and Protestantism was now, after act of war, declared official. The vineyard was torn up and the papal parties had to recognize it.

CALVINISM

Calvinism progressed apace after 1536, the year of Calvin's first *Institutes*. Calvin himself was just beginning his career; he was twenty-six at the time of this publication. Almost against his will he became the leader of Swiss reform. In

July 1536 after a trip to Italy he was returning to the north, perhaps to Strassburg and a quiet life, when he had to detour through Geneva to avoid the Emperor's troops. The detour was planned to involve only one night in the Swiss city; it turned out to imply the beginning of a career and a turn in the road of Christian history. He was virtually terrorized by collegial pleas to become active as the man of the hour to build the new Christian commonwealth at Geneva.

He responded by forming the Genevan theocracy, the city of God among men, where the new teachings could be put into effect in the civil and personal lives of men. A gateway city in the Alps, much desired by Savoyans and French, Geneva was strategic. Having developed a measure of freedom as early as the fourteenth century, Genevans formed an opposition party to rebel against Bishop John of Savoy (—1522); after early defeat the revolutionaries took over power in 1526 and held it despite raids by the Bishop in 1530. Bern, which had become Protestant earlier, came to Geneva's aid; the good turn led Genevans to examine the possibility of accepting the Reformed position. Through much violence and opposition, the anti-Catholic party developed. It was to this setting that Calvin came in 1536; here was a petri dish for his new culture. Previous acceptance of Protestantism had been an external matter; Calvin was to deepen it.

"The Frenchman" first assumed the post of reader in the Genevan church; he turned, like Luther, to the Book of Romans for resource. His star rose rapidly over the Alpine city. His triumph over Catholic debaters brought him fame and helped him cast Geneva and much of Switzerland beyond it in the Protestant die. A tight system of discipline and a broad program of education furthered the cause; laity and clergy joined in governing through a consistory which successfully fused functions of church and state. With the establishment of the Genevan Academy to round off the efforts

> Calvin had achieved his task: he had secured the future of Geneva . . . making it at once a church, a school and a fortress. It was the first stronghold of liberty in modern times.[4]

The honeymoon was brief. Theological factions countered the Calvinists, even if they were to be abruptly bested in debate. Anabaptists rose in rebellion and were suppressed. But aristocratic families who resented clerical authority carried the day under one Jean Philippe. Calvin and his sponsor Farel were repudiated and eventually were denied their pulpits. When they broke the ban on Easter of 1538 they nearly lost their lives. Exiled, they consolidated reform in several Swiss cities. Calvin settled at Strassburg in Germany, where Bucer befriended him. During this time Calvin married a widow, and consigned his word to print: his theological output now was formidable. He participated in several irenic discussions with other Protestants, including the Regensburg Colloquy of 1541.

When opportunity presented itself that year to return to Geneva, he did so and recovered his ground; with a man-sized career already behind him, he had reached the age of thirty-two. In this second round, as a sort of local hero he had more freedom in determining political life than previously. He had learned from Strassburg. He had read his Old Testament, which reinforced his theocratic ideal. But his career reveals the difficulties of ecclesiastical attempts at temporal control within the Protestant picture also. Tiptoeing at the edges of legalism at all times and plunging in at others, the consistory passed multitudinous petty moral laws against the theater, dancing, and playing cards. The third of these was a mistake. It roused a vested interest, just as Paul had done among the Ephesian silversmiths and Savonarola among the Florentine craftsmen. Pierre Ameaux, a playing-card manufacturer, rallied a party of opposition. Calvin's only popular achievement of this time was his part in the execution of a heretic.

The heretic's name was Servetus; the act makes the blackest page in Protestant history. Servetus we have met in Spain as the medical expert (who discovered much about the circulation of the blood) and anti-trinitarian. Rather foolhardily the unfortunate Spaniard went to hear Calvin preach, was spotted and apprehended. Soon he was to burn. The council which tried him, wearied by theological niceties, attempted a different tack: criticizing him for

subversion. When it decreed death by burning, Calvin inter-
vened, but only to the point of asking for a milder death.
Servetus died heroically, shouting with theological precision his convictions in his dying prayer addressed to
"Jesus, Thou Son of the eternal God." Calvin was doing
what the Roman church had often done, but "at the period
of the Reformation mankind had begun to know better
and so charity of judgement upon the Reformers begins
to wear thin." [5] It wears most thin on Calvin in his arroga-
tion to himself of God's judgment: "He who has trampled
under foot the majesty of God is worse than a brigand who
cuts the throat of a wayfarer." From the Lutheran side,
Philip Melanchthon concurred.

The execution of Servetus illustrates the triumph of
Calvinism in civil affairs and the temptations it was heir
to. Geneva became a mecca for Protestant exiles, a magnet
for commercial and mercantile interests. Calvin broadened
his reform to include schools, particularly the Genevan
Academy, founded in 1559 and taught by excellent scholars,
notably Theodore Beza (—1605). While Genevan capital-
ists developed their theories, Calvin enlarged his theology
through many versions of the *Institutes* down to 1559. The
Reformed movement on the continent was consolidated in
:he Zurich Consensus of 1549 when the Zwinglians merged
with Calvinists (Bullinger meeting with Calvin and Farel),
and in the Second Helvetic Confession of 1566. After about
the time of the Lutheran Concord of 1580 these parties
came to be lumped together consistently as the Reformed
Church.

Lutheran, Reformed, Anglican, Anabaptist, with plentiful varieties of each, confronted the church of Rome during the sixteenth century. In 1517 Leo X was still consider-
ing the entire Western church his vineyard, bothered at
times by alien growths and weeds that could be uprooted.
Now organizational unity in the West dissolved. The impact of this change on Rome was staggering. It eventuated
in what is usually called the Counter-Reformation or Catholic Reformation. Perhaps the former term is preferable, for
it recalls that the effort was more a reaction to Protestantism
than it was a resumption of continuity with pre-Protestant

reform as we encountered it in Spain under Ximenes or in France after Bourges. Panic was a factor. The Bull of 1520 describing the horticulture of the vineyard stands at its beginning; the Council of Trent represents its formal achievement.

COUNTER-REFORM

Roman Catholicism brought reserves to its reaction. It attracted humanists who, in the long view, remained faithful to Rome as often as not. While they were introducing many secularizing elements, they were useful instruments for a papacy seeking new respectability. The same resources of piety on which Luther drew in the Brethren of the Common Life, the preachers and late medieval mystics, were also Rome's; the Roman church nurtured this piety, and kept its contemporary spokesmen loyal to the system whose color and emotional richness was more attractive than the often barren forms of Protestantism. The centralized government was an organizational advantage; the loyalty of the right religious orders provided a reservoir of energies which maddeningly diffuse Protestantism could not share. And Rome could always count on the occasional support of political factions, offering relative stability to the insecure in a time of Protestant turmoil.

If we begin with Italy after the reaction to Savonarola we can see a flowering of counter-reformers that centered in the Roman Oratory of Divine Love, founded in 1517. Dedicated to prayer, selfless devotion, and service, the Oratorians attracted artisans, scholars, common people and theologians to work together. During the decade of its life-span it helped produce scholars and a climate in which scholarship thrived. Both helped formulate the opposition to Protestant dogmatic formulation. Best known among these are Bishops Jacopo Sadoleto (—1547), Gian Giberti (—1543) and Gian Caraffa (—1559), who advanced Bible study and sought to repress Protestantism. Also in this group, Gasparo Contarini distinguished himself as a conciliator at Regensburg.

The Inquisition and consistent imperial watchfulness obliterated the pockets of Protestant sympathy throughout Spain in the sixteenth century. If Italy provided the moralists and scholars, Spain produced monks and mystics. Best known of these was St. Teresa (—1582), a noblewoman who, with St. John of the Cross, developed a mystic quietism that has appealed to Christians of many persuasions. Scholasticism was fostered at the famed University of Salamanca.

In Germany counter-reform centered in efforts to stifle Lutheranism. Most of this response came from Italy, but we have already met John Eck (—1543) and the extravagant Cochlaeus (—1552). Hieronymus Emser (—1527) had called forth Luther's scorn for his naive and primitive attacks. While Germany saw defection of more humanists than did Italy, it retained the services for Rome of some Erasmians.

The papacy, of course, had most to lose. At times it responded blindly and desperately. At others its reform from within made it more attractive to an enlightened Europe. Many of the popes were still bewildered by the storms of the north, confused by political particularism and confessional novelty. Clement VII (from 1523–34), a moral and well-intentioned Pope, was unable to accomplish much because of his heritage of political involvements and because of the inadequacy of the counsel he received. He lost ground and was even disgraced in his vacillation between imperial and Valois fortunes. Charles was pressing for a reform council to strengthen the Empire and to lift the papacy out of embarrassment. Under Paul III (1534–49) hopes for reform were dimmed on the conciliar level, because the Pope's personal purity of character removed some of the sting of past attack. Surrounded by Contarini, Pole, Caraffa, and Sadoleto, he could anticipate criticism and formulate reply. Despite his reluctance, a council was called in 1536; at first it commuted from Mantua to Vincenza and elsewhere before Trent was chosen. Trent was acceptable to Charles V because it was on German soil, even if it leaned on the leeward side of the Alps toward Rome. The Council got underway in 1545, almost a third of a century after the Protestant movement had begun to break the Roman hold. Lutherans no longer saw point in attending.

Trent dates from 1545–63, but it did not convene consistently. Charles V and Paul III first looked over the issue of the character of reform; few hierarchs attended during that period. Contarini and Pole were gradually seen as conciliators, while Caraffa wanted a purge of Protestantism. Three popes later the Council completed its doctrinal formulation and succeeded in tightening Roman discipline. By 1563 it was all over and Rome ruled with new strength, possessing inner unities. Trent had set as its goal to preserve, not to regain, the "purity of the gospel," admitting little fault in the past. Late-medieval innovations were spurred along with the Reformation. The council regained for Rome much of the prestige long lost. Pius IV sealed Trent with the Bull *Injunctum nobis,* which made matters clear for Romans then and converts until now:

> I recognize the Holy Catholic and Apostolic *Roman* Church [emphasis added] as the mother and mistress of all churches; and I vow and swear true obedience to the Roman Pontiff, the successor of blessed Peter, the chief of the Apostles and the vicar of Jesus Christ.

But the papacy had also lost. The West was divided; past corruptions were exposed. *Cuius regio eius religio* prevailed as a political principle. This reduced the pope to a bargainer. The assumptions of a millennium had come tumbling to lie in the shambles of the torn vineyard. Historians ever since have had to see the Roman church as a "denomination" (a poor but accurate term) among others, however much it might dominate or predominate.

And the churches went their separate ways as efforts at union failed. This was a trend that hardly reversed itself until recent times. A church historian would need fuchsia-colored eyeglasses to pretend that, as he looked out on the Church that was ideally one, he saw anything but a welter of confusion, division, and disparity after the storms of the sixteenth century.

12

THE COMPASS OF THE FAITH

The story of the movement of Christianity in its catholic or world-wide sweep involves us in a paradoxical century. The concerns over apostolic doctrine, the holiness of Christian teaching, and the unity or disruption of the Western church monopolizes the scene so dramatically that we hardly notice that in the same sixteenth century the Christian message was for the first time carried around the world. Indeed, the lines of communication were weak, were strained almost to the point of nothingness. Most of the outposts of the faith were mere outposts, threatened with isolation and neglect. Much of the work was superficial.

But a new world was born in the years after Columbus sailed westward; during the sixteenth century the Roman Catholic Church had established a beachhead wherever explorers or colonists went in the western hemisphere. Jesuits also took another route around India and up the coast of China to Japan. The beginning of a world-wide mission that would unfold in the nineteenth century was made. It will be convenient to speak of the Roman church's work as *mission,* for it entered territories not yet Christianized; the word for the Protestant move is *expansion,* for it is usually the act of converting territories from Catholic to Protestant or at least plural profession. In the heat of reformative concerns Protestantism was directing its energies inward. It held neither the position nor the vision necessary for authentic missionary activity.

THE EAST

Profiting from the advances in navigatory arts in the time cf the modern world's dawn, we can take the mariner's compass to find the measure of the faith: East, in Orthodoxy; West, in Roman Catholic missions; North, in Protestant expansion. A view toward the East, the land of sunrise and cradle of the faith, is not encouraging. The Orthodox churches had been least touched by the Reformation, but they did not possess enough vitality or motivation for expansion beyond existing borders. Moslem dominance limited their horizons; if "the Turk" disturbed the pope, the emperor, and the reformers in the West, it is not difficult to imagine the terror in the East.

If there was little expansion, there was a dramatic shift of weight within the East, from the southern churches to Russia. Russia had expanded nationally during the rule of Ivan IV, "the Terrible" (—1584). Fierce autocrat that he was, Ivan moved to dominate the Urals in the south, Kazan in the east; he had less success against Swedes and Poles in the west. Peasants were subjugated and new subjects terrorized. Yet under Ivan's ruthless exterior was a perceptive religious nature and an alert mind; this was dissipated into madness and caprice in his later life. During the years of his conquest the church had opportunity to extend itself geographically and in prestige by attaching itself to Ivan's fortunes. Makary, the Josephite Metropolitan of Moscow, held a sufficiently powerful post to enable him to work with Ivan and to give his own patriarchal office sufficient grandeur that there could be some plausibility in references to Moscow as "the Third Rome." After Makary's death in 1590, Moscow was ranked with the ancient patriarchates of Jerusalem, Constantinople, Alexandria, Antioch—names that once were written large upon the Christian map but had now fallen toward obscurity. Moscow had more power than any of these. The new territory of

Kazan was granted archepiscopal status and became the center of conversion of newly conquered people. Ivan aided the cause until his time of madness by encouraging the monasteries. By the end of the Reformation century the "Russian Orthodox Church" was master of the East.

The need to tell the story in relation to a ruler like Ivan is a clue also to the fact that this was a troubled church. Though it had no Luthers or Calvins, its centrality was subjected to trial through tension and schism. Westerners, addicted to private vices of their own, have been mystified in their attempts to understand Eastern division: shall the *Alleluia* be chanted twice before the *Gloria,* as the Greeks do it, or three times as the Russians do? (The Greeks won.) More important was the severance of Uniatebodies from eastern control. Mention of the Uniates implies the clearest reference to Western issues. Through Polish national and Jesuitical religious influences, the western borders of the church flirted with Rome; they were wooed by a Jesuit college at Vilna (1570) where Western ideas could be promulgated.

At the end of the century several bridge-builders toward Rome were active; some of them seceded but were not to be pressed into conformity. While they acknowledged Roman authority they were allowed their private practices. The schism damaged "the Third Rome's" hold, but it did inspire some new Orthodox aggressiveness and vitality. To follow the story it is necessary to move with the controversy into the seventeenth century. To counter Cyril Lucar's (—1638) flirtation with the West (particularly the Reformed churches) Peter Mogila (—1646) prepared an Orthodox confession of faith that became normative for Russia and provided a rallying center.

Catastrophe came to the catholic claims of the East in another form; front-line priests and people in poverty and plainest peasantdom resented the noble higher clergy living in fatness. Attempts to reform monasteries and redistribute wealth, to trample power centers, and to retain familiar forms of worship against innovations of the higher powers characterized their attack. They shared no theological idea like the West's "justification by faith," and their revolt is in no sense causally connected with Western reform. At the heart of the confusion was the great Patriarch Nikon (—1681) of Moscow. Against his will he had acceded to the high office. Once there, he knew that success depended upon a sweeping view of its authority. He distinguished himself by liturgical reform. Again, there seems to be preoccupation with trivialities. Textual criticism had been developed; when a revisionist dropped the part of the phrase concerning sanctification "by the Holy Spirit and by fire" because "fire" did not have sufficient textual warrant, this offended those who believed that the Holy Spirit was Himself fire. And with how many fingers shall the sign of the cross be made?

Despite the people's conservative resistance Nikon forged the revised liturgies; he improved the educational and moral level of the clergy. His methods were extreme: he could exile opponents without a qualm. At his height he resembled the great Popes Leo, Gregory, or Innocent; but he overreached as they had done. He lost favor with the Tsar and saw his star falling after 1658. When he withdrew in a huff, his exiled opponent Avvakum was returned as people's hero with people's service-books. By the time Nikon returned to Moscow in 1664 it was too late for him to regain favor. Only after death did honors come.

Nikon's work had come to prevail, however; the Old Believers who held to the old ways were organized as Raskolniki, and were persecuted as schismatics. Sectarian movements sprouted on every hand. Not until the time of Peter the Great would the "Third Rome" concept gain new credence. The Russian church had seen expansion, had weathered schisms, had been enlightened from within and from the West; its versatility should have poised it for modernity under Peter. It was, as we shall later see, poorly prepared for the test.

THE WEST: LOYOLA AND THE JESUITS

The characteristic movement of missions from Rome begins with monastic impulses; in most instances the missionaries were aggressive counter-reformers, the products of a purged and revitalized church. They refused to stay at home, as their predecessors had, with their version of good news. The outstanding cell for this vision was the Society of Jesus. Born in the period of the Reformation, a hated symbol to many including later Catholics, it was to dominate Roman Catholicism until its suppression in Enlightenment times. To know the Order one must be introduced to the one Catholic who shares pedestals with Luther and Calvin among the century's greats: Ignatius Loyola (—1556). A Spanish noble converted from adventurous uselessness to military discipline to vital Christianity, this great activist produced one of the classics of devotion. While recovering from battle injuries he resolved to do battle for the cross. Going through a period of torment and doubt, he emerged with iron will and discipline, a zeal that he never relaxed. His resulting *Spiritual Exercises* became a manual of arms for Jesuits.

Not a book of devotion so much as a pattern of discipline, the *Exercises* were marvelous calisthenics for the task of a century. How useful was a man trained to think in this fashion!

> Always be ready to obey with mind and heart, setting aside all judgment of one's own, the true spouse of Jesus Christ, our holy mother, our infallible and orthodox mistress, the Catholic Church, whose authority is exercised over us by the hierarchy. . . . To uphold especially all the precepts of the Church, and not censure them in any manner; but, on the contrary, to defend them promptly, with reasons drawn from all sources, against those who criticize them.

Needless to say, here was a man untouched by the Protestant principle. The Jesuit appeal lay in the fanatic loyalty to Roman authority which it bred; it attracted those who would willingly bind their own wills, delivering themselves to another.

Like many another who had a late vocation, Ignatius had much homework to do; he studied at the great universities of Alcala, Salamanca and even Paris. But during this mastery of theology he was no bookworm. He channeled his energies and eventually attracted a remarkable circle of friends. In 1534 they formed the greatest of the modern orders with Francis Xavier, Peter Faber, and others. Most of the friends were laymen. They were by no means anticlericals; in a stroke of genius they appealed to the Pope for sanction. The Pope was reluctant to grant this because of charges of heresy against the Society. Yet when he studied their plan he is said to have remarked, "The finger of God is here."

No wonder. The plans were very flattering to the papal office. Theirs was no half-hearted appeal; they surrendered themselves absolutely to its needs.

> Let us with the utmost pains strain every nerve of our strength to exhibit this virtue of obedience, firstly to the Highest Pontiff, then to the Superiors of the Society; so that in all things, to which obedience can be extended with charity, we may be most ready to obey his voice, just as if it issued from our Lord . . .

The Society made no attempt to accommodate itself to the modern world in its administrative structure. The hierarchies were comparable to military ranks. They wore no special garb; they denied female membership; they would not waste their time with typically monastic specialties and virtuosities like chanting choirs. As a matter of fact an anti-Jesuitical Pope like Paul IV found it practicable to harass the Society by assigning to it choir offices.

Under Ignatius the Jesuits soon found a groove in reform, in education, in spiritual discipline, and in missions. They are still known for their highly organized educational system. In many respects their methods countered the modern development: they drummed into the ears of students the idea of ecclesiastical authority. Catechetical instruction was normative for the young; this did much to reduce the pitiful ignorance which the Reformers had confronted. But in the context of this chapter the Jesuits distinguished themselves by following the path of Francis Xavier (—1552), the greatest Catholic missionary of recent centuries. When nineteenth-century missionaries recovered lost territories for the faith they found many traces of Xavier's earlier work.

An acquaintance of Ignatius Loyola from Paris days

and an original Jesuit, Francis was obsessed by the idea of bringing as many people as possible into the circle of redemption, if necessary by marginal means with minimal goals. He claimed to have baptized hundreds of thousands of people as he sailed along the Asiatic coast from Goa in India after 1542. In the days before dramamine or benadryl he carried a cross whose weight only others affected by it can appreciate: he was constantly seasick. Yet he left the seas behind him; to Travancore, the Molucca Islands, Ceylon he went; on to Japan by 1549, and after a return to his Goan headquarters in 1552 he was off to China, where he died. It was fitting that Pius X should name him the patron of foreign missions. Attacked in his time for his Jesuitical practices of adaptationism, Francis has been faulted by moderns for his ties with government at Goa, his use of the Inquisition, his approval of persecution, and his shortcomings in the field of comparative religion. But he had enlarged the boundaries of Christian vision immeasurably.

He was not alone. Wherever explorers and exploiters went, there were Jesuits, Dominicans, or members of other orders prevailing upon shipowners, giving themselves to death for the cause they advocated. Sometimes they succeeded in gaining rights and humane treatment for the Indians of the Americas; sometimes they served as the conscience to men who lusted for power and plunder. Always they left behind missions. Since their fortunes were tied to the Iberian powers, their effectiveness was hampered by later defeats handed Spanish navies.

In Asia the faith encountered high religions instead of the vacuum it had met in American Indian country. But in both thrusts the attempt was usually made to gain mass conversions, even if this meant little understanding or nurture. Within a decade Franciscan Observants claimed to have baptized millions. The religion thus promoted often permitted retention of superstitious elements; its adherents were poorly informed, neglected, and exploited. But it was represented, and in the faintest glimmers of understanding new compass points were appearing for later missionaries to follow.

The church of later centuries was poorer for forgetting men like the Jesuit Pedro Claver (—1654), a noble who earned himself the title of patron to Negro Christians for his opposition to the slave trade in Columbia: he called himself "the slave of the Negroes forever" and championed their cause, baptizing perhaps one third of a million of them. Francisco de Vitoria, a Dominican, was similarly moved to promote Indian rights at great expense to his person. Or Bartolomeo de Las Casas (—1566), the son of an associate of Columbus who commuted across the Atlantic for Indian rights and for European interest in their cause. A peacemaker, he risked his life to settle armed conflict between exploiter and exploited; nor did his part in new laws that restricted colonists' greed make him popular with them.

With French Catholicism entering northern North America to balance the Spanish southern thrust, it looked for a time as if the Protestant faith would be unrepresented in the New World. In Canada, around the Great Lakes, along the St. Lawrence and the Mississippi, the Jesuits, Franciscans, and Sulpicians had their outposts. Many missionaries paid in blood for their conviction and their daring. The blood of Isaac Jogues and John Brebeuf colored the church, drawing it from parochial self-inversion toward the universal vision. The torn and stormed Rome of the sixteenth century was learning to realize anew the essential missionary character of the faith. It was learning from explorers; it was profiting from the prodding of Reformed Christians. The immediate expression of its new health was the desire for expansion.

PROTESTANT EXPANSION

Most Lutheran and Reformed growth was in continental Europe and the British Isles. Just as Catholicism thrived during its battle for survival by extension, so Protestantism enlarged its provinces even in the moment when it was struggling to exist. In the modern world perhaps 213,000,-000 Protestants balance 423,000,000 Roman Catholics and

160,000,000 Orthodox and Coptic Christians. The cast for this ratio was developed in the earliest years of the Reformation era when Protestants consolidated their gains, establishing themselves in the European countries from which later colonization of the New World and later missionary endeavor were to come. Much of the gain was not on the grounds of individual conversion but followed the pattern of *cuius regio, eius religio:* religion followed provincial and princely patterns of acceptance.

After Luther's death in 1546 his cause swept beyond Germany to consolidate its strength in Scandinavia. In 1337 the Union of Kalmar had united the nobility of what is now Sweden, Norway, and Denmark under Danish predominance. The union was never authentic because of governmental chaos in Sweden. The Danish royal family declined while other dynasties were rising. Petty princes were powerful, particularism of the German pattern was the vogue. Ecclesiastically the situation was confused by the presence of foreign-trained clergy who were often alien in their outlook, often reduced to vicious competition with secular nobles.

Change came in roughshod fashion under the rough Christian II (—1523) who tried to rise above the nagging nobles. As he gained power in Sweden he showed his tyrannical nature. In Denmark his gains were more fruitful; he was able to apply codes which limited churchly corruption. The clergy were to marry; ecclesiastical ownership of property was limited. Real reform began with the encouragement of education by Paul Eliae, a humanist Lutheran at Copenhagen. At his request Martin Reinhard and Carlstadt, both poorly equipped, were invited to introduce Lutheranism. As soon as the political situation changed they saw what a fool's paradise the Protestants had been inhabiting. Christian found it profitable to gain favor with his relative, Catholic Charles V. Soon after this he met political misfortune. His successor, Frederick I (1523–33), who had been influenced by Lutheranism, saw the opportunity to use the influence to advance himself. He invited Hans Tausen (—1561), a Wittenberger, to teach. Tausen was often in trouble for heresy, but his teachings made their way. Bible translations in Denmark became popular. Frederick hitched his wagon to the star of the Reformation, paralleling Henry VIII in many of his practices. Johan Bugenhagen, a colleague of Luther, prepared church orders for the northland. By 1530 it was clear that Denmark would become Lutheran; by 1539 a Lutheran Church Ordinance was the rule. The king was head of the church.

Out of the chaos of Swedish particularism rose Gustavus Vasa (—1560), who produced both modern Sweden and Lutheran Sweden. Brothers Lars and Olavus Petri from Wittenberg gained prominence in education and theology and won over the abler members of the native clergy to the program of reform. With Lars Andersson, they promoted a New Testament translation which was completed in 1526. Education and dynastic fortunes combined to advance the Lutheran cause; by the end of Vasa's career Sweden had become Lutheran; later kings—Eric XIV (1560–69), a Calvinist, and John III (1569–92), a Catholic—could not shake its Lutheranism. Iceland and Norway followed, though in Norway the imposition of reformed religion was not very popular at first. Finland chose Lutheranism under the influence of Michael Agricola (1508–57).

So much for the north. To the east the sweep soon included the Baltic states and parts of Poland, where it was blunted by princely particularism as in Sweden. No single form of Protestantism dominated there. Poland did become a center of the Unitarianism of Sozzini and his followers at Racow. In this divided state Roman Catholicism countered with some recovery toward the end of the century. Hungary was attracted to Lutheran influence because it was swayed by German culture. Many reform leaders like Matthew Devay (—1545) were evangelicals trained at Wittenberg who used the schools to advance the cause. Tensions with Germany, however, led many anti-Catholics to the Calvinism that was not associated so closely with the German cause. Transylvania came under Lutheran and Unitarian influence. Beyond this was the Orthodox front line in the East.

Czechoslovakia presented its own picture because of

the succession of Hussites. Hus's conservative followers (Utraquists) were not rabidly anti-Roman. The Bohemian Brethren were somewhat more radical. Urbanites and nobles leaned toward Catholicism. But all three groups saw some attraction in Lutheranism. The faith that filtered out from Wittenberg made little impact on the British Isles, the Romance lands, or the New World.

Reformed Protestantism was also on the move. Only in Poland and Hungary did it experience major gains in nations where Lutheranism had made its way. In a generalization that is so wide it verges on shallowness, we might say that it swung west into France and crossed the channel into Scotland and England while making gains in the Lowlands; Lutheranism began at that point of the arc and swept northeast and southeast. Neither compass pointed south. The early strongholds were Geneva, Strassburg, the cities of southern Germany. In the Palatinate Elector Frederick III (1559–76), who dabbled in theology, became convinced of the correctness of Calvinism and installed several professors of that adherence in the University of Heidelberg. Out of this circle came the Heidelberg Cathechism of 1563, as fine and coherent a statement of Reformed theology as we shall meet.

Calvin was not sufficiently aggressive to desire to step on Lutheran toes. But some of his followers, particularly exiles, crossed paths with the Wittenbergers. Laski worked in Poland and eastern Germany; Beza worked aggressively to establish Reformed strongholds in "Lutheran" areas. More dramatic were the advances in stormy France. Calvin, naturally, retained an interest in that troubled country. Protestant fortunes were often tied to the vagaries of the Hapsburg-Valois feuding. Henry II was strongly anti-Protestant; he set up a French form of the Inquisition in the *Chambre ardent* in 1548, and promulgated new laws to suppress Protestant literature. But since he had to keep one eye on political adversaries he could not concentrate on oppression, and the Reformed faith flourished. Some of his own family defected to the "Huguenot" side.

During the 1550's Calvinism became formal and open in France with the organization of congregations and the writing of confessions. Self-defensively Calvinists carried on war against the Guise family, which represented the new monarchical claims. The story of Calvinism's spread becomes an amalgam of religious and political motives at this point. Calvin himself opposed the purely political side of the movement and refused to enter the intrigues; he regretted to see religious wars taking shape. The Low Countries also became Reformed partly through political intrigues; they offered a convenient stopping-point for exiles commuting between the British Isles or France and the Swiss refuge. Even though the court supported the Inquisition, Swiss theologians braved the atmosphere. This was the home of Erasmus; here humanism fused with Reformed insights into a fine flowering of Protestant intellectual endeavor.

We have already followed Calvinism's early career in Scotland and England. It progressed through Cranmer and under the influence of the ubiquitous Laski and of Bucer, Ochino, and the "Marian exiles." John Knox out-Calvined Calvin in Scotland.

RELIGIOUS WARS

Into the details of religious wars from the Peace of Augsburg to the Peace of Westphalia we cannot go. These properly belong to military and political history, though religion was webbed with the events at most points. But enough must be told to describe the summation of the first wave of the Protestant movement beyond its first repulse in the Catholic Counter-Reformation. After the death of Luther and then Calvin their followers expanded the impulses, providing pillars in confessional statements and strong political alliances. Rome was not asleep; it began to make gains in Bavaria. When Protestants began to violate the terms of the Peace of Augsburg early in the seventeenth century the Catholics demanded that they be put down. Maximilian, Duke of Bavaria, took over the free city of Donauworth in 1607 and repudiated Protestantism there. This explosive situation attracted Protestants into forms of unity, specifically the Evangelical Union of 1608.

Ten years later war broke out between the parties in Bohemia, where Protestantism had gained on Hussite foundations. The "defenestration" (a rather impolite ejection from a window) of two Hapsburg emissaries by Protestants touched off the bloody events. Ferdinand, Archduke of Styria, attempted to put down the subsequent Protestant anti-Hapsburg revolt, and with the help of the military genius Tilly and the aid of Spain and Bavaria he advanced on Frederick, the Protestant leader, plundering Protestant lands. Rome gained through this first flurry (1622–23).

In its second stage the conflict grew again out of violations of the Peace of Augsburg. Again Tilly led the attack to triumph in northwest Germany and Denmark. But potent Catholic forces fell into internal division and met new opposition in Lutheran Gustavus Adolphus of Sweden. He wished to circle the Baltic; fearing Hapsburg advance, he went out to meet it in 1630 with the alliance of Cardinal Richelieu—religious lines were becoming entangled. He seemed to be well in advance in 1632 when he was killed. From this time on the war was indecisive; Catholics could not gain the north nor Protestants the south. Power more than religion preoccupied participants.

When peace came at Westphalia in 1648, Europe took a turn to the modern power picture and the age of the Reformation was ending. Rome could never again determine the political life of western Europe. Protestantism had seen the limits of its military capabilities. Modern states were being defined. Catholicism was busy redefining its purpose; Protestantism was plagued with disunity. Some had come to see that political *fiat* would not lead to permanent reunion of Christians. Negotiations of the sixteenth century had failed. Some, in the Erasmian tradition, wanted to gloss over minor differences in favor of greater unities, demanding assent to "those things alone which are clearly expressed in the Holy Scriptures or without which we see no way to arrive at salvation." Hugo Grotius among the Reformed and George Calixtus among the

Lutherans championed such views. Calixtus collided head-on with the most orthodox scholars Lutheranism has produced, men like Abraham Calov and others who would have no dealings with those of other confessions. Low Country attempts by Jacob Arminius and John Andreae (—1654) failed because they did not resolve basic theological difficulties or were, like Andreae's *Christianopolis,* too utopian.

FAITH AND CULTURE

We have followed the compass of the faith in Catholic mission, Lutheran and Reformed expansion, and the shattering of religious war. A summary comment is in order on the other dimension of catholicity: the pervasion of realms of culture by the faith. This progressed despite a process later to be described as secularization. But the informing of the culture by religion was stymied by "anti-Catholic" movements in both Catholicism and Protestantism.

The Catholics had to deal with a perversion of Gallicanism called Jansenism, named after Cornelius Jansen (—1638), who rallied pious commoners and the middle classes against the moral laxity of the Church. This movement is often described as Catholic Calvinism. Jansen, headquartering at Louvain, attacked most of all the Jesuits. Under his successor Arnauld, the overstress on the Eucharist and too-easy reliance on penance came under attack. Attempts by popes to suppress the ascetic and anti-cultural heresy failed; Jansenism was attracting fine minds like that of Blaise Pascal (—1662), who contributed to the cause through his *Provincial Letters.*

PURITANISM

More important was the reaction to Anglicanism's too-ready acceptance of temporal culture in what is called Puritanism. This became formal during the reign of James I and the rule of Archbishop William Laud (—1645) in the church. Laud's quasi-Roman position in liturgical matters alienated those who desired stress on simple Christian virtues. In the 1560's arguments had erupted over the use of vestments; official harassment by the Anglicans encouraged the party. Color, music, sensuous appeal, the liturgy—all these seemed to be leading back to Catholicism at the expense of biblical morality. Attacks centered on the episcopacy: "Either must we have a right ministerie of God & a right government of his church, according to the Scriptures set up (both whiche we lacke) or else there can be no right religion, nor yet for contempt thereof can Gods plagues be from us any while deferred."

Puritanism spread across class and party, gaining in Parliament and through preaching. The aggressions of James I through his insulting *Book of Sports* of 1618 (it advocated levity on Sunday) brought further reaction. Revolts broke out against the crown, which had underestimated the Puritan hold. Laud and King Charles I were executed; civil war raged from 1642 to 48 under the Puritan ironsider Oliver Cromwell, a man of steel fist and biblical faith. Splinters from Puritans were as socially aggressive as they were anti-cultural: the Ranters, who shouted down religious services; the Fifth Monarchy men who opposed Cromwell militarily on apocalyptic grounds; the Levellers, who stressed communitarian existence; and the Diggers of Gerald Winstanley, who were communist in their approach to common and public land use. Related to Puritanism's anti-catholic view of culture but completely opposed to its military predilections was the gentle new movement of the inner light, typified by George Fox and his Quakers or Society of Friends. Fox began preaching around 1647, attacking all externals, all sacraments, even churches themselves. Christ lives in the inner man—only there.

The spread of sects meant toleration for all. Puritans were often advocates of religious liberty. But Puritanism, later crushed by the restoration of the monarchy and exiled to Holland and America before it became recognized as a persistent emphasis, is most important to us for its outlook on Christian culture. For all its fineness of moral emphasis it usually had a negative cast, described by H. L. Mencken as the haunting fear that someone somewhere might be having a good time. (By the way, many Puritans themselves had a fairly good time.) A mistrust of the created order, a desire to serve God by emphasis on verbal expression at the expense of art and music, a completely moralistic approach to civilization characterized the Puritan state of mind.

But not all Puritanism was or remained anti-catholic in respect to penetration of culture. The work of John Milton or even the primitive John Bunyan, the fine sense of political responsibility developed by the dissenters—these were signs of positive approach to culture. Lutheran music, Lowland art, English literature illustrated the survival of positive and catholic approaches to creative expression. This was the age of Bach and Byrd and Handel, of Rembrandt, of Dürer and Holbein. And Roman Catholicism has had few hours so grand in cultural expression as it did in the time of Michelangelo, Velasquez, Murillo, El Greco.

Perhaps Protestantism's ultimate cultural impact was made more in the social than in the esthetic realm. The political involvements of the movement have been all too obvious in these chapters. Luther believed in separation of the two realms of church and state, both ruled respectively by gospel and law, but involved in each other because the same God is Lord over each and because the same men belong to each. He never saw opportunity to put his views into consistent practice. His stress on Pauline doctrines of obedience to existing power and his fear of anarchy led him from the side of the angels in many issues of social justice. Calvinism got into a different set of difficulties because it entangled the gospel in the legalism of the theocratic state. But Calvinism outstripped Lutheranism in its stress on the social responsibilities of Christians.

All forms of Protestantism: Lutheran, Calvinist, Anabaptist, or Puritan, stressed the sovereignty of God in the civil realm and the transcendence of the religious over the secular in its claim to the allegiance of Christians. In the face of rising absolute monarchies, this position forced many Protestants to die for their convictions. In the doctrine of vocation that grew from this situation, it also helped them to live with their convictions. They found meaning in their callings, fulfilling Christian love by purposeful service. (Many have pointed out that capitalism and Calvinism were entangled; each prospered where the other predominated, because of this serious view of life.) The home was elevated to higher status than celibacy in Protestantism. It displaced the monastery as the workshop of Christian love and virtue. The stress on education from childhood through the universities illuminated this life in Protestant lands.

1648: the date of Westphalia marks a turn to a new world. Divided Christendom was prepared for modernity after the shocks of two centuries; what was past was prologue. A shaken Catholicism looked ahead still singing the virtues, haunted by new facts, of one Holy Catholic and Apostolic *Roman* church. And troubled Protestants whistled in the dark, in the prospect of new light, and in the words of the first great Reformer they sang:

> *Take they then our life,*
> *Goods, fame, child, and wife,*
> *When their worst is done,*
> *They yet have nothing won:*
> *The Kingdom ours remaineth.*

The Kingdom, in the "secular" centuries, was to face a test; for there were other kingdoms bidding for the attention of men.

PART IV: *The Test*

13

WALLS OF SEPARATION

"Everyone regards all times as fulfilled in his own, and cannot see his own as one of many passing waves." [1] The historian Burckhardt frequently complained about the tendency of peoples to see their own time as a culmination, "just as if the world and its history had existed merely for our sakes!" While this is the instinct of people, including those swept up in the Christian movement, and while it is true that historians are frequently guilty of such a fascination, the charge is hardly fair if directed against church historians. Here the tendency is to look back to the "midpoint" in history, to the event of Jesus Christ, or to indulge in various forms of cosmic nostalgia. Roman Catholics like to make of the Middle Ages a Golden Age; Protestants regard the Reformation as a time of restoration of pristine purity to the Church.

Meanwhile, "modern times" suffer. Comprehensive church histories frequently trail off after the seventeenth century. The boundaries between church and world are no longer neat; it is more difficult to isolate the Church, to deal with it as a massive monolith; so it is hardly dealt with at all. Everything in the modern world seems to splinter and fissiparate. With good reason men have accepted the familiar words of W. B. Yeats as the perfect parable of these times:

271

Turning and turning in the widening gyre
The falcon cannot hear the falconer;
Things fall apart; the centre cannot hold;
Mere anarchy is loosed upon the world,
The blood-dimmed tide is loosed, and everywhere
The ceremony of innocence is drowned;
The best lack all conviction, while the worst
Are full of passionate intensity.
(From "The Second Coming")

Not all moderns have felt this, of course. Not the men of progress or the theologians of nature; not the religionists who see in evolution an upward spiral of "God's way of doing things." But those who have seen the tests to which Christianity was put conventionally complain of the loss of coherence and tangibility of reference.

This short history of Christianity assumes a somewhat more equilibristic stance. Listening to Burckhardt, we must remember that in the unfolding of the ages the time since about 1650 is but a moment, a passing stage, with unpredictable fulfillments ahead. Yet we cannot apply Yeats' parable of despair to Christianity, because Christianity has weathered many tests, because it still possesses resources in the contemporary world. If we ask the same four questions of the churches in these times (the plural, church*es*, carries its own significance), we shall receive different answers, but they will not be unanimously answers of failure and despair. The disparity between ideal and reality is gross as always, but plausibility of some sort remains as the Church asserts its unity, its holiness, its catholicity, its apostolicity. We may have to scrape below the surface, yet the energies are rewarded.

To provide the setting for "the modern world," we ask first the question of the career of Christian holiness. Here as always the reference to personal morality is secondary to the ascription of its objective and positive holiness derived from its divine institution. In that sense the Church is holy primarily as recipient and custodian on earth of "the means of grace." [2] The sanctifying power in it is God's power. The Church is *kadosh*, "set apart by God as his very own." Yet this Church, whose lineaments may be known in the language of devotion or of theology, is hidden to the eyes of the historian. The Church is set apart; yet it is thoroughly involved and constantly tested. "The Church stands in darkness, in this time of her pilgrimage, and must lament under many miseries" (Augustine). In no respect is it more dramatically tested during this pilgrimage than in its impingement on various realms of culture and social life, particularly in affairs of state.

SECULARIZATION

The word for the test which the world has presented in the past three centuries is *secularization*. The term in this sense is diffuse and imprecise—therefore it gains in usefulness. For it is employed to imply that Christianity is no longer the motivating or impulsive center of Western life; that the religious question is consciously or unconsciously pushed from the center of men's concerns; that the institutional forms of Christianity undergo revision at the hands of the "world." This movement will occupy most of this chapter.

Few contemporary Christians are conscious of the fact that the basic institutional or administrative cast of church life had changed in the past 150 or 200 years for the first time since the fourth century. From the era of Constantine and the Christianization of the Roman Empire to the latter days of the eighteenth century Western men assumed that religion was to be established by law and sanctioned by the legal arm of the state. Since that century nation after nation has been a party to the extrication of the Church from civil life in the legal or formal sense. What was often directed against the churches was, however, a favor in disguise: for the extrication left them free once again to assert their potentialities for holiness, less involved in dynastic intrigues, monarchical politics, and the petty play for power. This change, according to American church historian Winfred E. Garrison, is one of the "two most profound revolutions which have occurred in the entire history of the Church."

An American President who championed religious freedom on other than Christian grounds, and who in the process made a major contribution to the disestablishment of religion in his country, also provided a term which can apply broadly to the diagrammatic extension of this activity elsewhere. Thomas Jefferson averred that he would see built and retained "a wall of separation between church and state." He wrote those words to the Danbury Association of Baptists in 1802; he described a situation which perhaps a majority of the world's Christians now regard as normative. When he wrote them, however, the words were considered revolutionary and almost subversive of any possibility the churches might have of letting their holiness infiltrate human affairs. The churches were being progressively excluded from political, economic, and social life in the official sense.

The process, of course, was neither instantaneous nor without its marks of exception. It was not comprehended in the single and sudden action of any man's stroke of pen or sweep of sword. There was to be a rhythm of revolution and reaction, with the Church often as passive rider on the pendulum. But the pull of the decades is all in one direction; the Church was being set apart, often by its enemies; but as this involved a shift from compulsion to voluntaryism in men's response, new forms of holiness were possible and realized. From the middle of the seventeenth to the middle of the eighteenth century the foundations for separation of "church" and "state" were being laid; the next century saw its building; the past century has seen the arch and the capstone laid.

If the Peace of Westphalia is the end of an era, an uneasy settlement of the political disruptions resulting from the era of the Reformation, its religious resolutions of 1648 were not to endure. It still clung to the already obsolete principle of *cuius regio, eius religio,* in which the prince was to select the religion for an area and dissenters were forbidden public worship. Europe was in ferment. The principle which governed in Reformation times was itself a "secularization" if viewed in the light of the past. No longer did the religious institutions compel the choice of rulership; now the ruler chose the religion. With the emergence of a new, autonomous man this settlement would be unsettling. The day would come when each man wished to choose his response for himself.

ENLIGHTENMENT

Two movements that flourished in the century after Westphalia served to doom Christianity's chances to gain new dominance in the "secular" realm. One was the Enlightenment, an intellectual current which undercut Christian particularism. Its emphasis on natural religion countered the Christian belief in particular revelation. Its emphasis on toleration forced political adjustments upon an intolerant religious movement. Its organizing center of resistance to Christian presumption made it a convenient impulse for aggressive anti-Christian activity. The French Revolution near the end of the eighteenth century provides an illustration of the political effect of the clash of ideologies. And in one side of its own political theory (Hobbes is the prime example) the Enlightenment offered a supreme state as a "new Leviathan" whose interests would override those of individuals and competing institutions, among them the Church.

PIETISM

The other movement, to be detailed elsewhere, was itself in part a reaction to orthodoxy and to the Enlightenment, as well as an escape from modernity. Called Pietism, it compensated for Christianity's failure to assert its holiness in the social realms of life by stressing personal devotion. For all its glories, Pietism was one of the major strides of Christian retreat from responsibility as it had been viewed in the past.

In Pietism, the Christian "institution" fell; in the Enlightenment, it was being pushed. Various intellectual justifications appeared to parallel Hobbes' *Leviathan* (1651). Within decades Spinoza and Bayle would plead for tolerance and attack the wresting of conversions from unwilling men. These were pillow-punches compared to the brass knuckles of a later period when Voltaire, Diderot, d'Holbach set out to "crush the infamy" of organized Christianity, particularly as it intruded in the political realm.

NATIONALISM

With these two movements a third factor cannot be discounted: the quest for recognition by modern national states and the thirst for power of new absolute monarchs. In these centuries there emerged men like Frederick the Great, Peter the Great, Louis XIV, Charles I, and Napoleon. Each welcomed whatever theories would enhance his interests, at the cost of the temporal interests of Christian institutions. Whenever the Church allied itself with reaction to revolutionary ferments, it inhabited a fool's paradise out of which it would again be ejected.

THE EASTERN CHURCH

The story can begin with Eastern Orthodoxy, which lived a life apart, but in this respect experiences a fate similar to that which befell the West. To speak of Orthodoxy in the modern period within brief compass, we can safely pick up the story in Russia, concentrating there on the fortunes of "the Third Rome" after the times of Nikon (—1681). Having no time for a movement we must focus on a symbol, Peter I (the Great), who ruled from the year after Nikon's death (and exclusively after 1689) until 1725. The shaper of modern Russia who introduced Western fashion and learning, at great expense to traditional Russian culture, Peter's prime innovation in ecclesiastical life was the retreat he forced upon the churches as he set up the religio-political constellation which would persist, with minor variations, down to the Bolshevik Revolution of 1917, when "disestablishment" of Orthodoxy would become complete and final and the highest wall of separation in Christendom now existing would be built.

When Peter found weakness among the existing patriarchs he seized the moment: "I am your Patriarch." He reorganized monasteries and schools, reformed the parish life of the vast nation, infused religious instruction with a polite and subtle rationalism gleaned from his Western tour. Even less fortunately, the revenues of the church came under state control and the clergy became little more than stooges for the state. The marks of a priestly calling in a holy church were blurred. The priests became a governmental caste—low-caste at that—of unimportant and untrustworthy stewards. In the eyes of the people they often seemed to be no-caste stewards of slovenliness and sloth. Peter did away with the patriarchate in 1721, establishing a synod of bishops under the rule of a layman, the Procurator of the Holy Synod, called "the Tsar's eye." With its hopes tied to the hopes of the Romanov dynasty for decades to come, the church was embarrassed by every revolutionary anti-Romanov excitement. Before night fell on the Russian church in 1917 there were but two decades of relative freedom of determination. In 1905 religious liberty was proclaimed. It was too late. The Christian community had stagnated on its side of the wall built by Peter and was confused when a gate was finally battered through the wall. We need look to the East for very little in the way of creativity in the life of religious institutions during this period.

ROMAN CATHOLICISM

Because of its long record of involvement with the destinies of Western nations, the Roman Catholic Church was tossed most of all by the storms of the times. The papacy had weathered the Reformation with considerable temporal power still in its hand; the pope was still in the center of many monarchical disputes and power thrusts. Dramatic new political alignments in the last three centuries required an artful strategic retreat on most fronts.

The test case was France. There those who looked over the mountains for authority from the Vicar of Christ ("Ultramontanes") tangled repeatedly with the Gallican tradition of relative independence from Rome that had roots in the Pragmatic Sanction of Bourges in 1438. The French church, which for a millennium had been the flower of the Roman church, had for much of that time been growing the thorn which would afflict the flesh of the modern papacy. From both sides Rome was embarrassed: fanatic Ultramontanism was static and absolutistic. This limited the popes in their heavy-footed pavannes of adjustment to modern monarchical tunes. The Gallican line allied itself with French self-assertion. The revolt of the Catholic kings was applauded from within the church.

Crisis came with the Four Articles of 1682 adopted by the assembled clergy of France: 1) pope and church have no power over temporal princes; 2) Constantinian decrees on the superiority of General Councils to popes remain; 3) local tradition demands care on the part of the papacy when it exercises authority; 4) the church must ratify papal decrees on matters of faith before these become permanent and absolute in their binding character. Professedly fending off both extremes, those who "are striving to overthrow the decrees of the Gallican church" and those who "have the audacity to attack the supremacy of St. Peter and his successors," the Articles were more useful in aiding battle against the first type of attacker.

The papacy was not accustomed to taking affronts such as this by Louis XIV and the responsible clergy lying down; Alexander VIII condemned the Articles in 1690. But the papal office had been forced to embark on a losing cause. Embarrassment now becomes the key word: embarrassment at the authoritarian challenges, at the stiffness of overardent friends and the eagerness of ardent foes within the church; embarrassment by reform from within (as in the case of Jansenism) and by the new ideologies of Enlightenment. The path to the French Revolution was lit by the glow of the papal blush.

Gallicanism had its parallels in non-Gallic lands and in post-Revolutionary France. The Germanic counterpart was

Febronianism, after the penname of von Hontheim, Bishop
of Trier, who in 1763 substantiated German complaints
of 1742 against the residue of medievalism in papal dealings with Germany. His findings appealed to German civic
leaders as did Gallicanism to Louis XIV; but the onrush of
the French Revolution limited the German critique. In
Austria it was called Josephism after Joseph II, Holy
Roman Emperor from 1765 to 1790. Joseph asked for limitation much as "Febronius" had, along with positive pleas
for religious toleration. In 1781 the Josephists granted
general religious freedom and limited some Roman orders.
While the movement tottered into oblivion after the Emperor's death, another corner of the modern world had
seen another kind of example of straining at the papal
leash.

The high-water mark of papal retreat was the dispersion
"forever" of the Society of Jesus which had, in its fourth
oath, professed its absolute loyalty to the papacy. As ruler
after ruler, in France, Portugal, and Spain, issued demands
or began deporting Jesuits, Clement XIV acceded, and in
1773 abolished the Order which had been a symbol of
counter-reform. Jesuits continued to work in Germany and
Austria, but their expansive wings were clipped. Though
they were resurrected by Pius VII in 1814 to rise to greater
glories, their suppression meant a vital defeat in an hour
when modern nations were hemming in the papacy. The
Roman Catholic historian Philip Hughes has observed that
by 1790 the Catholic religion was free to exert itself as it
chose *only* in the Papal States and in the United States.

The worst shock was yet to come. The French Revolution
(1789–99) held terrors for Catholicism seldom matched in
its long history. The events of the decade served as catalyst
for many ideological and popular discontents; many of
them were directed against the "Christian cult." Both the
papal church and the revised standard version of French
Catholicism, the Constitutional Church, were under pressure and suffered from the radical revolutionary intent to
substitute the goddesses of reason and the altars of Enlightenment for the historic faith of France.

Reaction came with Napoleon, who picked up the pieces

in a new restoration; the church rode to ascendancy with him, not realizing the degree to which it was simply being used by its weak son. Pope Pius VII, who had been Bishop of Imola in Bonapartean territory, attempted to play along; though it pained him he had advised his people, torn between the faith and Napoleonic "democracy": "Be good Christians and you will be good Democrats." Napoleon would later speak frankly of his high, holy attitude toward holy Church: "My political method is to govern men as the majority of them want to be governed. That, I think, is the way to recognize the sovereignty of the people. It was by making myself a Catholic that I won the war in the Vendee, by making myself a Moslem that I established myself in Egypt, by making myself an Utramontane that I gained men's souls in Italy. If I were governing a people of the Jewish race I would rebuild the Temple of Solomon." Thus "his Catholic majesty" Napoleon: he has never been canonized.

Napoleon and Pius VII entered into several concordats; the most important, on July 15, 1801, was a treaty between "His Holiness Pius VII and the French Government." Bonaparte picked and chose cafeteria-style what pleased him to honor in these agreements. His patronizing favor shown the church at such hours, and the papacy's pathetic accession, dragged the holy name lower and lower. Worst of all, by tying itself to reaction under Napoleon in France, under Metternich in Austria, and again under Louis Napoleon, Romanism placed itself in a compromising and unlovely light to the revolutionaries that rose across the map of Europe in 1830 and again in 1848; to them the church was the fattest target in sight. Widespread disaffection with religious claims accompanied these revolts.

Nor did all the stress come from without the church; after the fall of Napoleon who had put the Pope in his place with an "I am your Emperor," there were many within the church who came to argue for separation of church and state, often making concessions to the new liberal currents. Montalembert, Lamennais, Lacordaire, men like these are remembered for their spearheading of tactical liberalism. They knew that the ultimate good fortune of the church lay in identification with the new currents of reform and that separation of church and state would actually make possible a greater Catholic impact on the fortunes of France. The Pope, attracted by the Ultramontane strategy, was at first ready to shake their hands; soon he was embarrassed and shook his fist in the encyclicals *Mirari Vos* and *Singulari Nos* (1832 and 1834), aborting their moves. He had ridden at first with the next liberal wave, but by 1848 he was reacting against himself, and during his, the longest papacy, the church came again to be tied to reaction. 1848: the Communist Manifesto, the Socialist front, the workers' uprisings, the European revolts—these were to set the tone for the next century. Each left Rome's temporal claims behind. Pius IX's defensiveness against liberalism is to be found hardened in the *Syllabus of Errors* of 1864, which attacked the heresy "that the Church ought to be separated from the State, and the State from the Church." Too late.

Mention need only be made of a final retreat from temporal authority in Germany's *Kulturkampf,* a "battle of civilizations" between Bismarck and the Pope. The Prussian Protestant statesman saw Catholic investment in Germany to be an intrusion on German national claims; harassment reached its peak with the anti-Catholic education May Laws or Falk Laws of 1873. But Bismarck had been too aggressive, and through the Centrist party under Ludwig Windhorst Catholicism regained much lost ground. With all exceptions in mind, however, we can safely generalize that the modern trend has been toward the disestablishment of papal religion, removing from it political sanction and forcing it to make its way on a voluntary principle among the other denominations and religions.

PROTESTANTISM ON THE CONTINENT

Established Protestantism fared little better. The picture is, of course, confused by Protestantism's lack of an organizing center; but the outline is clear. From 1650 through 1950 the movement on all fronts is toward a lessening of official (though by no means necessarily moral) influence by Protestants in the political sphere. Most of them had as much difficulty as Catholics in seeing that their disestablishment did not stain the Church's holiness—but rather enhanced it by disentanglement. At the beginning of the period Protestantism was favored or established in much of western Europe, the British Isles, America, and many colonies. The establishments tumbled one by one or they became little more than hollow symbols.

Continental Lutheranism suffered as did Romanism under the Enlightenment. As England had its Hobbes and France its Voltaire, so in Germany Spinoza and Lessing were outlining in an age of reason views of toleration and the irrelevance of theological distinction that were incompatible with the old formulas. No one shares center stage with Frederick the Great, a towering political figure imbued with the Enlightenment spirit, intent on imposing it on Protestantism. Preaching and exercising toleration, he refused to suppress the Jesuits and was in general patronizing toward most religious movements. The Landrecht of 1794 is clear evidence, posthumously, of the direction of his policies. Rationalistic Lutheran ministers were favored and the court preacher symbolized sycophantic sanctity. The unresolved tensions in Luther's thought on church and state were now being resolved—all in the direction of uncritical acceptance of secular pronouncements through ready acquiescence by fawning and flattering theologians.

The apex of governmental involvement as an illustration of the church's retreat was the Prussian Union of 1817, which Frederick Wilhelm III baked as a birthday cake for the 300th anniversary of the Reformation. Under the influence of Enlightenment ideas and the theology of romantic Christianity of his theologian, Friedrich Schleiermacher, Frederick set out to convince Lutheran and Reformed parties that they should forget their differences in the broader interests of German religion. A liturgical dilettante, he fashioned prancing antiquarian liturgical orders, imposing them on reluctant churches.

He grievously underestimated the degree of reluctance.

Claus Harms (—1855) replied with a new Ninety-Five Theses which contended that issues which separated Luther from Zwingli in 1529 were still live; forced agreement was unsatisfactory. Reformed opposition was also surprisingly organized and heated. The "Union" endured; so did the opposition. Pockets of severe resistance in Silesia and Saxony issued large numbers of migrants to America. Most grievous of the Prussian Union's aftereffects: its precedents set for groveling churchmen to be identified with state paternalism and upper or middle-class interest in the revolutionary century of the rise of the lower class. The common parson saw his fortune, his prestige, his vocation decline. Not until the social experiments of Christians decades after the ferments of 1830 and 1848 did German Lutheranism again begin to develop a distinct message for society. The wall of inclusion built by the state in this case was a wall of separation not from state but from society. The gospel of Bismarck and his court preacher Stoecker was unattractive against the relief of the gospel of Marx, Engels, Lassalle, and St. Simon. Continental Protestantism was in retreat.

GREAT BRITAIN

In the British Isles a somewhat different picture presents itself. A more tolerant establishment had less to lose, showed more room for coexistence with "free church" competitors. Sometimes, as in the Scottish Disruption of 1843, disestablishment was abrupt. More often amiable latitudinarianism gave way before brute disestablishmentarianism needed to rear its ugly head. After the Puritan Revolt and after the settlement in 1639, while Anglicanism achieved an enduring legal sanction it had to recognize (indeed it often nurtured) toleration as an enduring factor on the political and religious scene. Free churches, nonconformists, and various intra-Anglican parties criticized the establishment and usually made their point with methods short of drama or revolution. The variety of acceptable religious factions in England did reduce the impact of the state church, and for the past three centuries the most creative impact has been made by "rebel" movements within the establishment or by the free churches. Voluntary societies, or prophetic ministries like those of Thomas Chalmers (—1847) or the layman William Wilberforce (—1833), spread Christian holiness in the social realm with no dependence upon legal ties between church and state. Anglicans from Frederick Denison Maurice (—1872) down to William Temple (—1944) often gained their results in spite of their established positions.

Establishment did have its defenders from Hooker's line, carried on by Warburton (—1779) who argued in 1736 for *The Alliance between Church and State,* down to twentieth-century conservatives. But deists, rationalists, and natural religionists were always on hand to reply on their premises; free churchmen frequently allied themselves with the critique. By the 1870's the Evangelical party had come to such prominence and the Anglo-Catholic party had so embarrassed Anglican claims that anti-establishment forces were in position to make gains, particularly in the field of education. Non-conformists profited from liberalizing measures. In 1867 the franchise was greatly extended. This aided the people of less favored churches and gave them a new voice. In 1868 they were helped by the cessation of revenue collection for church rates. In 1871 Oxford and Cambridge were opened to dissenters. The Forster Act of 1870 was a new high point in educational realignment, providing more local autonomy in "board" schools which were neither specifically Anglican nor Roman Catholic: schools were to teach a sort of undenominational and broadly acceptable "evangelical religion." However, it did awaken the established parties, who regained some loss in the Education Act of 1902. Soon the ball would bounce again in the other direction. After two centuries of post-revolutionary life England recorded a still existent but largely impotent establishment.

THE NEW WORLD

The accounts of Gallicanism, Febronianism, Josephism and the Kulturkampf symbolize the declining fortunes of official Catholicism. Enlightenment patronizing, the Prussian Union, the sway of court preachers illustrate changes in continental Protestantism; secular intrusions in the field of education in England signal a change in assumptions in a secularizing modern life. The most significant reversal of assumptions occured in the New World, which at the time of the change had been settled, in its North American sector, largely by people of Anglo-Saxon provenance. In the United States voluntaryism and the "wall of separation" were predestined by the variety of religious representations. Yet the achievement is dramatic. Viewed in broadest perspective, the early example of popular disestablishment of religion there may be its greatest national contribution to religious history.

When the new nation was born its Constitution asserted:

> Congress shall make no law respecting an establishment of religion, or prohibiting the free exercise thereof; or abridging the freedom of speech, or of the press; or of the right of the people peaceably to assemble, and to petition the government for a redress of grievances.

What is now obvious and taken for granted was then a revolutionary departure from Christian precedent. Official disestablishment began in Virginia (of Anglican establishment) around 1776; its law was formed in alliance of "Enlightened" statesmen like Thomas Jefferson and James Madison with dissenting Baptists and Quakers:

> No man shall be compelled to frequent or support any religious worship, place, or ministry whatsoever, nor shall be enforced, restrained, molested or burthened in his body or goods, nor shall otherwise suffer on account of his religious opinions or belief; but . . . all men shall be free to profess, and by argument to maintain, their opinion in matters of religion, and . . . the same shall in no wise diminish, enlarge, or affect their civil capacities.

Words like these of 1786 were startling to Christian ears. But they were nothing more than an acknowledgment of the "secularization" which had already taken place in the Western world, and they were a surprising new charter for religious advance on a voluntary basis.

This solution was not the intent of most colonists, who, in coming to America meant by religious freedom, freedom for themselves in their own new establishments. But many complicating factors clouded the colonial period. From early landings at Jamestown after 1607 down to the forming of the nation in 1787, the religious colonists had done a poor task in religionizing the new lands. Perhaps only one tenth of the population had religious ties. Religious establishment was more a symbol of a way of life than a vital spiritual force. "Enlightened" ideas were making their way among the Founding Fathers, most of whom found the particularity of Christian revelation offensive. Couple this disaffection, tired establishment, and rationalist challenge with several other factors. First was the discontent of dissenting groups like the Baptists and Quakers, who were forced to support religions other than their own. Second was the cross-fertilizing influence of America's first Great Awakening of the 1730's and 1740's, when the preaching of the great Jonathan Edwards (—1758) and George Whitefield (—1770) crossed colonial lines and presupposed the voluntary acceptance of religion. Only one other factor was needed; no doubt it was the overtowering one.

How simple and obvious it was as a predetermining element! The word: incompatibility of varying claims. Anglicanism was established at Jamestown in Virginia; the Reverend Robert Hunt introduced religious services immediately, and the precedent was followed in the Carolinas as well. These southern colonies were under the jurisdiction of the Bishop of London who, at a distance, could not give effective counsel or care. Genteel Anglicanism was part of the southern way of life; most of the First Families (the Washingtons, the Randolphs, the Masons) produced vestrymen of light religious passion. The Church of England was established by law. It held glebe lands and received tax support. Even Maryland, which had begun as a commercial venture by the Calvert family (Roman Catholics, for whom religious toleration was not uncongenial), was soon to fall into Anglican providence.

From England to New England came the very people who were running away from Anglicanism, the dissenting Pilgrims and Puritans of Massachusetts Bay and Salem, who began colonizing in 1619, all with most serious religious intent. Their religion, often "separatistic," committed them to a more vigorous participation in affairs of the body politic than did southern Anglicanism. What Calvin hoped for at Geneva they realized in the Holy Commonwealth of Massachusetts. Those who went on the errand into the wilderness were aware with Governor Winthrop: "Wee must Consider that wee shall be as a Citty upon a Hill, the eies of all people are uppon us." Later Americans have often reread this history as a quest for religious freedom for all. On the contrary: when Anabaptists attacked the Massachusetts Bay government in 1681, arguing that the founders were nonconformists like themselves, builders of a refuge, Samuel Willard of Boston's Third Church corrected them:

> I perceive they are mistaken in the design of our first Planters, whose business was not Toleration; but were professed Enemies of it, and could leave the World professing they *died no Libertines*. Their business was to settle, and (as much as in them lay) secure Religion to Posterity, according to that way which they believed was of God.

"That Way" would clash with other establishments. Of course, it was also challenged from within by Roger Williams (—1683), Baptist hero of religious tolerationists, who was impolitely invited out of Massachusetts to found Rhode Island. The establishment long considered this Rogue's Island, for it attracted others who resented legal religion. Similarly the strange Anne Hutchinson was buffeted for preaching peculiarities of religious freedom.

Separation of church and state was not the way of asserting the Church's holiness or influencing social life in the express intent of the founders of nine of the thirteen original colonies. Chinks in the theocratic stronghold appeared in Rhode Island, among dissenters in the nine establishment-favoring colonies, and in the immediate pluralism of colonies like Pennsylvania. Founded by William Penn (—1718), it attracted many continental groups, too varied to permit uniformity; nor was uniformity sought by Quaker Penn.

The act which made one nation of thirteen colonies spelled the end of establishment. Which religion would meet legal favor? Not Anglicanism, averred the northerners; not Congregational-Presbyterianism, argued the southerners; a plague on both their houses, shouted dissenters, Pennsylvanians, and rationalist founding fathers. What was implied in the instrument of 1787 came to be explicit in the young states after that time, down to final disestablishment in Connecticut in 1829 and Massachusetts in 1833. The epitaph was provided by James Madison in his *Memorial and Remonstrance* as early as 1784:

> During almost fifteen centuries has the legal establishment of Christianity been on trial. What have been its fruits? . . . Pride and indolence in the Clergy, ignorance and servility in the laity; in both, superstitions, bigotry, and persecution.

> Establishments have been seen to erect a spiritual tyranny on the ruins of Civil authority; in many of political tyranny, and in no instance have they been the guardians of the liberty of the people.

The test was over, the trial completed; the pattern of fifteen centuries was reversed. A wall was built.

At first despair for the churches and their ability to influence society was widespread among the disestablished. But with characteristic ingenuity Americans adapted, and soon came to see an explosion of new possibilities on voluntaryistic lines. In one of those personal confessions that flash as an image of an age, Lyman Beecher, the theocratic leader of New England, who was to become the most perceptive of the denominationalists, described his conversion:

> "I remember," said his son Charles, "seeing father, the day after the [disestablishing] election, sitting on one of the old-fashioned, rush-bottomed kitchen chairs, his

head drooping on his breast, and his arms hanging down. "Father," said I, "what are you thinking of?" He answered solemnly, "THE CHURCH OF GOD."

Beecher later confessed: "It was a time of great depression and suffering . . . It was as dark a day as ever I saw. The odium thrown upon the ministry was inconceivable. The injury done to the cause of Christ, as we then supposed, was irreparable. For several days I suffered what no tongue can tell." Yet, later, he knew. It was "the best thing that ever happened in the State of Connecticut." It cut the churches loose from dependence on state support and threw them wholly on their own resources and God.[3] Later Christian experience affirms that this disentanglement which reversed fifteen centuries and set a pattern for the modern world was a declaration of independence for the Church in its assertions of its holiness while it walks as pilgrim in the City of Man.

HOLINESS MOVEMENTS

We have never been content to mark the path of holiness only in the social and societal relations of church and world; the objective holiness of the Mystical Body of Christ has from time to time been revealed in the lives of individuals and groups of Christians. This is, as always, difficult to document in the prosaic parish life and among the secular vocations of the millions of Christians in the modern age as in past ages. But a brief summary of modern movements toward holiness must be provided. If in ancient and medieval times monasticism provided this outlet, in the modern period the eruption of myriad sects was the characteristic pattern. The sects were the products of religious mass movements in reaction to established patterns of church institutionalism. Fanatic, radical (often in the good and profound meaning of the term), they were able to extricate themselves from many staining power-political attachments to which churches were bound. Disturbing as they were, they could at least set an example of a higher call.

They did erupt all over the Christian world. Whether they existed to change society or to keep themselves un-spotted from the world, "holiness" was always to be their mark. While the Christian movement was in retreat, they were conscious of advance. In Eastern Orthodoxy, in re-action against the official theologizing of the liturgical innovator Nikon or the politicizing and Westernizing of the church under Peter the Great, a brilliant floriation of sects grew. Earliest were the "Old Believers" whose indi-viduality was marked by the fervent hope that the world would end, preferably somewhere around 1669. The old evil foe was the heretical hierarchy and the institutionalized church. Peter the Great was the true anti-Christ. When the world failed to oblige by coming to an end, the first ferment quieted. Division resulted: the radicals, "priestless ones," rejected orders and sacraments; the conservatives adhered to forms of the past. Both looked in hope beyond history in a riotous splash of messianisms. In the meantime, they occupied themselves by forming Christian communities which recall the patterns of the Middle Ages and the Puritan period.

There were also creative evangelical movements in Russia, among them that of the Baptists, who survive there to this day. Legalistic Judaizers countered these. A Union of Evangelical Christians formed in the nineteenth century gathered old Stundist and Molokan sects; they appealed to the mystic depths of the Russian soul and to the activistic fires which quickened it. More radical were the Khlysty, the Skoptsy, the Dukhobors, uncontrolled and uncontrol-lable flagellants, ecstatics, and even *castrati*. Dukhobors ex-aggerated the dualism of flesh and spirit, even to the point of repudiating traditional morality. Holiness, strained, can snap; few Christians would find biblical or theological warrant for Dukhobor excess in its deliberate provocation of civil authority, its arch rejection of "traditional" morality.

Sects built walls against worldliness in other Christian traditions. We have already been introduced to the moral rigorism of the Jansenists, for whom penance, asceticism, holy living outranked sacramental life. Later deviations included the perfectionist movements which ended in libertinism, notably the Quietist heresy originated around 1685 by the Spanish priest Michael Molinos. The spiritual life must not be activated by man; this violates God's sovereignty. Man must wait passively for the movement of God upon his life. In France one Madame Guyon picked up the skewed sectarian emphasis but made it less extreme. In the same lineage, Pasquier Quesnel (—1719) introduced a moralistic version of the New Testament and attracted some of the French hierarchy to oppose official Rome on behalf of his "heresy." While we are dealing with France, it is well to have an aside on the patterns of holiness that were congenial to the official church. St. Alphonsus Liguori (—1787) is an example of this for his Redemptorist order and its hearty missionary objectives. Famed for his zealous vow never to waste a moment of his life, he chalked up impressive achievement. Over-taxed librarians, in the face of his voluminous literary output, could breathe a grateful sigh that his vow was not copied by too many other Christians! The fruit of his labors was a rigorous monastic mission movement and an answer to Jansenism within Catholicism.

The Passionists were founded in this period by St. Paul of the Cross, a mystic devoted to the wounds of Christ. They provided a similar alternative to heretical holiness movements. Devotion to the Sacred Heart of Jesus was instituted by St. Margaret Mary Alacoque, who was convinced she had seen apparitions of the wounded Christ and heard his voice calling her.

Protestant holiness in the post-Puritan period reached nearly normative forms in continental Pietism and in England nonconformity and Wesleyanism. Each of these will receive further treatment in the discussion of the Christian mission, but their impulse bears examination here. Each resisted compromise with the world on the part of officially established churches; each sought to live the Christian life within the walls of new communities, in cells or in patterns of individual response. From each grew new desire to win the world for Christianity.

Pietism is of interest to historians and social scientists for its sectarian reaction to institutionalism; in the midst of a rationalistic-scientific world it evaded the theological question through emphasis on personal piety. Church and state questions? Both could be offensive or irrelevant to Pietists. In its original form, Pietism was a Lutheran and Reformed movement on the continent. The term appears in 1689 as a rebuke to Lutheran holiness movements. The patriarch was Philipp Jacob Spener (—1705) of Alsace-Lorraine. In his *Pia Desideria* he argued for a converted ministry and an increase in devotional life. Like many parallel movements, his introduced an apocalyptic note, which was also picked up by the founders of "pious colleges" such as August Hermann Francke (—1727) of Halle. The usual shape of the movement was conventicular, again implying the building of a wall of separation—in this case of a "little church" within the larger church. Frustrated by the official church, harassed by the government, persecuted by fashionable society, Pietism grew to become an effective force in European religion.

Reformed Pietism had an easier time of it than its Lutheran counterpart because its moralism was somewhat more congenial to Calvinism and Arminianism. In the time of rationalistic apathy, concerned Christians picked up earlier strands of Dutch and English Puritan holiness movements; combining mysticism with an appeal to the lower classes, a group of covenantal theologians in Holland attracted wide attention. Neander in Germany, Doddridge and Watts in England can be seen in this context. Most familiar of all these movements was that of the Moravians under Count Nikolaus Ludwig von Zinzendorf (—1760). Influenced by Spener and Francke, wealthy and spiritual, he fused his interests and infused the spirit of a colony of Pietists at his estate called Herrnhut, after 1722. This refuge for the persecuted became a sort of Protestant version of Redemptorist or Passionist concentration on the suffering body of Christ. From the walls of Herrnhut an impressive stream of mission endeavor was to flow.

Yet no Pietist movement ranks with the path of holiness prescribed by Wesleyanism or Methodism, a movement within the Church of England which was to stamp Protestantism in the nineteenth-century era. Growing out of "holy clubs" at Oxford, it burst to fire in the warmed heart of John Wesley (—1791) to spread in a mighty mission wherever Christians were establishing themselves in the great century of expansion. Eventually severed from Anglicanism, it became a great world-wide denomination which understressed dogma and stressed holiness of living. Its story properly belongs to the later narration of the nineteenth-century Christian movement. Finally, mention should be made of the American Great Awakening after 1734 which erupted within the established churches and was to prosper dissenting churches in their reaction to religious apathy in the colonies shortly before the nation was born.

As the churches were forced to retreat during the wall-building period, and as they evaded the theological question in the various holiness movements, they were being set up for two new tests. Could Christian theology substantively adapt itself to the modern world's new assumptions? Could the Christian mission compensate for its exclusion from affairs by a growing "secularism" by winning the hearts of individuals around the world? These are two of the three remaining questions of this book. For now it is enough to glance backward at the century and a half after Westphalia to remark: Holiness is dead, long live holiness. The assumption that the churches could reform the world by official involvement in societal life was seriously questioned. The assumption that they could reform the world through the experience of devoted individuals was being seriously tried. Through all the relativities and ambiguities of human existence and churchly shortcomings it was still possible for Christians to assert, "I believe in . . . holy . . . Church."

14

THE ACIDS AND ASSETS
OF MODERNITY

The fourth "note" of the Christian movement in its churchly form is a confession of its apostolicity. We have seen this in its early translation from the missionary idea (the apostles were sent out) to the ideological or doctrinal reference. In this light apostolicity refers to the rejection of heresy on the basis of reference to an assumed unity of the antique apostolic tradition. This rubric has guided us repeatedly in a review of the course of Christian thought in its enduring witness to God's work in Jesus Christ amid changing views of the world around and in the Church. The term, therefore, shall again imply not so much the outreach of the Church (which can be discussed in the scope of its catholicity) as its continuity of message and meaning.

THE SCIENTIFIC OUTLOOK

This continuity met two basic challenges in the modern world. While each of these is quite obvious to the student of religious and intellectual history, two references by one witness, Alfred North Whitehead, may provide them with a more memorable setting. The first is from "without," in what may conveniently be called the scientific outlook which has marked the last three centuries; this is vastly different from the setting of the Church's intellectual life in its first sixteen centuries. Says Whitehead:

> The mentality of an epoch springs from the view of the world which is, in fact, dominant in the educated sections of the communities in question. There may be more than one such scheme, corresponding to cultural divisions. The various human interests which suggest cosmologies, and also are influenced by them are science, aesthetics, ethics, and religion. In every age each of these topics suggests a view of the world. Insofar as the same set of people are swayed by all, or more than one, of these interests, their effective outlook will be the joint production of these sources. But each age has its dominant pre-occupation; and during the three centuries in question [the last three] the cosmology derived from science has been asserting itself at the expense of older points of view with their origins elsewhere.[1]

This cosmology would confront Christianity with crisis, for the faith too made cosmic claims. It spoke of neither death, life, angels, principalities, things present, things to come, powers, height, depth, "nor anything else in all creation" as being able to separate men from the love of God in Christ Jesus as Lord (Rom. 8:38–39). The assertion was put to test in the countering cosmology described by Whitehead.

THE INTELLECTUAL RETREAT

From within the apostolic question was put to test in the great evasion raised by the Church's fumbling adaptation to modernity in Pietism or Methodism (here referred to not in the denominational sense, but as characterizing an era).

> The great Methodist movement more than deserves the eulogies bestowed on it. But it can appeal to no great intellectual construction explanatory of its modes of understanding. It may have chosen the better way. Its instinct may be sound. However that may be, it was a notable event in the history of ideas when the clergy of the Western races began to waver in their appeal to constructive reason.[2]

In the centuries when the assault was intellectual, Christians chose to reply with weakened intellectual equipment. It is as if a boxer were doped before his most important match, so that he will feel it less—if he falls.

There is a double-sidedness to this response. When Walter Lippmann spoke of the "acids of modernity" he could well have been describing the process of corrosion which affected the vessel of apostolicity. But we may also speak of some assets of modernity, even going beyond Whitehead's reference that the Methodist movement "may have chosen the better way. Its instincts may be sound." The buffeting this message received, the challenge to its core, the residue remaining, the awakened and renewed response in faith—this pattern of survival suggested anew the validity of Paul's awareness: nothing could separate Christian men from Christ Jesus as Lord, through the apostolic witness.

SCIENCE AND PHILOSOPHY

The change in the scientific cast of cosmology has been well described in the title of a book by Alexandre Koyré, *From the Closed World to the Infinite Universe*. A galaxy of bright scholars lit up the scientific sky. Astronomers looked into the distance: Nicholas of Cusa (—1464), and then Copernicus (—1543), and Bruno (—1600); they enlarged the heavens and met condemnation from the Church for disturbing the coziness of the three-story universe. Galileo (—1642) and Descartes (—1650) went further, pondering the quasi-theological significance of infinity of universe. To men like Newton (—1727) and Bentley, Berkeley (—1753) and Leibniz (—1716), was left the task of relating time and space to God and His world. Near the end of this process, before it quiesced only to re-explode in the twentieth century, the English philosophical theologian Dr. Samuel Clarke (—1729), perhaps "fronting" for Isaac Newton who had still theologized space, countered Leibniz, who was subtracting the idea of personal deity from the discussion. Clarke complained, asking Leibniz why "so great

Concern should be shown, to exclude God's *actual* Government of the World, and to allow His Providence to *act* no further than barely in *concurring* (as the Phrase is) to let *all Things* do only what they would do *of themselves of mere Mechanism*." But Leibniz and his colleagues had already created a distant, limited, personless God. Says Koyré in summary:

> The Divine Artifex had therefore less and less to do in the world. He did not even need to conserve it, as the world, more and more, became able to dispense with this service. Thus the mighty, energetic God of Newton who actually "ran" the universe according to His free will and decision, became, in quick succession a conservative power, an *intelligentia supra-mundana*, a "Dieu faineant."

And the infinite Universe of the New Cosmology "inherited all the ontological attributes of Divinity. Yet only those— all the others the departed God took away with him." [3]

After the departed God had packed His personal baggage and left but the trace of divine artifaction, other sciences also waved good-bye. The age of Descartes and Hobbes (—1679), of Bacon (—1626) and Browne (—1682), produced a new kind of theology of the Divine Artifex. In England this was called Deism; in France, Rationalism or Naturalism; in Germany, "Enlightenment." Congenial to religion without passion and to God without person, the rationalistic sentiment worshiped a God of nature and reason, who was universal in the responses of the religions of men—among them, Christianity. Lord Herbert of Cherbury (—1648) had outlined perfectly the God of the next century and a half and prescribed a new theology in five creedal statements. 1) "That there is a Supreme Power." 2) "That this Sovereign Power must be worshipped." 3) "That the good ordering or disposition of the faculties of man constitutes the principal or best part of divine worship, and that this has always been believed." 4) "That all vices and crimes should be expiated and effaced by repentance." 5) "That there are rewards and punishments after this life." In a word, rationalism was simply outraged by what Soren Kierkegaard called "the scandal of particularity." Emotion beyond this rage it hardly knew.

A host of Christians would rise to reply, many of them men who fell into the timeless error of Christian apologists: they granted so much to the presuppositions of the antagonist that they could not really win the case. Richard Baxter (—1691), George Berkeley (—1753), and Joseph Butler (—1752) would reply in England to the deist challenge. In general they also pointed to a natural religion, which in this case paralleled the revealed. But their concessions were less effective to counteract deism than was the blunt attack on natural religion itself by the philosopher David Hume, who tore from reason the ability or the right to establish or derive truth from itself. The deist proofs for the existence of God were abolished. In his radical empiricism Hume rejected causality and substance and was skeptical of the mind, which had been the one eternal entity in earlier deism. Christians rose in rage at him, not realizing the ways in which he was doing them a favor in disguise.

French Christianity produced few antagonists of naturalism so effective against the crushers of Christian infamy as had been Berkeley or Butler in England. There Voltaire (François Marie Arouet, —1778). Holbach, Diderot (—1784), Rousseau (—1778) stormed the Catholic citadel. Clever and mocking, Voltaire, like the deists, claimed to be on the side of true religion against atheism. The Age of Reason had arrived, the God of reason ruled. Voltaire attacked with glee all belief in miracles and mystery, often popularizing scientific findings more sophisticated than his own; he illustrates the extremism of French rationalism, attacking Leibniz himself for conciliating too much between rational and revealed religion. The German philosopher became the example of eighteenth-century Babbitry and boobery in Voltaire's *Candide*.

THE GOD-KILLERS

To detail this philosophical picture is not our calling; it is necessary, however, to pay one more visit to the kingdoms of reason, which drew on the resources of the new scientific cosmology a century later for another massive assault on the

Christian scandal of particularity. If the earlier round of "natural religionists" was eventually defeated or rendered obsolete (though never completely so), the second cycle remains to plague the Christian world or to create problems for it. If the Enlightenment was to meet its best refutation from within, the later wave is too new to see a similar reply. Four mid-nineteenth-century "god-killers" could be named.

The most potent of these was the father of a movement which had grown to be perhaps the greatest antagonist the Christian tradition has known, at least since Mohammedanism of the eighth century. The obvious reference is to Karl Marx (—1883), the German socialist revolutionary who was a second-generation descendant of the Enlightenment *via* the philosopher Hegel. Essentially an economic thinker, he combined this thought with a view of history which echoed the fervor of early Christian prophecy and apocalypse and paralleled its proclamation of a common life and brotherhood in suffering, looking to an "end" in which all would be new. His messiah was an impersonal historical process; his offspring was the communist movement. Much of his ammunition was gained from his observations of ecclesiastical disregard for the common man, the sop it seemed to throw him in its sacramental system and the promise of a better life hereafter. In the time of the spending of the Christian movement, Marxism began to fill a vacuum on a world-wide scale. The beginning of the end of its struggle with the Christian faith is not yet in sight.

Somewhat more containable in scope is the work of a second antagonist, Friedrich Wilhelm Nietzsche (—1900), the son of a German Lutheran pastor, who prophesied the end of the Christian era. He would "transvalue all values" in his philosophy of life and his view of the will to power. "God is dead, He spoke to us and now is silent." Nietzsche chose to designate himself as the anti-Christ; he lets a madman speak of the death of God:

> We have killed him—you and I. All of us are his murderers. But how have we done this? How were we able to drink up the sea? Who gave us the sponge to

wipe away the entire horizon? What did we do when we unchained this earth from its sun? . . . Are we not plunging continually? Backward, sideward, forward, in all directions? Is there any up or down left? Are we not straying as through an infinite nothing? Do we not feel the breath of empty space? Has it not become colder? Is not night and more night coming on all the while? [4]

In the night that followed were new atheisms that ranted against the servility of Christ's "slave morality"; these were concretized in several modern totalitarian movements, particularly in German National Socialism.

Another giant was Sigmund Freud (—1939), a man of later time, whose assault on Christianity was a by-product of his new view of man's place in the cosmos. Decades after his first winds blew Christians began to learn to pitch their tents and find the climate congenial. But for a time the new view of "animal man" seemed to be potentially more devastating to Christian claims than had been any other attacks on the faith. In many ways the ground had been prepared for this view of man by the other great "god-killer," Charles Darwin (—1882), who had not set out in his theory of evolution to refute the Christian faith explicitly; yet in his hypotheses concerning the origin and descent of the species he attacked the particularity of the Christian doctrine of man's creation and further corroded its distinctiveness. Fumbling adaptations to the Darwinian world by Christian theologians helped matters little.

In the face of these attacks Christians felt called to "take a stand." With little experience at self-defense in the millennium of their ideological monopoly in the West, they often staggered as they stood. In each case there were accommodationists who accepted the new dogmas fairly uncritically and, with more enlightened optimism than Christian warrant, saw possibilities for new syntheses. Others reacted in belligerent counterattack or through isolated withdrawal. After the acids of modernity had eaten their way, there was never again to be a cozy containment of the apostolic message.

The age of response to modernity in Christian thought produced few theological giants of the stature of Origen and Augustine. Anselm and Aquinas, Luther and Calvin.

Yet names like Schleiermacher and Ritschl must be reckoned with; the apostolic question produced men of stature even in the age which found it difficult or unnecessary to make an "appeal to constructive reason" for Christianity.

ORTHODOXY

A survey such as this can largely bypass Eastern Orthodoxy, which until the twentieth century was relatively unexposed to the corrosions of modernity's acids. The Eastern church was less theologically articulate than the Western, finding less necessity to justify itself intellectually, and living a more quiet internal life. It drew nourishment from renewed patristic studies; the review of past glories rendered it conservative if not static. Those Western philosophical currents which did make their way to Russia were usually idealist: Schelling (—1854) and Hegel (—1831) seemed to fit glove-on-hand over the philosophy long acceptable there. No doubt the most significant theologizing was done not by professional theologians but by novelists like Dostoievsky (—1881) and Tolstoi (—1910) near the end of this period. Alexis Stepanovich Khomiakoff (—1860) was known as a critic of Aristotelianism and the more fashionable idealism of Hegel and Schelling. He opposed Protestantism's "freedom without unity" and Catholicism's "unity without freedom," advocating Orthodoxy's organic union of both, "freedom in the spirit at one with itself." Near the end of the period Vladimir Solovieff (—1900) flourished as an advocate of Christian reunion. He favored the idealist tradition which Khomiakoff had attacked, fusing its pantheism with the Christian view of incarnation. His modern Gnosticism, despite its influence on literature and philosophical thought, was not widely accepted in the Church; eventually he became a Roman Catholic.

ROMAN CATHOLICISM: FOUR SOLUTIONS

Roman Catholicism provides several excellent opportunities to review its stance toward the apostolic question, the problem of the continuity of the Christian message in reference to the original witness. We shall review Rome's innovations and additions to apostolic· doctrine; the adjustments of Roman Modernism; the revival of Thomism as normative philosophical theology; the theological effect of national thought in France, Germany, and England; the renewed concern for intellectual justification of social Christianity.

Two of three Roman additions to the doctrine of the apostles in modern times were drawn from traditional sources in mid-nineteenth-century decades. The first of these was the Dogma of the Immaculate Conception. Debated in Roman circles for many centuries, this concerned itself with the problem of Christ's birth. If Christ was born without the agency of a human father but through the Virgin Mary, did not his sinlessness depend upon her own? Yet, in Catholicism, the act of conception is seen to bear the taint of sin. Was the Virgin conceived, then, without sin? Earnest theologians had long pondered this. Anselm denied it; the Dominicans, following Bernard and Aquinas, drew the conclusion that, conceived in sin, she had been made holy in the womb. The Franciscans pushed the frontier of speculation a step further: requests to reinforce this latter view, already popular in Reformation times, that she was conceived without sin, came frequently during the times of Roman reaction in the nineteenth century. Pius IX responded with the Bull *Ineffabilis Deus* of 1854.

> We, with the authority of our Lord Jesus Christ, the blessed Apostles Peter and Paul, and with our own, do declare, pronounce and define that the doctrine which holds that the Virgin Mary was, in the first instant of her conception, preserved untouched by any taint of original guilt . . . is to be firmly and steadfastly believed by all the faithful.

No reference was made to biblical authority; the act itself reveals the brashness with which Pius IX met the modern world, making embarrassingly explicit what properly had been mysterious.

A more blunt affront to other Christians was the ultimate step in the elevation of the papacy as the absolute guardian of apostolicity. From Rome as first among equals, to supremacy: this had occurred a millennium and more earlier. But in a time of insecurity Rome reacted with a blatant trumpet blast: the pope's authority lay also in his own official infallibility. Over the opposition of many concerned Roman Catholics, the Vatican Council of 1870 imposed upon the church the view that the pope was infallible, as defined:

> The Roman Pontiff, when he speaks *ex cathedra* (that is, when fulfilling the office of Pastor and Teacher of all Christians—on his supreme Apostolical authority, he defines a doctrine concerning faith or morals to be held by the Universal Church) . . . is endowed with that infallibility, with which the Divine Redeemer has willed that His Church—in defining doctrine concerning faith or morals—should be equipped . . . If any one shall presume (which God forbid!) to contradict this our definition; let him be anathema.

A few did. John Doellinger (—1890) of Munich opposed the move on historical grounds, was excommunicated, and attached himself to the Old Catholic churches which also rejected such papal authority.

With this weapon to solidify its opposition to modernity went Rome's stamp on a convenient official theology. In this it chose well, turning to the golden age of Catholic thought, to the glory that was Thomas Aquinas'. The papal encyclical of 1879, *Aeterni Patris,* made the "prince and master" required reading at all Roman schools of higher learning. Resistance to this tendency to absolutize a moment in history and to put all the eggs of Roman development in the scholastic basket was effectively frustrated by papal strategy; it found its outlet in Thomist variations. With the rise of the new and intellectually respectable Thomism French scholarship came to new prominence.

But France more than any other nation reflects the difficulties of Catholic thought in the social unrest of the times. We are familiar now with the background of confusion in Jansenism and Quietism, in Gallicanism and Ultramontanism. The Roman See used the nineteenth century to strengthen its position after it had lost ground in the revolutionary age; but revolution refused to die young. The *Syllabus of Errors* of 1864 condemned most "modern" sentiment: toleration and indifferentism; socialism, Bible societies; pantheism, naturalism, rationalism, liberalism. The *Syllabus* defined the last of these as the belief "that in the present day, it is no longer necessary that the Catholic religion be held as the only religion of the State, to the exclusion of all other modes of worship . . . that the Roman Pontiff can, and ought to, reconcile himself to, and agree with, progress, liberalism, and modern civilization."

What was this despised liberalism? Distinguished from the later Catholic Modernism, this made its greater impact on social life of western Europe, particularly in France. The excitable and emotional Abbé Lamennais (—1854) is an excellent representative of the theological side of this political ferment. Attached to the revolutionary movement in 1830, he urged the church to cast its lot with democracy. The lower classes were emergent: the gospel should be made appealing to them. At first he saw hope in attracting the papacy and making it his tool, or his ally. He was a slave of Rome, an Ultramontane who blamed the papacy's later failings on Josephism and Gallicanism. A stronger, really free Catholicism would aid the working man. Ally pope and people. Repudiate the alliance of pope and monarch. It would be as simple as that. In *L'Avenir* he argued the case with a cogency that makes it still attractive to some Catholics. To his great surprise, the papacy did not appreciate this new elevation. In 1831 Lamennais and his friends took their case to the Pope, Gregory XVI. They were frustrated; separation of church and state, even if to enchance the church, was "absurd," "perverse," "ludicrous," "execrable." Catholic liberalism received a death blow.

Catholic Modernism forced a different kind of test. It reflected the spirit of accommodation to modernity, of compatibility with biblical and historical criticism, and of hope for continuity with secular culture. The foredoomed movement began to appear under the church historian Duchesne (—1922) in the 1870's. His collaborator and student was the famed Alfred Loisy (—1940). By 1886 Loisy had trampled on his old beliefs, but remained within the church. By 1892 he was questioning biblical authority;

he was condemned by the Pope's *Providentissimus Deus* in the following year. Between 1888 and 1900 the Modernists held a variety of scientific meetings which turned out to be another form of adjustment to the post-Darwinian age. Baron von Hügel (—1925) spearheaded the movement in this period in England, where George Tyrrell (—1909), an Irish Jesuit, was also influential. The movement spent itself early under the formal attacks of the Pope in 1907–08. By 1910 Roman Catholicism had closed ranks, less corroded in its theological distinctiveness than Protestantism would be. The neo-Thomist fence-posts have since partially corralled Catholic theological caprice. One Modernist had said that the age of partial heresy was past; it was.

PROTESTANTISM

Protestant theology and apostolic reference is much more complicated. No pope could say, "I am tradition," "I represent the authority of the apostles." No uniformity guarded it as the Orthodox tradition could hold the East. Exposed on all fronts by its divisions, by its participation in more of life, by its competition of principles, and by its openness to God's larger revelation, Protestantism was vulnerable to upset by many "winds of doctrine." Here it will be possible only to outline several main currents. In the discussion of Reformation history we pointed to the seventeenth-century development of Lutheran and Reformed thought: it preoccupied itself scholastically. System builders fitted all the square pegs into the square holes, the round pegs into the round holes. Everything was as neat as that, and the systems served well for their day.

The later seventeenth century and the eighteenth century found Protestant theology most involved in response to the scientific world view, in the bewilderment at the infinite universe, in the reply to those who delineated the Great Artifex; here we encounter the apologists to rationalists whose own religion had to be "reasonable." The fine art of brinkmanship was carried to tantalizing extremes; Christian witness verged on complete concession. Meanwhile as a parallel current the "Methodist movement" or the "Pietist era" made the dogmatic questions somewhat irrelevant. Quoth John Wesley: "I believe the merciful God regards the lives and tempers of men more than their ideas." And was not sterile dogmatizing what Neander and Zinzendorf, Spener (—1705), Francke (—1727), Teelinck and the other Pietists were rebelling against? Theologically their movement was conservative; it resisted the modern winds by sheltering itself.

GERMAN THOUGHT

It was in response to the German philosophical Enlightenment that the more important theological strains of recent times grew.

> It was . . . natural that modern theology should begin in Germany, where also post-Kantian philosophy had its beginning. And indeed unquestionably ever since the years of the nineteenth century down to the present time German theology has had the primacy over all other. Its hegemony in modern theology resembles that of Greek patristic theology in the Ancient Church, and is grounded on a similar reason. Just as Greek philosophy furnished the framework of the traditional dogma, so philosophy as transformed by Kant has furnished that of modern theology.[5]

Immanuel Kant is a starting point (—1804). Professor at East Prussian Königsberg, he lived one of the more prosaic physical and more dramatic mental lives of modern times. His deviation from Lutheranism, around 1792, brought him into difficulties with officials, but this did not prevent the continuance of his publishing efforts. The scientific shock described above motivated him to attempt to relate human understanding to the natural laws then under study. He held that knowledge contains an element from nature; thus the traditional proofs for the existence of God, following the lines of traditional metaphysics, were destroyed. There went twelfth- and thirteenth-century Protestant systems: on Kantian lines, an entirely new approach was called for.

Kant himself provided that new beginning by associating the validity of ideas not with nature but with the conscience of man. The moral law predominated. He adopted theological terms at some points compatible with Lutheranism. Men are radically evil. Good and evil are in conflict around and in men. In the victory of the good, the Kingdom of God is established. But Kant's moralist-base cut at the foundation of Lutheran theology, which stressed God's free gift in Jesus Christ. History as history was without place; the distinctiveness of revelation in Christ disappeared. Prayer was irrelevant to the moral man; miracles were offensive to Kant. From Kant flowed the idealist stream represented by Hegel, Schelling and Fichte (—1814); in England later by Bradley (—1924) and Bosanquet (—1923). Various theological schools grew out of these strains with their anti-metaphysical and pro-moralistic approaches. Here was a coquette to Christian theology in quest of a new mistress. Idealism infiltrated Christian life; the heir of Reformation thought, it wooed the sons of the Reformation.

The Kantian line is made more complex by Hegelian deviations. Hegel removed the last remaining Kantian stricture against the possibility of constructing a universally valid comprehension of reality in one great system. Hegel begins by affirming that reality, reason, and thought are in their absolute senses the same. The rational is the real and the real is the rational. God is introduced into the system in a dialogue with the developing rational process and the life of history. In this process and history Christianity was the most perfect form of religion; but after Hegel had finished with Christ, he was little more than an idea. Apostolic Christianity tended to become a great rational idea. The world process was deified: Hegel verged on pantheism.

It is easier to trace Hegelian theology to its dead end than to explore the pervasive ramifications of Kantianism in Christian thought. The more dramatic of the Hegelian schools was its left wing, typified by David Strauss (—1874), Ludwig Feuerbach (—1872), and Karl Marx. Strauss strained the remnant of agreement between philosophy and history to an immediate breaking point and came to the heart of the matter, rejecting the Gospels as history. His *Life of Jesus* represented an extreme of historical skepticism: hardly a kernel was left. Was the apostolic witness itself a romantic fabrication? Feuerbach went further (if that is possible) by inverting divine revelation into human fabrication, seeing in the idea of the deity a projection of human consciousness. Only Marx in his secular messianism could carry this still further, making a deity out of the historical process. For relief, we might backtrack to Ferdinand Christian Baur (—1860) of the Tübingen school, who took Hegel's historical framework and asked the critical questions of development in the New Testament and early Christianity. With Adolf Harnack (—1930) he is usually remembered as the great church historian of the century.

A generalization of limited usefulness is in order. The Hegelian school concentrated on history and philosophy to elevate and bring into the Christian orbit the concerns of earlier Pietism. In this latter context appears a theologian who overshadows his century with the mark of greatness, Friedrich Schleiermacher (—1834). Had Germany seen such a theologian since Luther, or Protestantism such a systematizer since Calvin? Profoundly influenced by Kant, Schleiermacher was sufficiently the child of his century to react extremely against the cold moralism of Kantianism: his stress was on "feeling" in religion, on intuition in spiritual response.

Some of his color came from his attachment through Schlegel to the Romantic movement; much of it came from the palette of his own personality. He was interested in regaining for Christianity the lost ground of the rationalist period. For him the locus of religious authority was not in apostolic teaching or the tradition of the Church, but in the religious intuition and experience: "religion is the feeling of absolute dependence" which is heightened in monotheism. Christianity is the best, though not the only true religion. Not until the time of the First World War, at the hands of Karl Barth, was Schleiermacher to meet a reaction worthy of his stature.

This was romantic Christianity; but it was still romantic

Christianity; Schleiermacher was much moved to witness to the classic faith. "Christian doctrines are accounts of the Christian religious affections set forth in speech." His obsession with affections led him to interest in the doctrines. Sin is the troubled harmony between man's own powers which disturbs his relations to God. Redemption implies Christ's influence on the believer. Christ was in this sense a redeemer or even *the* redeemer from sin. The Holy Spirit is the working, spiritual force proceeding from Christ, produced by and emerging in the life of congregations. The Christian life is the ethical response to Christ's example. As Jesus lived in perfect consciousness of God, freed from consciousness of self, so the Christian moves beyond moral uncertainty into new, full life.

Despite the magnificence of his achievement, the forming of the vocabulary for a new century's theology, Schleiermacher raised more questions than he solved in the matter of apostolic reference. The shadow of all the doctrines was there, but the psychologizing which makes them plausible also gives one a slippery feeling; little anchor is there in Scripture or history. But Schleiermacher, of course, contended that Scripture and history were confluent with the feeling he described. But it is experience that becomes deified; the consciousness of the Church is normative. Man-centered religion did not have to await Karl Barth in our time for reaction. By the middle of the century Protestant biblical theologians were "mediating" and confessional theologians were reacting against this expression. But these were relatively minor theologians, who attracted less attention. Names like Beck, Cremer, Kuebel, or the Erlangen school mean little today. They could not reverse the tide. And they were susceptible to tendencies toward static dogmatism and a too-contented reference to the past.

Institutional, confessional, mediating, and biblicistic theologians did not hold the field for long. More important in the perspective of the decades were the transformed Kantians led by Albrecht Ritschl. Their version incorporated a positivism or empiricism that learned from the scientific method advocated so confidently at that time. Ritschl (—1889), one of the few whose name can be mentioned in the same breath with Schleiermacher, did not think of himself as a rebel. In his focus on the historical witness, he concentrated his high theological endeavors on those apostolic questions which sometimes eluded Schleiermacher. Ritschl still is respected among thinkers who stress the particularity of Christianity. With Kant he placed emphasis on the will of man; theology came to be a sequence of judgments of value. The original sources for the faith were most important in this study.

Ritschl's ethical sense led him to prepare a theological justification for social Christianity. His theology revolved around an ellipse with two foci: the relation of man to God as His son and to the Kingdom of God. Helping usher in this kingdom among men became the Church's task. Ritschl was a modern among moderns in theology in his sense of need for reconciliation on the level of society's concerns, in his pragmatic-utilitarian nuances and his ethical reference. His successor Wilhelm Herrmann (—1922) picked up the moralism and anti-metaphysical bias and carried them to subjective extremes. Ritschlianism would also produce the great church historian Adolf Harnack (—1930), famed for his criticism of the Hellenization of Christianity in the form of dogma.

The later decades of the century witness the constant confrontation of the basic questions of apostolicity in the authority of the Scriptures. Biblical criticism, the application of scientific and literary methods and canons to the Bible, was in vogue. The school of Comparative Religion studies, which tended to set original Christianity in a syncretistic pattern, rose to prominence. Finally, we must mention Ernst Troeltsch (—1923), who brings us full circle "back to Schleiermacher" as a historian stressing the subjectivity of response and the relativity of Christianity among the world religions.

DENMARK

Less noticed than German theology were several Danish trends which have attracted attention in recent decades.

Two extremes are represented. Nikolai Grundtvig (—1872) was a romantic ecclesiastic, a nationalist obsessed with promulgation of Danish culture in fusion with Christian witness. In this context he is important for his naively simple question: Would not agreement on the Apostles' Creed satisfy the apostolic question? The living word of the Church outranked the written word of the Bible: the book rests on the altar. Uncritically accepting the idea that the Creed antedated the New Testament, Grundtvig promoted his discoveries up and down Denmark. Parallels in his churchly concern to Britain's Oxford Movement will be obvious.

The radical solution belonged to Soren Kierkegaard (—1855), who enjoys a cult a century after his death. He posed the question in an "existential" framework which appeals in our time of resistance to metaphysics, and of religious discontent with other philosophical options. Kierkegaard belittled the life of the Church and social Christianity to the point of intense and isolated religious individualism. His *Attack upon Christendom* was occasioned by the comatose state church of his day. The apostolic question is in a sense beside the point: there can be no disciple at second hand; in Christian history the sense of continuity is pointless. The stress lies with contemporaneousness with Christ, on personal confrontation in the *now*: the present moment is weighted, freighted.

Kierkegaard began with a devastating critique of the Hegelian system because it attempted to comprehend the incomprehensible. Finding man in anxiety and God in remoteness, he allows for a bridge in Christ. Christian experience is discontinuous; the Church by relying on its stewardship of the mysteries and by glorying in the "cloud of witnesses" buffers the drama of confrontation. The rigor of response called for an ethical Christianity with a view of man so perceptive that a later century picked it up as the most accurate depiction of human plight in a blighted day.

A survey such as this cannot do justice to the full sweep of continental thought; it neglects the neo-Calvinism of Abraham Kuyper (—1920) in Holland, the New Testament research of Godet (—1900), the churchly "feel" of Wilhelm Loehe, and many others. But we must pretend once again that we are standing a great distance from events, and seeing them only in broadest outline. On this cavalier pretext we embark for Britain to sketch its theological development.

GREAT BRITAIN

British and American thought produced few men equipped to deal with "basic questions" of the root and ground of the Christian faith; no shapers like Schleiermacher and Ritschl, no rebels like Strauss and Feuerbach, no individualists like Kierkegaard. The moderation of the British temper, the church-centeredness of thinkers, and a mediating interest characterized the main stream. To some this has seemed the strength of Anglican thought; to others there is little room for congratulating what seems to be but a sophistication of "muddling through"; still others dismiss mediation as the end-product of the Anglican principle of comprehensiveness and indifferentism.

Yet British thought did parallel many continental concerns in its immediate alertness to the challenge from science and natural religion, from the time of Newton to the time of Darwin. Idealism was also represented, particularly in the school of Samuel Taylor Coleridge (—1834). British thought outstripped continental efforts, apart from Ritschl's, on the place of Christian social thought. The Oxford Movement shared similarities with the theology of Grundtvig or Loehe as it sought to reestablish continuities with the apostolic past. Here we shall look at four solutions: evangelicalism, Oxford Tractarianism, social Christianity, biblical research.

Evangelicalism as a term can include both the Methodist movement and the pietism of nonconformity within Anglicanism, along with the British free churches. The strength of the evangelical party, William Wilberforce (—1839) produced little of theological substance to match the greatness of his ethical activity, particularly in the warfare

against slavery. Nonconformity produced Andrew Fair-
bairn (—1912) as the greatest Congregationalist scholar of
the times. His central interest was Christology. In the main
this lineage attempted to work with theological steam
generated in the past, avoiding more profound intellectual
questions. Much of its specific theologizing was directed
to providing a rationale for its polity and its critique of
high-church parties.

The High Church resided in the nineteenth century in the
Oxford Movement; here was a concentrated attempt to
let the doctrine of the church settle the question of doctrine itself. Elevating tradition and the Church beyond
Protestant bounds, the Movement, also called Tractarianism, experienced some leakage to "mother" church, Rome.
In its exaggeration of the apostolic succession and tradition, the critical principle which motivated nineteenth-
century Protestant thought was allowed to slip. Perhaps it
is unfair to the genius of the men of Oxford to include
them in a chapter discussing adaptation to a new day. As a
churchly (and in some sense political) movement it is more
a comment on the British situation than a concession to
continental ways of theological response. Gathered around
several leaders like Hugh James Rose (—1838) and
Alexander Knox (—1831), a group of young churchmen
became attracted to the idea of comprehensive Anglicanism
as a "middle way" between Romanism and Protestantism.
The liturgy would safeguard continuity and catholicity;
succession offered the key to the apostolic doctrine of the
Church.

The younger men developed these ideas: John Henry
Newman (—1890), John Keble (—1866), Richard Froude
(—1836), and Edward Pusey (—1882), after whom the
Movement is often called Puseyism. Pusey brought high
Anglicanism in its sacramental life to a point near Romanism. It remained for Newman, however, to cross the
bridge. Converted from Calvinism, as he put it, in his
early years, he was repelled by Wesleyanism and Lutheranism at Oxford; seeking a "rock" he veered next toward
Rome, approaching it with the fanaticism of the convert.
In political reaction against Whig intrusions on church life,

the "Tractarians" responded with a series of pamphlets which aimed to pull the church above politics, back to the apostles. They were awed by the mysteries of the faith; their devotional expression is most impressive and their sacramental piety noteworthy against the pattern of scientific matter-of-factness. Beyond the tracts and Newman's own scholarship, the Movement produced little of theological moment.

The tendency for liberal Anglicans to look at social questions as an outlet (and sometimes as a theological evasion) is a third nineteenth-century characteristic. The giant of the impulse was Frederick Denison Maurice (—1872) who came from Unitarianism to the Church of England in 1834. His thought coupled Platonic influence with Christ-centered theology. Jesus Christ, the divine son of God, stands at the head of humanity; he helps man overcome his divorce from God by revealing the Father's love. Every man is "in Christ" who heads the race; if this is true, the human race's concerns are intimately bound up. Christianity can act in two ways upon the human situation. Polemics add to the breaches between man and man. Positive affirmations can restore the unities and provide a circle of inter-influence and sharing. Maurice's refined sense of Christian community and social responsibility helped his school of social Christianity to counteract Pietism's individualism and Anglo-Catholic formalism. Some Ritschlian ideas find parallel here: the Kingdom of Christ was a key.

Finally, the modern period saw in Britain the development of a high tradition of biblical scholarship that continues to our time. Many of these scholars were Anglicans who chilled at the Oxford Movement's diversions from the critical questions of New Testament witness. Stressing the importance of linguistic study, men such as Brooke Westcott (—1901), and Fenton Hort (—1892) or Joseph Lightfoot (—1889) preoccupied themselves with philology, with preparation of new editions of the Scriptures, with biblical commentaries. A more critical scholarship associated with names like Driver, Jowett, Sanday, and Hatch is evidence of the pervasiveness of concerns such as those activated on the continent by Wellhausen.

No single line triumphed in England: the acids of modernity were at work. Evangelicalism and social Christianity evaded by altering concerns; conservatism went about its business not noticing the corrosion of the sacred vessel—postponing, pretending; "modernist" theology conceded; high-churchism lived in uneasy psychosomatic imbalance between ecclesiastical security and the nag of critical questions.

AMERICAN THOUGHT

In this context we can do little more than characterize American theology as a whole. Its concerns moved from the development of the Calvinist "federal" theology in New England to a justification of the conversionism in the Great Awakening down to the adaptation to modern concerns. It began in high dogmatism and ended in an historical relativism learned from Europe, coupled with the empiricism that so suits the American temper. For the most part we can safely generalize with historian Jerald C. Brauer that "Protestantism in America can be characterized in terms of a full, free experimentation and an enduring Biblicism." [6] The two major exceptions were the drift toward Unitarianism in New England in the afterglow of the "Enlightenment's" natural religion and the drift toward Modernism at the end of the nineteenth century in accommodation to the world of Darwin and his successors, Huxley and Spencer. Most American Protestants would have characterized themselves, throughout this period, as "evangelical" in sympathy. Both Protestantism and Roman Catholicism came into fuller flowering in scholarship in the twentieth century, which falls beyond the scope of this chapter.

Protestant thought, more Reformed and Arminian than Lutheran or Anglican, largely contented itself on the apostolic question by accepting uncritically the biblical witness and acquiescing in the Reformation; the American experience was also included as being somehow redemptive and revelatory. Other modern developments and the entire medieval direction were largely repudiated as ages of atheism or superstition. If we wish to keep a consistent perspective and distance in evaluating theologians, perhaps only Jonathan Edwards (—1758), the theologian of the Great Awakening and as fine a philosophical mind as this continent has produced, should be mentioned in the same breath with most of the Europeans who have gone before. For the most part Americans were preoccupied with filling up a continent, winning men to Christianity, establishing churches. Substantive theology was neglected; creedal affirmation of the past was largely taken for granted. The real genius of American thought has been seen in its pragmatic adjustments to the problems and possibilities of a new world. Theological pace-setting has been associated with Europe.

"I believe in . . . apostolic . . . Church" meant to men of the modern period several things: to biblicists and confessionalists or Roman dogmatists it meant that a certain deposit had been prepared for saving men with its truth; the acids of no time could destroy this. To others it meant that the flux and change of a new day could eat toward its very vitals. But the God who had more truth and light to break forth from His holy word would guide men into new and fuller truth. If this group made more mistakes of clumsy adaptation, theirs was the more difficult task, the greater risk.

15

GREAT THINGS FOR GOD

The story of the Church in the modern world brightens after the accounts of a secularizing world and an idea-buffeted Church in the eighteenth and early nineteenth centuries. Two encouraging themes present themselves, one centrifugal, the other centripetal. The first is the story of mission expansion in the nineteenth century, "the great century" in the words of Kenneth Scott Latourette, mission historian. The second is the story of the drive toward reunion among the divided churches which has characterized the twentieth century. Each suggests some of the resilience and residue of energy left in a movement which, apart from them, has often seemed to cling by a fingerhold at the edge of an abyss of obscurity in a new age.

THE STORY OF MISSIONS

First, mission expansion: this is the story that will take us around the world. The last glimpse, in the sixteenth century, found Roman Catholicism establishing outposts of minor importance around the world while Eastern Orthodoxy expanded within its own borders and Protestantism consolidated its gains in western Europe. The Reformers were guilty on two fronts of failing to realize and actualize their missionary obligations. On the one hand the toehold of survival was sufficiently demanding of energies. Second, they misread Christian history in their preoccupation with the near at the expense of the remote. In discussing the New Testament's charge, a modern scholar has faulted early Protestantism:

> The Reformers took a false attitude when they believed that they could do away with the mission to the Gentiles by saying that the gospel had already been offered to all Gentiles by the apostles. It belongs rather to the nature of the sign that to the very end it *appears in every generation* that belongs to the present intermediate period in the final phase of redemptive history. From this, however, it follows that the missionary obligation also must fill the entire time that still remains until the unknown final limit, and that every generation must proclaim the gospel anew to the nations of their time, without being troubled by the opportunity to hear it. On the basis of this Primitive Christian conception, therefore, the Church must proclaim the gospel to the entire world in every generation.[1]

If the generations following the Reformation still misread the signs, something was to happen soon to change this. Call it what you will; a new outpouring of the Spirit, a new dash of adventure, a new grasp of vision—in any case, Christians soon had a world-wide view of their task. Their hymns reflected the new sense of geography:

> *From Greenland's icy mountains*
> *To India's coral strand,*
> *Where Afric's sunny fountains*
> *Roll down their golden sand;*
> *From many an ancient river,*
> *From many a palmy plain,*
> *They call us to deliver*
> *Their land from error's chain.*

"Error's chain" might mean that the "heathen in his blindness bows down to wood and stone." This was most dramatic in spreading the impulse. Other heathens were experiencing a period of the decline of world religions: Hinduism, Buddhism, Mohammedanism were relatively quiescent in the nineteenth century—their resurgence would come later. Christians sensed that they could fill a vacuum;

this was made particularly easy by the fortunate coincidence —it seemed to them—of Western colonialism's interest in forming the entire world on Western lines. Had they had time to think, the nationalist-missionaries would have foreseen some of the difficulties their efforts would raise. Few had time; and their achievements were too impressive in other senses to warrant their being severely judged in this.

Because the Kingdom of God which Christ had announced had "the tendency to become a universal religion" (Holtzmann) from the first, it is difficult for contemporary Christians to picture that only a century and a half ago the movement was still identified with Europe and western Asia, and with new outposts in the western hemisphere. Africa, Australia, the greater part of Asia were hardly touched. Should we seek one word to characterize the nineteenth-century rebound from the defeats of the modern world, it would have to be "surprise!" It was surprising how little Christianity had done to become, according to its own profession of its genius, universal, realizing its catholicity. It was surprising how much it did in so little time. It was surprising that the expansion came when it did. Christianity was experiencing deep anxiety and insecurity. But the mission literature, the diaries, the records of promotional societies, the tracts—these hardly reflect hesitation. From the storms of the time the ship of the Church was being battered as never before; yet it sailed as never before since the days of persecution and bare survival.

The modern Christian mission movement was born in the 1790's, its patriarch the cobbler William Carey (—1834), who inspired others and outpaced the followers. On May 31, 1792, he preached a missionary sermon on a text from Isaiah which included a call to "expect great things from God and attempt great things for God." To attempt great things for God—an evangelical, Methodistic sentiment filled hearts with consuming love. Men were often nearly lost and forgotten in fastness of forest and darkness of jungle and expanse of desert. There were others who would follow, conscious of a new call, a new destiny, a new vision. Though our perspective judges them because they tied this vision to "the American way of life" or because they wanted to guarantee that in the corner of many a foreign field there should be a spot that was forever England, this does not explain the impulse, the sacrifice, the courage, the obscurity that revealed itself. There was still operative the explanation Paul had given as he undertook his work: "For though I preach the Gospel, I have nothing to glory in, for the necessity is laid upon me." This was the divine *must* that seemed to make the difference.

These were the catalysts: a time of discovery and national expansion, a theology of activism, the novelty of outreach, the opportunity presented by quiescent world religions, a simplicity of method (evangelize, educate, give physical aid). If what follows takes on the character of a whirlwind tour of the globe, even this will be faithful to the breathlessness of the movement. But we must pause for three preliminary generalizations as chart and road map.

First, expansion was least dramatic in areas of earlier repudiation or where Christianity was waning, or in the lands that were nearer, more familiar (in the cradle of the three great religions, among Jews, and in nominally Roman Catholic countries). Conversely, expansion was most dramatic in the areas of fresh contact on the part of the faith and in areas which were more remote, less familiar with historic Christianity (in southeast Asia, the Far East, and all but the north of Africa). Third, the older "catholic" churches tended to show less initiative than did the younger churches which passed on the fire when they first received it. Orthodoxy's expansion was hardly significant; Roman Catholicism followed older patterns; young churches created younger churches. These generalizations provide an outline to which we shall also add a brief survey of the societies and men who were in vanguard, a discussion of several factors that help account for the slowing of pace after a century. Special emphasis will be placed on expansion within the United States—a factor not yet accounted for.

A GLOBAL TOUR: THE CRADLE

To begin, then, with that region which cradled three great religions, where advances in the nineteenth century were least dramatic. Palestine, the eastern and southern rims of the Mediterranean, the Near East, and North Africa had been scenes of the earliest spread. Today hardly a single nation in the area is nominally and principally Christian. The Canary Islands are Roman Catholic; Egypt and Ethiopia have respectable Coptic churches; Syria and Lebanon have representative Uniate Christian bodies, distinctive groups with Roman ties. But with the exception of Jewish Israel the remaining lands of the area are predominantly Moslem. The nineteenth century failed substantially to change this millennium-old configuration.

The Jews had been largely dispersed from their homeland. Christian endeavor to attract them was halfhearted, not localized in Palestine, and it met with little success. After centuries of repudiation and oppression by Christians, in outcaste status partly because of race and partly because of faith, the Jews were hardly predisposed to the faith which had been nurtured among them, for "salvation is of the Jews." Several notable Jews became prominent scholars after their Christian conversion. But numerical gains were insignificant. In the 1830's several Americans undertook work in Palestine, but neither they nor the Church of Scotland achieved much. Some German Lutherans and English evangelicals made sporadic attempts in Jewish circles at home. The modern world has seen little restoration of a Christian movement among the Jews.

Almost equally unsuccessful were efforts among the Moslems who shared the lands of Christianity's birth. Opposition was more formal and rigid. A century of effort in the arid lands of North Africa tallied little. What successes there were belonged largely to the Archbishop of Carthage, Lavigerie (—1892), whose "White Fathers" in Moslem-type garb made serious efforts.

ROMAN CATHOLIC NATIONS

Lands of past nominal attachment to Roman Catholicism presented a special' problem. The attachment was often formal and undeveloped, yet Protestants were unwelcome and often harassed. Areas where Roman Catholicism was far below standard, where its practices seldom elevated people above the ignorance and superstition they had known, were virtually unchanged. Nearly every land in Central and South America belonged in this category in the nineteenth century except for British and Dutch Guiana and later the Canal Zone. Protestants entered Mexico at mid-century. A Miss Rankin was the first Protestant missionary; she obtained aid from nondenominational organizations. Converts from Catholicism aided the cause further, and several denominations from the United States entered the field. Some German Moravians worked in Nicaragua around 1849. From the Protestant viewpoint vital Christianity established a minimal hold.

Argentina and Brazil dominated Latin America; they had been Christianized by Iberians in the sixteenth century. Protestant influence began when Robert Reid Kelley opened British work in Brazil in 1855. American Methodists settled there in 1867. James Thompson, a Baptist from Scotland, initiated work in several South American countries, including Argentina, around 1820; this met with Roman suppression. At mid-century Captain Allen Gardiner engaged in dramatic exploits around Argentinian shores. His party met privation and eventually starvation in their Patagonian extension. If the story were confined to Latin America, the new triumphs of the faiths in a semi-Christianized land would hardly have earned the name "The Great Century."

FRESH OPPORTUNITY

A different story entirely begins in the lands of fresh opportunity. To this day none of the lands of southeast Asia is predominantly Christian: Hindu, Moslem, Buddhist, Confucian, Taoist, Lamaistic, and tribal religions prevail, while Western communism makes its way threatening each. But in most of these countries Christianity made substantial inroads. India could serve for illustration. A Hindu and Moslem nation that developed under British rule, it is the home of 375,000,000 people. From 1757 to 1947 it was under the British; its culture felt the impact of the West more than did that of other Asiatic lands. The religious customs of caste, polygamy, child marriage; the amalgam of religions; poor social conditions—all these impressed those who came into contact with Indian life. The Danish-Halle Mission had done preliminary work there, but lasting effect came with the "Serampore Trio," Carey, Marshman, and Ward. Carey had attempted great things for God out of his own religious experience, first by writing and preaching in England, then by forming societies to support mission work, and finally by going into the field himself. He landed in Calcutta in 1793. With his colleagues he set out to learn the languages, to translate, to work for reformation of Indian law, and to gain converts until his death in India in 1834. He never returned home. Anglicanism soon became active. The East India Company discouraged missions, but its chaplains often broke barriers. Henry Martyn (—1812) is best known. He announced that he was ready to burn himself out for Christ. He did, by the age of thirty-one and after a life of achievement. Reginald Heber (—1826) was most famed among early Anglican bishops of India. British and American societies entered the field. Continentals continued their work through the Gossner Mission, the Basel Society, and others. Substantial Christian communities grew to form what are now mature "younger" churches, among them the Church of South India. Despite social difficulties and the problems of an awakening nation, efforts in India were in many respects the jewel in the crown of Christian achievement at the time.

Adoniram Judson (—1850), the Congregationalist who became a Baptist on the way to India, began the enduring work in Burma at great expense to his person. Despite the nobility of effort, this Buddhist land registered few Christian gains. Roman Catholicism predominated in Indo-China; Protestant societies recorded successes in Ceylon; Thailand has been particularly receptive to the Christian message. The islands of the South Pacific have in several cases been converted to Christianity. Roman Catholicism is prime in the Philippines, the Marianas, New Caledonia, and part of Polynesia. Protestantism holds sway also in Polynesia, the Hawaiian Islands, much of Melanesia and Micronesia and Indo-China. All of this occurs against a background of tribal religion (as in New Guinea) complicated by Moslem, Hindu, and occasionally Buddhist influences.

Anglican strongholds in Australia and New Zealand aided the work in the smaller islands. One of the most productive missions in this part of the world was that of continentals to the Bataks of Sumatra, where three quarters of a million people are Christians.

To Western eyes the "darkest" area was the mysterious Far East. Early traders and explorers beguiled and intrigued missionaries. None of these lands have become Christian and many have renewed their opposition. But for almost a century the door was open, and several nations registered visible gains for Christianity. Robert Morrison initiated the work of modern Protestantism in China in 1807. Frustrated by the East India Company, he entered Canton under United States protection. Gaining few converts, he succeeded in translating the Bible and opening other doors. The German Karl Gützlaff, a ubiquitous figure in the East, made inroads in China. Americans started missionary activity in 1829. Interdenominational societies became active, and Roman Catholicism marked new gains on older foundations.

The Christian endeavor met many reverses because of the vagaries of Chinese policies. The T'ai Ping rebellion at mid-century seriously damaged the cause. A novelty on the scene was James Hudson Taylor's (—1905) China Inland Mission, a daring venture that worked on faith, refused to go into debt, and by the 1890's had over a thousand workers in the field. One of the last setbacks before the Communist sweep was the Boxer rebellion of 1900, a reaction against "foreign" intrusion. Korean work was late and successful. American Presbyterians prospered most; since beginnings in the 1830's they could count within a half-century a church of 270,000 Christians. Korea has known awakenings and revivals of the Western type, and has developed its own rather rigorous ethos of prayer, sacrifice, and Christian observance. It has even produced missionaries to go to other countries.

Roman Catholicism had entered Japan in the time of Francis Xavier, but little trace of the Jesuit's work remained by the time the country was opened to the West in 1854. From 1859 the societies have been active there despite recurrent persecution. The first Japanese church was organized in 1872. After this time missionaries experienced greater freedom to open stations. The renascence of Buddhism and Shintoism as instruments of war and later the Second World War itself hampered the cause, but after the Second World War Japan would see a new beginning.

Africa, finally, presents the picture of Christian growth against the background, not of sophisticated philosophical and natural religions, but of primitive tribal cults. East Africa shares with the North a Moslem character, except for Coptic Ethiopia. Work in the Sudan, Eritrea, and the Somalilands has been largely unsuccessful under the sign of the crescent. Mingled with tribal religions in South Africa are several partly Roman Catholic nations, among them Mozambique and Angola, and even more with a partly Protestant character, notably the Union of South Africa, Southwest Africa, and Nyasaland. Both forms of Western Christianity are active in Northern and Southern Rhodesia and in Madagascar.

The Union of South Africa is most interesting from the viewpoint of this narrative. Protestant work there began with George Schmidt, who entered under Moravian sponsorship in 1737. He was soon banished. The most remembered pioneer was Robert Moffat (—1883), a Scot sent by the London Missionary Society, who experienced great success in transforming the lives of natives. David Livingstone (—1873) is the first name known to people when the word "missions" is casually introduced. He too pioneered in South Africa, following Moffat. A scholar and tireless worker, he was active at mid-century in fostering Christian work as an agent of the British government.

Central Africa also offers the mixed complexion of tribal and Moslem religion with vital influences by Roman Catholicism in French Equatorial Africa, the Belgian Congo; Kenya, Uganda, and Tanganyika are predominantly primitive in religion. For almost a half century the work of Albert Schweitzer (1875—) has drawn attention to French Equatorial Africa. Livingstone's name is associated with efforts in the Belgian Congo, Africa's heart. West Africa includes no nation of Protestant predominance, though Roman Catholics are well represented in the Azores and other island groups. Liberia and Nigeria show mixed Christian influences. For the rest, a Moslem overlay on paganism complicated Christian work. Africa, in the eyes of many, is still the continent of the future, also from the Christian viewpoint.

THE MISSIONARY IMPULSE

Another way to look at missions is not at their point of extension but of impulse. Eastern Orthodoxy had roughly the same boundaries at the end of the period as at the beginning. It recovered some lost ground in southeast Europe; it reached out somewhat into Japan and stirred in Korea and China. Orthodoxy's gains in the United States can be accounted for largely through migration, not through mission effort. An institute at Kazan was designed, in the latter part of the century, to provide initiative for educational and missionary efforts. For the most part, Orthodoxy had spent itself as an expansive force.

No remarks about Protestantism's novelty dare detract from Roman Catholicism's impressive achievement. It not only consolidated earlier gains and reshaped others, but it made inroads on every continent. As two centuries earlier it had found an outlet while besieged by insurgent Protestantism by going into all the world, so again it responded to defeats in western Europe by advancing elsewhere. But for inventiveness, adaptation to new opportunities, overcoming of obstacles, and dramatic suddenness, it was a "Protestant era."

What profited Roman Catholicism most in this period was that now it could begin to plumb the depths of its catholicity: what had long been an ideal now reappeared as reality. At the end of the development one of its sons could write:

> All peoples each with their special aptitudes, are her children and all bring their gifts into the sanctuary. The elasticity, freshness of mind and sense of form of the Roman combine with the penetration, profundity and inwardness of the German, and with the sobriety, discretion and good sense of the Anglo-Saxon. The piety and modesty of the Chinaman unite with the sublety and depth of the Indian, and with the practicality and initiative of the American. It is a unity in fulness, fulness in unity. . . . It is a great, supra-national tidal wave of faith in God and love of Christ, nourished and supported by the special powers of every individual nation and of every individual man, purified and inspired by the divine spirit of truth and love.[2]

"Great things for God" were accomplished by the Society for the Propagation of the Faith, which originated in Lyons, France, in 1822. The Leopold Association worked from Austria; in Bavaria it was the Ludwig-Missionsverein. Impulse came also from medical groups such as the society of St. Vincent de Paul. Women co-operated in the Franciscan Missionaries of Mary, while the German Society of the Divine Word, the English Society of Mill Hill, and the Belgian Congregation of the Immaculate Heart of Mary contributed notably through money, prayer, personnel and information.

One asset Romanism possessed was the firm papal grip on policy, control, and order. Coupled with this was a growing support on the part of the common people, who reflected their concern in financial endeavors for European foreign mission societies. It was handicapped by the papal tie with certain crowns, which made missionaries look like enemy agents in many colonies.

The nineteenth century, the century of Catholic losses and trials in all the Catholic countries of Europe is then, at the same time, the century in which the Faith has at last been carried to every part of the earth. Everywhere, now, it has at least made its appearance . . .[3]

Two illustrations of Protestant inventiveness in the century are the development of missionary societies and individual creativity. This creativity appears among "heroes" who have served some functions within Protestantism which the saints recall to Roman Catholics. Many societies found it necessary to bypass the official organizations of the churches on the continent and of the denominations in America. Larger institutions were often unable or unwilling to spread their concerns on a world-wide scale. The interdenominational agencies were usually the products of men of great vision who could rally others. It was not difficult to portray the horrors of paganism to a curious West and, later, to dramatize the heroic sacrifices of the men and women sent by the societies. With this background, financial support was relatively generous.

MISSIONARY SOCIETIES

William Carey's Baptist Missionary Society established precedent in 1792; the London Missionary Society was born in 1795. The following year saw the birth of the Scottish Missionary Society, and in 1799 the Church of England followed with the Church Missionary Society. Continental Protestantism repented for past neglect in the 1790's with the Netherlands Missionary Society, and soon the Basel, Berlin, and Rhenish Missionary Societies and groups from north Germany and Leipzig joined. The new denominations of the United States were not far outdistanced. During the early years of the new century, the American Board of Commissioners for Foreign Missions, the American Bible Society, the American Tract Society, the American Sunday School Union and several other mission agencies were born. Had missions depended upon the support of settled religious organizations, the missionary activity would no doubt have presented a less stirring story.

GREAT MISSIONARIES

The other aspect of creativity was in the heroic lives of the missionaries: even this brief record includes names like those of Carey, Moffat, Livingstone, Martyn, Gardiner, Morrison, and Judson. Most of these were men of common origins and uncommon evangelical experience which inspired them to attempt great things for God. The stories concerning their feats soon became stylized, and many of them grew beyond fact. The process resulted in their elevation toward saintly status. Few sermons of the times failed to include a missionary story. The field enriched Christian hymnody. Societies prepared great rallies to bring together Christians of various communions. In all these respects the mission fields engaged in healthy reciprocity with the home front.

The story of mission and expansion is not yet over. It has been blunted by Communist aggression, the revival of the world religions, the challenge of nationalist ideologies. Its original impulse is spent; its institutional forms are tiring. Apathy at the nerve-centers, selfishness in the prosperous nations have limited the work. The novelty is gone. Debris from past mistakes, for instance the shameful example of disunity on the mission field, must be cleared before new advance. Yet the shrinking of the globe and interactions of peoples make possible yet unforeseen new approaches toward the realization of the catholicity of the Christian faith. If the division is healed, if a theology of missions is developed, if Christians can extricate their proclamation from national and "way of life" ties which are offensive in a time of colonialism, this may not yet be the end of the missionary era which crested in "the Great Century."

THE UNITED STATES

It has seemed best for the sake of clarity to postpone the story of the American development and to provide isolated treatment; its expansion of the Christian message certainly belongs to the "great things attempted for God" in the nineteenth century. It is now necessary to fill a gap. No reader of these pages can fail to realize that Christianity in the United States and Canada has assumed significant proportions on the world Christian scene. In sheer activity and progress it ranks second to none in the past two centuries. Yet a reading of these same pages to this point would have told the reader little of how this came to pass. We have remarked on the early Spanish and French Catholic colonies; on the development of Anglicanism and Congregationalism on the eastern coast coupled with the admixture of religious forces in the middle colonies; on a Great Awakening of religion, and the significant achievement in the United States of separating church and state; on the absence of first-rate substantive theology. Between that point and the Christianity of modern America is a dramatic story in which words such as "expansion," "revival," and "frontier" loom large.

The drama enters because at least at two points religion in the United States narrowly missed taking a different cast than it did. The first: it could well have been Roman Catholic from the beginning, had not the seagoing fortunes of the Iberian powers been dissipated and had not Great Britain and northern European states risen to power in the American colonial period. The second: when the nation was born, Protestant Christianity had seriously ebbed in the United States. The "Great Awakening" was two score years past; it had not been great enough. The philosophy and circumstances which brought the states together were not Protestant Christian in orientation. They had learned from the Enlightenment, from rational latitudinarianism, and were imbued with a spirit of tolerant apathy which found theological and doctrinal distinctiveness irrelevant and partially obstructive to free life in a free society.

What changed these circumstances was the coincidence of the world-wide "Great Awakening" associated with the Pietist or Methodist movement of evangelicalism and the missionary fire that swept the world. When it was poised to advance, American Protestantism had assumed the "denominational" form. This was an exception to the European pattern of establishment with varying amounts and degrees of permissiveness for nonconformity and dissent. In America all the churches were "free," each independent and autonomous, and—soon—all disestablished from legal status. They grew out of certain confessions of faith or doctrinal positions, and rallied people by their program and their purpose. Most Old World religions were represented, though Judaism, Orthodoxy, and Catholicism were negligible forces around 1800. Theological lines were already eroding, and Americans divided themselves around two clusters. One was named "evangelical"—claiming that it held to what everyone shared in biblical teaching and Reformation thought. The other, called "non-evangelical" or "liberal," involved in particular the Unitarian and Universalist groups of New England which were being formed in this period. Evangelicals could unite on many causes: Congregationalists and Presbyterians in the Plan of Union of 1801, and most denominations in the great voluntary societies. They could divide on the slightest of pretexts. There seemed for a time to be a new denomination for every purpose.

WESTWARD MOVEMENT

This cluster of voluntary and independent "denominations" which made America unique was confronted with a unique two-fold task. First, they must build up religious energies in the settled parts of the countries; second, they must use these energies for Christianization of the opening western nine-tenths of the continent. The means for the first was revivalism, for the second missionary evangelism. Revivalism has come to be the characteristic pattern of religious response in America, where the quest for novelty permits the nation to pick up and drop movements with finesse and forgetfulness. This must be coupled with the religious assumption that men can do a great deal in furthering their own salvation (Arminianism characterized the century theologically) and with the understanding that "success" in religious life can be measured in external terms of statistics and progress. All of these forces came together in the "Second Great Awakening" at the turn of the nineteenth century.

In its eastern form this was a theological and educational reply to the inroads of rationalism and latitudinarianism. Timothy Dwight (—1817) at Yale and a host of others with him re-won a new generation to the neo-Calvinist glories of New England. Meanwhile the Lyman Beechers and their cohorts began to move west, keeping records of conversions and commitments. The "camp meeting" of revival and devotion was born in Kentucky around 1801. The circuit rider or nomadic evangelist was the characteristic religious leader. Old-line denominations like Episcopalianism and Congregationalism lost out to the more aggressive, activistic, and time-tempering Methodist and Baptist movements. At every crossroads of the west, new churches challenged the skies with their towers and beckoned the westward migrants. The voluntary associations of like-minded people who shared interest in evangelizing supported the moves.

So pervasive was this influence that by the middle of the nineteenth century America seemed well on its way to becoming a Protestant empire—who could refute the prophets who saw this to be so? A few minor problems remained: slavery, infidelity, rum and—oh, yes, the beginnings of Romanism. For at mid-century, after the abortive European revolts of 1830 and 1848 and after various droughts and depressions, migrants from the lower classes on the continent, men of "low habits and ideas, retaining supreme allegiance to a foreign pontiff" (according to one Protestant historian of the 1880's), began to arrive. Assertive but isolationistic Lutheran and Reformed p ies complicated the evangelical cause. Out of the "boil er" of revivals a flurry of esoteric "sects" emerged, which bewildered main-stream Protestantism: the Mormons, the Millerites, the Spiritualists. All were uncontainable by traditional Protestant canons. Despite this, Protestant religion and national culture tended to fuse and form the "national religion" of the nineteenth century.

Always there was the movement west, across seemingly limitless space. Men could practice the religion they chose, and when undesirable neighbors moved in there was always space: America did not yet realize the implications of its incipient pluralism. It could still be grasped virtually as a "whole," and that whole looked consistently Protestant. This Protestantism retained its sense of manifest destiny to convert the land and to spread scriptural holiness and works of social amelioration. Only after the frontier had filled and the cities were alienated did American Protestants begin to realize that their "Great Century" had ended and they would need to learn to live with other religions.

Meanwhile American Catholicism grew to amazing proportions as the immigrants came. They adapted well to the unfamiliar pattern of church and state in separation; nowhere in the modern world did Catholicism find a climate so congenial as in America. At the end of the period, 1908, the church was removed from the authority of the Congregation for the Propagation of the Faith to be a national body in its own right. It had weathered anti-popery attacks by Protestants, leakage of disaffected immigrants and their children, attempts by lay movements to gain control, and nationalistic battles within its fold, to spread across the land by the beginning of the new century.

MATURATION

After the first great immigrations, the divisive Civil War, and the bloated period of the Gilded Age, American Christianity was maturing. As the first great spurt of world missions was ending, American Christianity flexed its muscles, conscious of its numerical successes and its manner of informing all of culture. It saw a world to win and a manifest destiny to win it. As new denominations were developed in America, each took new responsibilities for the Church's world-wide mission. Optimism, a belief in progress, a faith in the future: these sheltered Americans from the reality of new international problems and a more complex life characterized by social discontent and religious pluralism. But if they sheltered, they also inspired. When at the end of the century men spoke of "evangelizing the world in this generation," they did so without tongue in cheek. All the facts seemed to be on their side.

But if we wish to tiptoe to the edge of the twentieth century and its peculiar problems, we can summarize the legacy of a century of expansion also in negative terms. The Christian Church was sorely divided; if this was true in the torn vineyard of post-Reformation Europe, it was never fully realized until America had been settled by competing immigrations and varying religions and until different missionary movements met each other on the field. Each presented to a bewildered world a picture of a universal faith which was one. Each claimed the truth. Each was divided from the other. Few had had time to notice yet that no sin of the Church could have been so offensive to the potential convert as the thicket of variant growths that were not simply diverse but disparate.

America is the field for observation, in its several waves. The first wave of immigration included Congregational, Presbyterian, Episcopal, Reformed, Quaker, Baptist, Roman Catholic, Swedish Lutheran, Mennonite, Moravian, Schwenkfeldian, and Methodist. The later immigration brought representatives of the largest Protestant denomination, Lutheranism, from Germany, Sweden, Norway, Denmark, Austria-Hungary, Latvia, Finland. The panoply of Orthodoxy was unfolded by Greek, Russian, Serbian, Syrian. Baptists, Methodists, Presbyterians divided. The Disciples of Christ, the Church of Christ, the Churches of God, and Christian Science were born.

At the end of the century (about 1890) there were in the larger families: of Baptists, 3,700,000 Americans; the Methodists counted, 4,500,000; the Presbyterians, 1,300,-000; the Disciples, 700,000; the Episcopalians more than

500,000. Each was growing and prospering, each was attempting great things for God, expecting great things from Him.

Around the world, men could confess with the centuries: "I believe in one . . . *catholic* or universal Church." Now there was plausibility to the belief. But they, the thoughtful ones, blanched as they also confessed, "I believe in *one* . . . Church." The Christian movement, an expression of faith and life in one Body of Christ, seemed to be denying its essential nature. At the end of the nineteenth century it appeared to many that the Christian Church was on the verge of gaining the whole world—and losing its own life. Perplexity over this problem has preoccupied most of the churches in the twentieth century.

16

THE GREAT NEW FACT
OF OUR ERA

Bishop Azariah of Dornakal, India, told the Edinburgh
Conference of 1937 on the Church's Witness to the World
Today of an incident which occurred in 1935. Dr. Ambedkar, leader of the untouchables in India, had denounced
the caste system. He had called upon his sixty million
fellow untouchables to renounce Hinduism with him, to
find another religion. Many of them were drawn to accept
Jesus Christ as the Way, the Truth, and the Life, but "when
Christianity is mentioned, they remind me of the many
divisions within the Christian Church. We are united in
Hinduism, say they, and we shall become divided in Christianity." And Bishop Azariah could only confess—"I had
no answer to give." The Bishop ended his speech moments
later: "We want you to take us seriously when we say that
the problem of union is one of life and death with us." [1]

The encounter was not an incident so much as a parable. The Bishop's plea illustrates the reason why among
the world's thoughtful Christians the centrifugal direction
of the faith in the nineteenth century has been reversed:
now it is centripetal. When these Christians looked for
signs that the Holy Spirit of God still brooded over their
bent world and their torn Church, they usually pointed to

the new worldwide stirring and striving for unity of the faith. The effects were the more remarkable because the century itself was a time of disruption, estrangement, alienation, and fear.

THE ECUMENICAL MOVEMENT

There are two ways to look at the historical entity which has now been baptized "the Ecumenical Movement." One can look with Archbishop William Temple (—1944) of Canterbury at its reality and summarize the age: the "world-wide Christian fellowship, this Ecumenical Movement as it has been called, [is] the great new fact of our era." It was great, for it involved men in almost every communion—separated for centuries—in every land. It was new, for not since the sixteenth century had Christianity shown such a conscience for its division. It was a fact, for men not only talked; they acted. This viewpoint grows out of the historical sense of Christian intention and the contemporary reality (with Bishop Azariah): this is a matter of life and death. Men will tolerate a schism within a movement; they may even relish the option of several varieties. But when Christianity overarches a world with a gospel which makes the claim that it unites even as it frees, yet hundreds of competing and often exclusivistic versions present themselves: then men will see that either Christianity is a lie, or its professors are faithless.

The other way to see the movement is to drop the historical sense and predetermine theological patterns for reunion which will absolutely frustrate all efforts at manifesting Christian unity. With this *a priori* one can formulate tests for the ecumenical movement which no other Christian movement could pass, were it not enhanced by the glow of historic distance. The pristine purity of the early Church, the golden glow of the Middle Ages, the brightness of the Reformation's evangelical thrust: each of these was in its day as stained by ambition, as confused in motivation, as faltering in direction, as unlovely and tired in some of its institutional forms as is the Ecumenical Movement of today. To obtain this perspective there is no substitute for the study of Christian history.

One: this was the image of the Church presented at the beginning of this narrative. One body, one Spirit, one Lord, one faith, one baptism, one God and Father of us all; "that they may all be one."

Many: the process had gone as far as it could go. The Church at the end of its Great Century was in need of pivot and reform as much as the Church had been at the end of its fifteenth century of night. Christianity was confused by a crisscross of migrations and often by competitive missionary endeavors; disunity had been inevitable or accidental. Ethnic, sociological, and geographical elements were non-theological factors too patent to all. Somehow solving these has seemed as knotty a problem as going to the heart of the quest, to have separated churches find each other by first finding themselves in Jesus Christ.

The reconcilers have had (and will have) no easy time of it; they have only begun. One has the chilly feeling that the first enthusiasm is over. But already, confirming Temple's acclamation, it is possible to see that the motif of the new age is reconciliation in the midst of turmoil and estrangement. In the long perspective of the ages this century, it is already clear, will be characterized by the ecumenical efforts just as the first was known for the act of founding, the twelfth for synthesis, the sixteenth for reform, the nineteenth for expansion. A few churches stood outside the new stream. They paid a high price for the defense of a truth as they saw it: they had to calculate the cost, to know that they were assuming the burden of proof, were isolating themselves from a massive historical attempt at regaining a lost dimension of the faith. To all the world, and to the rest of the Church, in the resulting breakdown of communications, they appeared as spoilsports, enemies within the camp.

Behind the movements that we shall survey (unfortunately for the idealist, these movements must take institutional form; they can be examined by historians only as finite, relative, broken entities) was the common assumption that the effort for reunion could not create fellowship; it could only recognize it. When one recognized that Jesus Christ was somehow formed in another person or church body, he must somehow put that recognition into action. Indeed, there were still sentimentalists, good fellows who would find "union at any price" in the dying line of "Erasmianism." Most of their colleagues had learned of the difficulties painfully and early (the Movement is but fifty years young, a mere moment in a history which saw less effort at reunion from the time of the Photian schism through a millennium of division than it has seen in those fifty years); the men of the ecumenical spirit have learned that the reunitive goal is marked by the highest denominator: oneness in Christ. Consequently, the Movement has begun to produce a theological flow and a haste to regain depths in biblical research.

The great new fact of our era and of what may prove to be, as theologian Leonard Hodgson has suggested, the beginning of a really new period in Christian history, will dominate these pages for the way it permits us to ask again the basic meaning of the story begun with Jesus, Paul, the Fourth Gospel, and the early Church after Pentecost. After a brief description of the organizational realities that grew out of the idea of reunion, it will be possible to survey several developments in the constituent communions of the world Church today.

There are those who have criticized the term "ecumenical" as being a vogue word, hard to communicate in the newspapers. Perhaps for the new fact we need a new term which reflects, in W. A. Visser 't Hooft's words: "that spiritual traffic between the Churches which draws them out of their isolation and into a fellowship of conversation, mutual enrichment, common witness, and common action" [2] Visser 't Hooft has listed seven historic meanings for the term from its reference to the whole inhabited world, to the whole of empire, to the whole of the Church; then "ecumenical" was redefined to include that which has universal ecclesiastical validity; then it referred to the missionary outreach of the Church. Now it pertains to the relations between churches or confessions, or to the consciousness of belonging to the world-wide Christian fellowship and a desire for unity with other churches.[3] As a movement it had roots in the Evangelical Alliance of the nineteenth century and in that era's interdenominational co-operative organizations. But it was near the end of the century before organizational fruition that would endure appeared.

THE CHARACTER OF THE MOVEMENT

The emphases of this first fruition reveal a great deal about the character of the Movement. First, it was young. It stirred the hearts of men who could still dream dreams, even so wild as this: to evangelize the world in their generation. This youthful spirit is evidenced in the fact that the first great contributing organizations were student groups. With origins around 1886, and guided by the American John R. Mott, the Student Christian Movement set a pace for enthusiasm for the world mission on the part of young men. Out of the Young Men's Christian Association of the nineteenth century came the World Student Christian Federation in 1895. These two, with the Student Volunteer Movement, paved the way for theological conversation and missionary enthusiasm; they were the training grounds for the men who matured to lead in reunion, men like Mott, Temple, Visser 't Hooft, whom we have already met.

As it attracted younger men, so the Movement drew younger churches. The missionary character of the organizations was solidified in conferences at the turn of the century, culminating in a great meeting on missions at Edinburgh in 1910. Mission fields came to be recognized as "younger churches" on their own. Out of the conference grew the International Missionary Conference. Jealous of their identity yet unitive in spirit, participating churches here, as in parallel organizations, resisted any idea of a super-church. They preserved their distinctive character, but they wanted to converse and work in a way to remove the scandal which offended most on the faith's frontiers.

In 1928 the International Missionary Conference met at Jerusalem and in 1938 at Madras. Whoever reads the resultant documents today will see them as milestones in the theology of missions.

Third, the early efforts were activistic. Life and Work emphases preceded those of Faith and Order. But not by much; it was natural that the activism and optimism of the nineteenth century should carry over into the twentieth. Soon most participants felt the need for asking theological questions. Life and Work (Stockholm, 1925, and Oxford, 1937) has had an easier time of it—let each interpret as he will—but the Movement began to produce men also concerned with Faith and Order (Lausanne, 1927, and Edinburgh, 1937). Social questions and pronouncements resulting from Stockholm and Oxford inspired reform in many parts of the world; statements on faith at Lausanne and Edinburgh awakened scholarly activity.

THE WORLD COUNCIL

All the elements were on the point of consummating union when the noises of war in thunderous staccato drowned out the tentative legatos of the reconcilers. The universal catastrophe was a judgment upon the churches, and its horror alarmed them to new urgency. It seems fantastic in the perspective of centuries that only three years after cessation of hostilities men who had been thrust into opposing battle lines could face each other in assemblies to be reunited in faith. That is what did happen in Amsterdam, Holland, in 1948, when most of the persistent unitive forces joined in the new World Council of Churches:

> Here at Amsterdam we have committed ourselves afresh to Him, and have covenanted with one another in constituting this World Council of Churches. We intend to stay together.

They succeeded this affirmation which breathed the spirit of Life and Work with a confession that recalled Faith and Order; it was acceptance of "our Lord Jesus Christ as God and Saviour" that had brought them there, not to conclude but to begin reaching out to each other. This was a penitent assembly, anguished by past failures, aware of present difficulties of basic communication. But they stayed and worked and talked. Men from East and West, slavery and freedom, high Orthodoxy and broad evangelicalism; men who would find no basis for conversation in personal, national, or ideological interest, found a depth of religious communion. Six years later the World Council, which had its headquarters in Geneva, Switzerland, moved on from its Amsterdam theme, "Man's Disorder and God's Design," to the logical next step at Evanston, Illinois: "Christ, the Hope of the World." The new era had begun with its first faltering step. A stumbling-block remained: among the world-wide church bodies unrepresented were the great Russian Orthodox Church and Roman Catholicism.

REUNION OF CHURCHES

A related phenomenon, entirely different organizationally yet motivated by the same shame and the same creative spirit, was the achievement of reunions among separated churches. The younger churches set the example, moving from most brief but greatest separation toward greater unity. Was it not remarkable for five denominations to gather into a Church of Christ in China in 1927, in the midst of national unrest? Methodists, Presbyterians, and Congregationalists predominated: all confessed faith in Christ as Redeemer, in His Kingdom, in the Apostles' Creed. The same three denominations were forced to form the Church of Christ in Japan just before the great War; they also took part in forming the United Church of Christ in the Philippines in 1948, just after the War.

More significant was the formation of the Church of South India in 1947. It united an earlier merger of Congregational, Reformed, and Presbyterian churches with Methodists and Anglicans. Difficulties persisted in connection with Anglican insistence on the historic episcopate as a mark of the Church. Despite this, a nascent harmony was developing at the strategic moment when India was largely closed to missions from the West. North India was following in a similar pattern, attempting to void the stalemate of episcopacy.

These mergers in the younger churches were matched by efforts in the young Christian mission to North America. In 1925 the United Church of Canada was formed and acclaimed by thousands of tongues in a great hall that rang to Wesley's words, "Oh, for a Thousand Tongues to Sing." Methodists predominated in the union, which also included a substantial number of Presbyterians and some Congregationalists.

Those who live in the United States, which is the very paradigm of pluralism, with good cause are impatient. Yet the distance of a half century reveals an impressive record. Northern Baptists and Free Baptists merged in 1911. Several Lutheran bodies united in 1917 as the United Lutheran Church in America. Two Norwegian Lutheran groups seconded the motion at the same time. Northern Presbyterianism welcomed the Welsh Calvinistic Methodists in 1920. 1922: the Evangelical Church was born of two others. 1924: the Reformed Church in the United States absorbed the Hungarian Reformed Church. 1930: three Lutheran bodies became one American Lutheran Church. The Christian Church united with Congregationalism in 1931. In 1934 the Evangelical and Reformed Church was formed; 1939 saw three Methodist groups reunited. 1946 was the year of merger of the Evangelical Church and the United Brethren Church. In 1957 the Congregational Christian Churches and the Evangelical and Reformed Church united. 1958 saw the consummation of United Presbyterian and the Presbyterian Church U.S.A. as one body. Many other mergers were in sight.

It is impossible to predict where the Ecumenical Movement will go. Can it sustain itself as its institutions harden? Will other mergers occur? Most of those who worked for both refused to predict the forms that response would take: they spoke only of the imperative, to seek each other until they find each other in Christian unity. Sometimes confessional understanding growing out of negotiations forced earnest men to recognize that they had been farther apart than they had known. Sometimes familiarity bred contempt in world organizations. The way was inevitably slow. The chief reason was the passing of sentimentality. The Orthodox in the World Council made no secret of it that they did not regard other participants as churches in the full sense. They were there on the assumption that they had the full truth and were there to teach but not to learn. But they were there.

Anglicans insist tenaciously on apostolic succession and the historic episcopate as marks of the Church. It is to the credit of Anglicanism that while it would be the bridge church, it has the courage to cling to a distinction which is offensive to others because it believes it to be true. Lutherans, so deeply involved in the Movement, have made it clear that they did not come to compromise basic truth; they could not deny their commitment. But each group was concerned that in the "one body"

> something has gone wrong. The organism has somehow failed to function as one body. It has come to be divided into countless little bits of life, each person trying to be a quite independent cell, a self-sufficient atom, dancing on a pattern of its own, instead of joining in the great communal game of universal love. Each person makes himself the centre of his universe, caring little for the fellowship of the whole, but seeing things from his selfish point of view; becoming his own God, and worshipping himself.[4]

They grew tired of singing, and lying while they sang:

> *We are not divided, All one body we,*
> *One in hope and doctrine, One in charity.*

Of course, it would have been a mistake of judgment for the churches to expect too much of an instrument so frail as the young Ecumenical movement. There were other problems, other discontents; there were hopes which reunitive solutions did not fulfill. To sketch some of the scope of this, we shall conclude with a brief survey of the life and work of some Christian churches in the twentieth century.

ORTHODOXY

The Orthodox churches were divided in the twentieth century by their association with divisive political forces. All were invited to participate in the World Council of Churches, also for what they could contribute:

> The Eastern Churches have maintained a sense of the objective reality and the cosmic dimensions of the drama of salvation which the Western Churches need to recapture. They are today going through a crisis which may well prove a crisis into life and in which they must be able to count on the fraternal sympathy and help of their sister-Churches of other confessions,

explained W. A. Visser 't Hooft concerning their invitation. But the largest of the Eastern churches, the Russian, declined to participate from behind its curtain. The Communist hammer pounded at the wall of the church; its sickle cut at the tender shoots of faith nurtured within. Since the Revolution of 1917 the church has been beleaguered, finding its freedom and bondage tied to the caprice of national policy at each moment. The Soviet "five-year plans" after 1928 usually meant more and more state control of family life, education, public assembly, and religion. Only when it suited Soviet powers to woo the West during the Second World War did policy slacken, to be hardened again later.

So the church of the East, which likes to think of itself as the sole guardian of the whole Christian truth, sees its unity torn by contests between patriarchates, by Russian *versus* non-Russian national bodies, by pro- *versus* anti-Communists, by varying degrees of definition in distinction from the Western churches. Little constructive theology has appeared. One exception was Sergis Bulgakov (—1944), a contributor to the Ecumenical Movement. Another was that free spirit Nicolas Berdyaev (—1948). Inspired by central Christian affirmations, informed by existentialism, imbued with mystic fervor, intrigued with the questions of creativity, slavery, freedom, and the spirit of man and God, Berdyaev stirred many to re-explore Eastern values:

The Orthodox Church, like the Orthodox soul, is just the opposite of Gothic. Orthodoxy is neither cold nor passionate. Orthodoxy is warm, sometimes even hot . . . Christ comes down into the Orthodox Church and the Orthodox soul and gives them warmth.[5]

ROMAN CATHOLICISM

Ironically, the church which most stressed its catholicity and which was most dramatic in the way it offered a path to unity became a symbol to the twentieth century for the way it effectively blocked this path. The Roman Catholic Church suggested that all would be so easy if all would accept the papacy as a starting-point. This is the last thing the "separated brethren" would be willing to do. Pius XII (—1958), in line with his predecessors, continued the absolutistic claims for his office in encyclicals of 1943 and 1950. If he, the Vicar, is removed, "the visible bonds of unity [are] broken, the mystical Body of the Redeemer is . . . obscured and disfigured." No official participation in the Ecumenical Movement is permitted to Roman Catholics. At present the best hopes are minimal; they lie in irenic conversation. We might best characterize as "benevolent aloofness" the attitude of Rome in its un-Catholic stance.

So Roman Catholicism has lived its own life in the twentieth century, buffeted as never before in lands of Communist domination, leading an ambiguous existence in the cloudlands of concordats with totalitarianism, thriving in the American free climate. In Germany theologians like Karl Adam and representatives of the liturgical movement have yearned for restoration of the visible portrayal of the *Una Sancta*. Many Protestants have been warmed by the evangelical character of worship, as at Maria Laach Abbey, and in the mystery theology of Dom Odo Casel. In the United States many unofficial exchanges between Catholic and non-Catholic have shown the possibilities of dialogue.

But the most charitable historical judgment must lay the blame for further division at the papal door, for the pontifical widening of past breaches. It would be difficult to picture a more offense-giving wedge than the proclamation of papal infallibility in 1870. But to the Protestant world the innovations regarding the elevation of the Blessed Virgin Mary to co-mediatricial status with her son has been a scandal that cuts at the heart of the faith. This elevation reached its escalatorial peak in the Dogma of the Assumption, first proclaimed in the Marian Year of 1950. To non-Roman Catholics this act appeared to be a gesture of papal contempt.

External forces which besieged all of Christendom were most felt in this largest, most inclusive body, particularly because of its authority, solidarity, and comprehensiveness. The acids of modernity and the frustration of attempts to do great things for God forced many to yearn for medieval times when Catholicism held sway. This "cosmic nostalgia" was a clear misreading of history. Despite the setbacks, Roman Catholicism had never before known an hour such as the present. The enhancement and absolutization of the papal office provided an iron grip that made the church manageable, more efficient than "democratic" Protestantism. Pius XI (—1939) retreated on many temporal fronts. But his learning, piety, and uncanny ability to seek new fronts and to appear graceful in retreat made his holding operation effective until the secretary, Pius XII (—1958), assumed office. His self-chosen image as man of peace, his administrative abilities, and his vision should mark him among the remembered modern popes.

The central problems faced by the two popes was the denial of temporal claims by European totalitarians. This was doubly embarrassing in that almost without fail the dictators themselves had come out of Roman Catholic backgrounds: Franco, Tito, Hitler, Mussolini, Pétain, Dollfuss, Salazar, and in the western hemisphere, Perón. Most of these men remembered how to deal with mother church and to advance themselves through the proper rhythm of concordats, broken agreements, illusory encouragements and new suppression. Their example has confused the record of progressive Catholic Center parties in present-day Europe.

In Italy Pius XI's early approach to Fascism is repulsive to democratic men. The Ethiopian aggression had his blessing as a holy war; he excused much in Mussolini's rise to power. In the Lateran Pacts of 1929 he thought he had gained, and was giving Italy back to God when the Vatican was assigned minute statehood. The gain was illusory; soon Pius knew he had made a bad bargain. By the time Hitler rose to power he was more wary. The agreements with Nazism were worth little more than their paper and ink. In 1937 the papacy spoke out with tearful rage against Hitlerism. The pontifical coddling of Dollfuss in Austria and the comfortable liaisons with Dictators Franco in Spain and Salazar in Portugal have made the papacy a dubious symbol for the rallying of non-Roman Catholics in the West.

The redeeming feature of each concordat in the West's eyes is the fact that the alternative in each case would seem to have been Communism. From the first the church recognized in Communism an ultimate religious threat. In eastern Europe the sickle has cut at Catholicism. In Poland, Hungary and Yugoslavia men of God in the twentieth century have been martyred anew. In the West informed by Protestant history, Catholicism has surged forward. Its impressive gains in England are but shadows of its glories on many mission fields and in the United States. The resurgence of a strong eucharistic piety and a theological reconstruction under men like Jacques Maritain (1882–), Etienne Gilson (1884–), and other neo-Thomists, as well as the biblical theology of Henri de Lubac and Jean Danielou, have made it attractive. The new encouragement shown artists, architects, and writers; the adoption of modern means of communication; concessions to modernity—all these have attracted. A stream of noted converts has appealed to many. In the United States an extensive system of parochial schools and charitable institutions has given it strength and a center for outreach. Gone forever is the old information of the American ethos by Protestantism: now pluralism, with a heavy admixture of Catholicism, is doing the informing.

The two knottiest problems presented twentieth-century Catholicism in America are in the field of education and in church-state relations. Competing forces in the United

States are trying to win the Catholic and national ears. One sees acceptance of separated church and state and life in pluralistic society as abnormal and temporary; the other would encourage development in later Romanism of a democratic philosophy. American Catholicism, as its claims expand, has also had to begin to fight off united fronts of opposition in the form of "Protestants and Other Americans" who collaborate in negation. But for all its gains Roman Catholicism is haunted by its failure on the first front: to become a symbol of reunion; instead it is the greatest stumbling-block to reunion. In such an hour some Catholic scholars make defense of the impasse by what looks like rationalization to many ecumenicians. Thus Gustave Weigel, S.J., summarizing the rise of secularism, naturalism, and (sometimes) Catholicism, has written:

> The alarm occasioned by these facts has driven the Protestants to plug up anxiously the leaks through which their strength is flowing away. The biggest leak was the splintered multiplicity of churches. The reduction of this multiplicity to some amorphous kind of unity is the World Council. Hence to many a Catholic the World Council is nothing more than "Protestantism, Inc.," in spite of the presence of some Orthodox churches and the absence of the fundamentalists.[6]

All this would be true except for its misreading of Protestant motives and except for the fact that from the first Roman Catholics have been invited to responsible participation. Recently Pope John XXIII has planned his own invitations: he has announced an ecumenical council with the Eastern Orthodox churches particularly in mind.

PROTESTANTISM

So for the present the reunitive task falls to the section of world Christendom least obviously equipped to achieve it, Protestantism. Yet despite its inner divisions the Protestant movement still retains vitality. The heart of the Ecumenical Movement is made up in the main of a half dozen world-wide communions. The largest, the Lutheran, numbers around 65,000,000; three families of similar size, of about 40,000,000 members each, are the Anglicans, the Reformed and Presbyterian, and the Baptist. Not much smaller is world Methodism, while Congregationalism numbers perhaps 5,000,000: on this scale statistical niceties mean little, and anti-ecumenical exceptions in each family are dispersed toward insignificance.

Most of these communions, particularly the Lutherans, are active in both the free world and behind the curtains which cover oppression; most of them have representative churches in Europe, America, and in the lands of "younger" churches.

The oldest, largest, and in the geographical sense most catholic Protestant body, Lutheranism, has suffered most in times of catastrophe and suppression. Sorely tried in its German stronghold by the First World War and post-war disillusion, it was handicapped by a long tradition of accepted paternalism on the part of the state. Never working out a detailed approach to church-state relations, it held largely to a doctrine of acquiescence, always uncertain when the moment would come when one must forget penultimates for the superior: "We ought to obey God rather than men." Much of Lutheranism in Germany was therefore quiescent in the rise of Hitler. The extreme element rallied around the Nazi puppet, Reichsbischof Mueller. Some theologians tragically sold themselves to the German Christian Movement.

The other extreme rallied radically with Reformed theologians and churchmen in the Barmen Declaration of 1934. The movement produced an uncommon number of martyrs; most of the survivors of terror have seen the urgency for Christian solidarity and reunion. After the war Germany was divided but Lutheranism was not, emerging in a potent world Federation which was nurtured by common work and shared theological endeavor. Behind the Iron Curtain in Hungary and Poland, Lutheranism remains a symbol of resistance to Communism.

Anglicanism continued in a congenial climate in its birthland. Like Lutheranism, it was most equipped by its catholicity and virtual universality to lead in ecumenical participation. Lutheranism tempered its call by its insistence on theological particularity; Anglicanism was limited by its insistence on the historic episcopacy as an essential of the Church. But the Anglican view of succession opened it in another direction: through it was a more acceptable door to Orthodoxy. Anglicanism has compensated for its loss of popular appeal in England by vitality in social thought, in liturgical reform, and in literary appeal. Its participation in church union movements in India shows where its heart is.

Reformed churches on the continent were most notable for their theological contributions. The father of contemporary theology, the man who reversed the century-long theological trends associated with Schleiermacher and Ritschl, was Karl Barth, who around 1918 began to ring a bell for "The Theology of the Word," or crisis thought. The Reformed movement has suggested its strength by its prosperity in America and on mission fields. Methodists, Presbyterians, and Congregationalists have been central in forming several national United Churches.

Much of the overcoming of division in American life has happened through the efforts of Calvinist and Arminian or Reformed and Wesleyan bodies. In this most pluralistic nation, significant strides have been made, as through the Federal Council of Churches (1908) and its successor, the National Council of Churches (1950), toward cooperative activity and to "express the fellowship and catholic unity of the Christian Church," necessarily at this point on grounds of minimal doctrinal agreement and maximal cooperative activity.

The relative unity-in-diversity which marked American evangelism in much of the nineteenth century was shattered as an aftereffect of adaptation or resistance to Darwinism, biblical criticism, and other aspects of modern thought. This reached its climax in the controversy between Fundamentalism and Modernism during the 'teens and twenties of the century. The uncreative impasse was broken by a theological revival which made the questions of both sides largely irrelevant. Modernism has largely dissipated itself. Recurrent revivals of Fundamentalism have had a hollow sound, and appear to be more "politically partisan" in denominational life than are they basic approaches to re-affirmation of the churches' apostolicity. One legacy of the old controversy is this: differences in theology are often greater within each denomination than between denominations. This complicates the reunitive picture, and makes old divisions even less defensible.

American Protestantism at mid-century was haunted by its need to adapt to realized pluralism and to participate more profoundly in the theological quest; its assets were tremendous statistical successes and considerable popular appeal. The old activism and piety remained as strengths.

In Asia, Africa, and elsewhere the new watchword that has complicated efforts at Christian reunion is nationalism and its converse, anti-colonialism. Dissident elements have deprecated the Christian message by pointing to its frequent ties to imperialist and exploiting forces in the nineteenth century. Renascent world religions have seized upon this; combining with anti-Christian political ideologies, they have ushered in a new era for the younger churches who have been forced to ask for patience on the part of the Western establishments. It is difficult to picture what future Christianity will have in Communist China; it is impossible to superimpose a blueprint for Japan, India, Africa. But the Christian flock is still being gathered; the Word is preached, the sacraments are offered. This is all the Church has ever needed to have an even chance.

THEOLOGICAL RENEWAL

Before wrapping up the package of the twentieth century one other element must be included by mention. Partly as an outgrowth and partly as a constitutive factor of the Ecumenical Movement, and partly coincident with its rise, has come a profound theological recovery that bids fair to make this the most theologically conscious era since the Reformation. World problems grew so great that they could be treated only in soul-size; catastrophe and disillusion and anxiety helped men frame questions that glib and optimistic solutions would never satisfy. The transcendent dimension alone seemed to offer hope. The old theological liberalism and negative historical criticism had reached a dead end. Fundamentalist reactions to them were hopeless. Beginning in Switzerland around the end of the First World War, and spreading around the world, there has gone a word of judgment upon the churches, even in their act of reuniting, for their shallowness, weakness, and denial of divine truth. Men like Karl Barth and Emil Brunner and Rudolf Bultmann, Reinhold Niebuhr and Paul Tillich, William Temple and Anders Nygren—these and others called attention to the divine interruption of history in Jesus Christ. The only conceivable answers seemed to be biblical; the only language in which reuniting churches could make themselves understood was biblical. A fine flowering of scriptural study associated with names like C. H. Dodd and Edwyn Hoskyns, Vincent Taylor and Austin Farrer, Joachim Jeremias and Ernst Kaesemann, had new appeal. Americans, no longer content with their activist tradition, began to listen to the Niebuhrs and their fellow-prophets. A church-theology developed to balance the individualist preoccupations of existentialism. The report of a division at the North American Conference on Faith and Order at Oberlin, Ohio, 1957, summarized the fruit of the biblical movement:

> The emergence of biblical theology is one of the exciting developments of our time. As we acknowledge in common the authority and constraint of the Word of God we are brought into a new measure of agreement one with another.[7]

"Biblical theology" as such solves little: the question is what kind? Here immediate problems presented themselves. Literalists took courage that men were again returning to the code-book. Demythologizers stripped away much of the Scripture in order to make an appeal to modern man, often losing the man along the way. Between them a renewed witness to God's activity and his purpose in history as revealed in the Scriptures seemed to hold the field.

THE END—AND THE BEGINNING

These earliest gropings toward reunion and recovery were signs that the Christian movement was not yet ready to relax the finger-grip which holds it to the cliffside of continued existence. The Kingdom of God as it is active in the Christian movement faced great tests in the modern era; secularization, ideological challenge, a world yet unwon, its own divisiveness and division; these are the questions that have concerned us here. Even a fool would not be so absurd as to predict the future. In its loyalty to the notes of the Church and through them to the call of its Lord, the Christian thrust will be consistent in affirming the unity, holiness, apostolicity, and catholicity of the Church; its historians will always join the prophets in remarking on the disparity between these notes and the discordant sounds the Church actually emits.

The tests of the times remain; they are all potent. Out of their consistent center we can expect the churches to take the stance of W. H. Auden's *Double Man:*

> *Perched upon the sharp* arete
> *When, if we do not move, we fall . . .*
> *Yet movement is heretical,*
> *Since over its ironic rocks*
> *No route is truly orthodox.*

We come full circle in the short narrative. No, not full circle, for Christian history does not move in cycles: it marches toward an end. In that march are prophets, apostles, preachers, laymen, workers, priests, scholars, singers, servants: all stagger at the road and the rocks before them. They have received new life, according to their own affirmation, whenever they looked back at the cross of Jesus of Nazareth, the Christ. At their best they have been unwilling to relax whenever again they are haunted by the hint they recognize from his ancient prayer:

Ut omnes unum sint—that they may all be one!

REFERENCES AND CITATIONS

Chapter 1

1 Alfred Loisy, *L'Evangile et l'église* (1902), p. 11.
2 Daniel Jenkins, *The Strangeness of the Church* (New York: Doubleday & Company; 1955), p. 62.
3 Karl Barth, *The Doctrine of the Word of God* (New York: Charles Scribner's Sons; 1936), p. 188.
4 R. H. Lightfoot, *The Gospel Message of St. Mark* (Oxford: Clarendon Press; 1950), p. 103.
5 See Karl Löwith, *Meaning in History* (Chicago: University of Chicago Press; 1959), p. 183.
6 Rudolf Bultmann, *Primitive Christianity in Its Contemporary Setting,* trans. by R. H. Fuller (New York: Meridian Books; 1956), pp. 71ff.
7 Rudolf Bultmann, *Primitive Christianity in Its Contemporary Setting* (New York: Meridian Books; 1956), p. 93.
8 Edwin Clement Hoskyns, *The Fourth Gospel,* ed. by Francis Noel Davy (London: Faber & Faber; 1947), p. 85.
9 Thomas F. Torrance in *Scottish Journal of Theology,* Sept. 1954, p. 249.
10 Rudolf Bultmann, *Theology of the New Testament,* trans. by Kenrick Grobel (New York: Charles Scribner's Sons; 1951), Vol. I, p. 42f.
11 C. H. Dodd, *The Apostolic Preaching and Its Developments* (New York: Harper & Brothers; 1936), p. 17.
12 Paul Tillich, *The Protestant Era,* trans. by James Luther Adams (Chicago: University of Chicago Press; 1948), p. 31.
13 Oscar Cullmann, *Christ and Time,* trans. by Floyd V. Filson (Philadelphia: Westminster Press; 1950), p. 151.
14 Anders Nygren, *Christ and His Church,* trans. by Alan Carlsten (Philadelphia: Westminster Press; 1956), p. 96.
15 H. H. Farmer, *God and Men* (New York: Abingdon-Cokesbury; 1947), p. 167.

Chapter 2

1 Hans Lietzmann, *The Beginnings of the Christian Church,* trans. by Bertram Lee Woolf (New York: Charles Scribner's Sons; 1949), p. 73.

[2] For a discussion of this question see John Knox, *Chapters in a Life of Paul* (New York: Abingdon Press; 1950).

[3] Lietzmann, op. cit., p. 110.

[4] Knox, op. cit., p. 54.

Chapter 3

[1] Ernst Troeltsch, *Christian Thought, Its History and Application*, ed. by Baron von Huegel (New York: Meridian Books; 1957), p. 177.

Chapter 4

[1] Ernst Kaesemann, as quoted in Bultmann, *Theology of the New Testament*, Vol. II, p. 142.

[2] M. C. D'Arcy, *The Mind and Heart of Love* (New York: Meridian Books; 1956), p. 56.

Chapter 5

[1] Ernst Troeltsch, *The Social Teaching of the Christian Churches*, trans. by Olive Wyon (London: Allen & Unwin; 1931), Vol. I, p. 203.

[2] Quoted in Charles Norris Cochrane, *Christianity and Classical Culture* (New York: Oxford University Press; 1944), p. 327.

[3] Henry H. Halley, *Pocket Bible Handbook* (Chicago: Halley; 1943), p. 512.

[4] James Bryce, *The Holy Roman Empire* (New York: Macmillan Company; 1904), p. 201.

[5] C. H. Turner in *Cambridge Medieval History* (Cambridge: Cambridge University Press; 1936), Vol. I, p. 173.

[6] *De Civitate Dei*, in the translation by J. Healy, Vol. V, p. xi.

[7] W. E. H. Lecky, *History of European Morals* (7th ed.), Vol. II, p. 107.

[8] "Opuscula Varia" (Migne: *Patrologia Latina*, Vol. 145) as trans. by James Bruce Ross, *The Portable Medieval Reader* (New York: Viking Press; 1949), pp. 49 ff.

[9] "Exposition of the Lord's Prayer" in *Late Medieval Mysticism*, ed. by Ray C. Petry (Library of Christian Classics, Vol. XIII). (Philadelphia: Westminster Press; 1957), p. 120.

Chapter 6

[1] As quoted in *The Best of Modern European Literature*, ed. by Klaus Mann and Hermann Kesten (Philadelphia: Blakiston Company; 1945), p. 12.

[2] Roland H. Bainton, "The Ministry in the Middle Ages," in *The Ministry in Historical Perspectives*, ed. by H. Richard Niebuhr and Daniel D. Williams (New York: Harper & Brothers; 1956), p. 89.

[3] C. G. Coulton, *Art and the Reformation* (Cambridge: Cambridge University Press; 1953), p. 290.

[4] Emile Malê, *Religious Art from the Twelfth to the Eighteenth Century* (New York: Pantheon Books; 1949), p. 29.

[5] Arnold Hauser, *The Social History of Art* (New York: Vintage Books; 1957), Vol. I, p. 232.

[6] Malê, op. cit., 96–97.

Chapter 7

[1] Ludo Moritz Hartmann, *The Early Medieval State: Byzantium, Italy and the West* (London: Historical Association Pamphlet; 1949), p. 2.

[2] R. M. French, *The Eastern Orthodox Church* (London: Hutchinson University Library; 1951), p. 23.

[3] Walter F. Adeney, *The Greek and Eastern Churches* (New York: Charles Scribner's Sons; 1908), p. 262.

[4] As quoted in Routley, *The Wisdom of the Fathers* (Philadelphia: Westminster Press; 1957), pp. 115, 117.

[5] As quoted in Gustav Aulen, *Christus Victor*, trans. by A. G. Hebert (London: SPCK; 1931), p. 48.

Chapter 8

[1] For a brilliant discussion of the transformation of this term, see Albert Outler, *The Christian Tradition and the Unity We Seek* (New York: Oxford University Press; 1957), Chap. 4, "The Christian Tradition."

[2] *Summa Theologica*, Pt. I, Q. 1, Art. 8, Reply Objection 2, in Anton C. Pegis, *Introduction to Saint Thomas Aquinas* (New York: Modern Library; 1948), p. 15.

[3] See Henry Bettenson, *Documents of the Christian Church* (New York: Oxford, 1963), p. 149.

[4] Ibid., p. 149.

[5] Troeltsch, *The Social Teaching of the Christian Churches*, Vol. I, p. 228.

[6] Ibid., p. 232.

[7] Cyril Charles Richardson, *The Church through the Centuries* (London: Religious Book Club; 1938), p. 104.

[8] *No Cross, No Crown* (New York: Doubleday & Company; 1957), p. 103.

[9] George Burch, *Early Medieval Philosophy* (New York: King's Crown Press; 1951), p. 5.

Chapter 9

1 Henri Pirenne, *A History of Europe from the Invasions to the XVI Century* (New York: University Books; 1956), pp. 552–53.
2 Karl Adam, *One and Holy* (New York: Sheed & Ward; 1951), pp. 23, 25.

Chapter 10

1 Jaroslav Pelikan in *More About Luther*, ed. by Gerhard L. Belgum (Decorah, Iowa: Luther College Press; 1958), p. 50.
2 Albert C. Outler in *The Christian Tradition and the Unity We Seek* (New York: Oxford University Press; 1957), p. 36.
3 Martin Luther, *A Commentary on St. Paul's Epistle to the Galatians*, ed. by Erasmus Middleton (London, 1807), p. 330.
4 Luther, *Tischreden*, ed. by H. Borcherdt and W. Rehm (Munich, n.d.), Vol. 12, no. 19.
5 Heinrich Bornkamm, *Luther's World of Thought*, trans. by Martin H. Bertram (St. Louis: Concordia Publishing House; 1958), p. 45.
6 Ibid., p. 53.
7 Einar Billing, *Our Calling*, trans. by Conrad Bergendoff (Rock Island: Augustana; 1947), p. 7.
8 Philip Hughes, *A Popular History of the Reformation* (Garden City, N. Y.: Hanover House; 1957), p. 252.
9 *Calvin Commentaries*, ed. by Joseph Haroutunian and Louise Pettibone Smith (Philadelphia: Westminster Press; 1958), p. 52.
10 Ibid., pp. 41–42.

Chapter 11

1 G. M. Trevelyan, *History of England* (New York: Anchor Books; 1953), Vol. II, pp. 80–81.
2 As quoted by Guy Mayfield, *The Church of England* (New York: Oxford University Press; 1958), p. 5.
3 Yngve Brilioth, *Eucharistic Faith and Practice*, trans. by A. G. Hebert (London: SPCK; 1956), p. 158.
4 Charles Borgeaud as quoted by John T. McNeill, *The History and Character of Calvinism* (New York: Oxford University Press; 1954), p. 196.
5 Alfred North Whitehead, *Adventures of Ideas* (New York: Mentor Books; 1955), p. 57.

Chapter 13

[1] Jacob Burckhardt, *Force and Freedom*, ed. by James H. Nichols (New York: Meridian Books; 1955), p. 317.

[2] Robert L. Calhoun, "Christ and the Church," in *The Nature of the Unity We Seek*, ed. by Paul S. Minear (St. Louis: Bethany Press; 1958), pp. 73 ff.

[3] Winthrop Hudson, *The Great Tradition of the American Churches* (New York: Harper & Brothers; 1953), pp. 64–65.

Chapter 14

[1] *Science and the Modern World* (New York: Macmillan Company; 1927), p. ix.

[2] Whitehead, *Adventures of Ideas*, p. 30.

[3] Alexandre Koyré, *From the Closed World to the Infinite Universe* (New York: Harper Torchbooks; 1958), pp. 272, 276.

[4] *The Portable Nietzsche*, ed. by Walter Kaufmann (New York: Viking Press; 1954), p. 95.

[5] R. S. Franks, *The Doctrine of the Trinity* (London: Gerald Duckworth and Company; 1953), p. 162.

[6] *Protestantism in America* (Philadelphia: Westminster Press; 1953), p. 7.

Chapter 15

[1] Oscar Cullmann, *Christ and Time*, trans. by Floyd V. Filson (Philadelphia: Westminster Press; 1950), pp. 166–67.

[2] Karl Adam, *The Spirit of Catholicism*, trans. by Dom Justin McCann (New York: Image Books; 1954), p. 154.

[3] Philip Hughes, *A Popular History of the Catholic Church* (New York: Image Books; 1954), p. 250.

Chapter 16

[1] As reported by G. K. A. Bell, *The Kingship of Christ* (Harmondsworth, Middlesex, England: Penguin Books; 1954), p. 140.

[2] Ibid., p. 18.

[3] *Handbook of Christian Theology* (New York: Meridian Books; 1958), pp. 60 ff.

[4] D. M. Baillie, *God Was In Christ* (New York: Charles Scribner's Sons; 1948), pp. 203–4.

[5] *The Meaning of the Creative Act*, trans. by Donald A.

Lowrie (New York: Harper & Brothers; 1955), p. 308.

[6] As quoted in *Christian Unity in North America*, ed. by J. Robert Nelson (St. Louis: Bethany Press; 1958), p. 48.

[7] Minear, *The Nature of the Unity We Seek*, p. 168.

CHRONOLOGY

This sequence of events parallels the framework of the book; it places special emphasis on setting the more important persons into context. In many instances only the date of death is given (thus: –461   Leo the Great). Early dates are approximate.

PART I: *To* A.D. *451, Council of Chalcedon*

B.C.

168–	The rule of the Maccabees in Palestine
175–163	Rule of Antiochus Epiphanes
143–63	Period of relative Jewish independence
	Appearance of apocalyptic literature in this period
63	Pompey takes Jerusalem
37–	Rule of the Herods
27–	Augustus Emperor
6 or 4	Birth of Jesus of Nazareth

A.D.

6	By now Augustus assumed procuratorship
–14	Rule of Augustus, Tiberius becomes Emperor
27	The appearance of John the Baptist as preacher and reformer
30	Death of Jesus
c. 35	Conversion of Paul
44	Herod Agrippa persecutes early Christian Church at Jerusalem
–50	Philo
c. 50	First New Testament writings, Paul's letters begin
48 or 51	Apostolic Council at Jerusalem
64	Fire in Rome in time of Nero signals occasion for persecution
64	Deaths of Peter and Paul
65 or 70	Beginning of Gospel-writing period, St. Mark
68	Vespasian becomes Emperor
70	Destruction of Jerusalem
93	Writing of Josephus' *Antiquities*
c. 96	Literary production of Clement of Rome
–96	Domitian

c. 100 Period of Cerinthian heresy which denied full humanity of Christ

112 Letter of Pliny with reference to Christians

–117 Trajan Emperor

135 Jewish uprising ends after about three years of turmoil

140 Arrival of Marcion in Rome; spread of his heresy

155 *Apology* of Justin Martyr

160 Other apologists active at this time; Tatian

–160 Marcion

160 At about this time Valentinian came to Rome; spread of Gnostic heresy

180 Writings of Irenaeus detail early views of Church and episcopacy

195 Conversion of Tertullian; beginning of his apologetic activities

200 Shaping of canon well in process

–215 Clement of Alexandria; beginning of Eastern theological lineage

250 Decian persecution

–254 Origen, shaper of Eastern theological tradition

–258 Cyprian, "high church" theologian

304–313 Period of transition for Roman Empire: from persecutor of Church to officially Christian Empire

Edicts of toleration from 311 to 313

319 Activity of Arius

325 Council of Nicea, symbol of the period of great ecumenical councils dealing with basic dogma

–337 Constantine

340 Old Roman Creed dating from this period carries kernel of "Apostles' Creed"

–346 Pachomius and

–356 Antony represent beginnings of Egyptian monastic era

361–363 Rule of Julian the Apostate briefly causes relapse into anti-Christian policy of Empire

372 Martin of Tours begins missionary activity in Gaul

–373 Athanasius

–379 Basil of Asia Minor, spread of monasticism

381 Apollinarianism condemned

–383 Ulphilas; activity of Christian movement among barbarians

–397 Ambrose, Bishop of Milan

PART II: *To the Fifteenth Century*

-754 Boniface, great missionary in "Germany"

772–76 Victories of Charlemagne in Saxony consolidate his power and growing empire

781–96 Alcuin at Court of Charlemagne, Carolingian renascence of learning

787 Nicean Council

800 Charlemagne crowned by Pope Leo III, act symbolizing theocratic character of medieval empire

814–40 Reign of Louis the Pious

843 Treaty of Verdun prefigures modern European national picture

850 Pseudo-Isidorean decretals to substantiate papal territorial claims

858–67 Nicholas I Pope

-867 Ansgar, Scandinavian saint

867 Photian schism increases tension between churches of East and West

910 Beginning of medieval reform of monasticism at Cluny

962 Pope crowns Otto I (the Great)

c. 1000 Peace of God and Truce of God represent religious attempt at taking the sharp edge off the medieval ethos

1054 Schism between East and West in Christendom, Leo IX Pope, Michael Patriarch

1073–1085 Gregory VII Pope, represents pastoral ideal of medieval papacy

1077 Henry IV "humiliated" by pope at Canossa

1084 Carthusian Order, new monastic movements

1095 Council of Clermont; the Crusades

1098 *Cur Deus Homo* of Anselm at head of scholastic theological line

1122 Council of Worms

1145 Prominence of Gothic architecture after St. Denis

1198–1216 Innocent III Pope

1200 Innocent's interdict against Philip Augustus of France illustrates use of religious sanctions against secular rulers

1208 Innocent's interdict against John of England

1215 Magna Carta in England

-1221 Dominic de Guzman; Dominicanism

1232 The Inquisition established

1245 Thomas Aquinas at Paris; height of scholastic period

1294–1303 Boniface VIII Pope, makes extravagant claims for papacy which it can no longer enforce

1296 Bull *Clericis Laicos*
1302 Boniface' Bull *Unam Sanctam*
1309– Babylonian Captivity of the Papacy
–1321 Death of Dante
1337 Union of Kalmar, consolidation of Scandinavian nationhood
–1349 William of Occam; nominalist philosophical threat to realist position undergirding medieval Catholic thought
1377 End of "Babylonian Captivity of the Church," restoration of Roman papacy from Avignon in France

PART III: *To Westphalia, 1648*

1414–1418 Council of Constance, Hus burned as a heretic when Council fails to keep faith
–1431 Jeanne d'Arc
1431 Council of Basel
1438–39 Councils of Ferrara and Florence
1453 Fall of Constantinople
–1471 Thomas a Kempis as representative of new forms of piety in northern lands
1483 Thomas de Torquemada, Grand Inquisitor
1483 Pragmatic Sanction of Bourges, at head of French church's semi-independence of Rome
1483 Birth of Luther
–1498 Death of Savonarola for outspokenness against late medieval papal extremes
–1504 Isabella, whose marriage to Ferdinand made possible great hour of Spanish dominion; period of exploration of world encouraged by Spain
1509 Henry VIII accedes to throne in England; during his reign England undergoes "reform"
1516 Charles V Holy Roman Emperor during Reformation period
1517 Luther's Ninety-Five Theses symbol of beginning of Protestant Reformation
–1517 Ximenes, Spanish Catholic reformer
1520 Luther's treatises detail Protestant position
–1527 Machiavelli, representative of secularizing state
1529 Marburg Colloquy, breach between German and Swiss reforms
1529 Diet of Speyer, first use of term "Protestant"

1530   Diet of Augsburg, articulation of Lutheran position
−1531 Zwingli, Swiss reformer, killed in battle
1534   Act of Supremacy in England
−1535 Thomas More, English humanist
1536   Calvin's *Institutes* sophisticate Reformed position
1536− Beginning of sequence of meetings known as Council of Trent
1536, 1539 Ten Articles and Six Articles suggest difficulties of relating Protestantism to Roman Catholicism in England
1545   Actual beginning of Council of Trent
−1546 Luther
−1547 Henry VIII
−1547 Francis I of France, monarch during Reformation period
1547−53 Edward King of England, Protestantizing period
1549   Act of Uniformity in England
1553−58 Under Mary Tudor England again turns toward Catholicism
1553   Michael Servetus put to death by Protestants as heretic
1555   Peace of Augsburg
−1556 Charles V
−1556 Ignatius of Loyola, founder of Jesuits and spark of Catholic Counter-Reform
1558   Accession of Elizabeth, who brings about relative religious settlement in England
1559   Act of Uniformity in England
−1561 Menno Simons, founder of Mennonites, symbol of Anabaptist movement in Reformation
−1572 John Knox, Scot reformer
−1584 Ivan the Terrible, Russian ruler
−1600 Richard Hooker, theorist of Anglican position
−1603 Death of Elizabeth
−1604 Fausto Sozzini, "Unitarian," represents theological extreme of Protestant reform
1618   King James *Book of Sports* designed to antagonize "Puritan" movement in Church of England
−1632 Gustavus Adolphus, Scandinavian king killed in Thirty Years' War
−1638 Cyril Lucar, who bridged East-West theologically

−1638   Cornelius Jansen, leader of a "Puritan" movement in Catholicism

−1645   Archbishop Laud, high-church foil of Puritans

1648   Peace of Westphalia, end of Thirty Years' War, which had some elements of "Holy War" as culmination of breach within Western church

PART IV: *To the Present*

−1648   Lord Herbert of Cherbury, spokesman for Deist religious movement

−1650   Descartes, in many respects the father of modern theology

1651   Hobbes *Leviathin* outlines a secular state

−1681   Patriarch Nikon of Russian church

1682   *Four Articles* suggest relative independence of French Catholic church

−1683   Roger Williams, American pioneer for religious freedom

1689   Settlement after Puritan Revolt

−1705   Spener, who may be thought of as the father of pietism in continental Protestantism

−1725   Peter the Great, "Westernizer" of Russia

1734   American Great Awakening

−1758   Jonathan Edwards, great American theologian and preacher

1765–90   Joseph II, Holy Roman Emperor

1773   Abolition of Society of Jesus

1776   Virginia disestablishment begins American process of separating church and state in formal sense

1787   American nationhood

−1788   Voltaire, antagonist of Catholic Church in France

−1791   John Wesley, father of Methodism

1792–   Activities of William Carey and others lead to a decade of formation of missionary societies in England and on the continent

1801   Concordat between Napoleon and Pius VIII

−1804   Immanuel Kant

1807   Early efforts at introducing Protestantism into modern China

1814   Society of Jesus reestablished

1817   Prussian Union designed to unite Lutheran and Reformed churches

1822	Formation of Catholic Society for the Propagation of the Faith
1830	Continental Europe in social discontent and revolt
−1831	Hegel
1832 & '34	*Singulari Nos* and *Mirari Vos* directed by papacy against French political Catholic "liberalism"
−1833	William Wilberforce
1833	Disestablishment in Massachusetts culminates period of legally separating church and state in United States
−1834	Friedrich Schleiermacher, perhaps greatest nineteenth-century continental theologian
1843	Scottish Disruption; disestablishment of church
1848	Revolutionary year in Europe Communist Manifesto
1854	Bull *Ineffabilis Deus* heightens dogma concerning Virgin Mary
−1854	Lamennais, leader of French Catholic political "liberalism"
−1855	Kierkegaard, Danish theologian
1864	*Syllabus of Errors,* Pope counters modern errors
1870	Vatican Council, Pope now "infallible"
−1872	F. D. Maurice, British social Christian
−1873	Livingstone, famed missionary
1873	May or Falk Laws, part of German *Kulturkampf* with papacy
−1872	Ludwig Feuerbach
1879	*Aeterni Patris* makes Aquinian thought-pattern official in Catholicism
−1882	Charles Darwin
−1883	Karl Marx
1886−	Student Christian movements forerunner of Ecumenical Movement
−1889	Ritschl, German theologian
−1890	Newman, Anglo-Catholic converted to Roman Catholic
−1900	Nietzsche
1907−8	Papal attacks on Catholic "Modernism"
1908	Federal Council of Churches in the United States
1910	Edinburgh meeting on missions, another forerunner of Ecumenical Movement
1918	Karl Barth commentary on Romans begins revolt in modern theology

1925 Stockholm, first ecumenical conference on Life and Work

1927 Lausanne, first conference on Faith and Order

1928 Soviet Five-Year Plans harass churches

1934 Barmen declaration, Protestant reply to Hitlerism

−1939 Sigmund Freud

1948 World Council of Churches at Amsterdam

1950 National Council of Churches of Christ in the U.S.A.

GENERAL BIBLIOGRAPHY AND
SUGGESTED READING

For Reference

F. L. Cross, *The Oxford Dictionary of the Christian Church*. Oxford.

Henry Bettenson, *Documents of the Christian Church*. Oxford.

Kenneth Scott Latourette, *A History of Christianity*. Harper.

The volumes in *The Library of Christian Classics*. Westminster.

For Further Reading

The mysterious science of church history has been opened to all in recent years; more and more publishers have satisfied the demands of people who are asking questions about the faith by searching its past. The "quality paperback" book has become an institution which celebrates this new maturity. The list below is made up entirely of easily available permanent "paperbacks" which are capable of leading readers of first acquaintance with this field down various bypaths of interest. Readers of more technical orientation will know where to consult more technical bibliographies, though they, too, may be surprised to learn of the variety of standard works now accessible to everyone.

In many cases there will be a reference to both publisher (e.g., University of Chicago Press) and the name of the paperback series (e.g., Phoenix).

Preface (works of overall interest)

Karl Adam, *The Spirit of Catholicism*. Doubleday Image.

R. G. Collingwood, *The Idea of History*. Oxford Galaxy.

Christopher Dawson, *Religion and Culture*. Meridian.

Ludwig Feuerbach, *The Essence of Christianity*. Harper Torchbook.

Anne Fremantle, *The Papal Encyclicals in Their Historical Context*. New American Library Mentor.

A Handbook of Christian Theology. Meridian Living Age.

Philip Hughes, *A Popular History of the Catholic Church.* Doubleday Image.

Karl Löwith, *Meaning in History.* University of Chicago Phoenix.

H. Richard Niebuhr, *Christ and Culture.* Harper Torchbook.

Rudolf Sohm, Outlines of Church History. Beacon.

Ernst Troeltsch, *Christian Thought: Its History and Application.* Meridian Living Age.

Alfred North Whitehead, *Adventures of Ideas.* New American Library Mentor.

Charles Williams, *The Descent of the Dove.* Meridian Living Age.

Chapter 1

J. M. Allegro, *The Dead Sea Scrolls.* Penguin.

B. Harvie Branscomb, *The Teachings of Jesus.* Abingdon Apex.

John Bright, *The Kingdom of God.* Abingdon Apex.

Rudolf Bultmann, *Primitive Christianity in Its Contemporary Setting.* Meridian Living Age.

E. M. Cornford, *From Religion to Philosophy.* Harper Torchbook.

Morton S. Enslin, *Christian Beginnings* and *The Literature of The Christian Movement.* Harper Torchbook.

Austin Farrer, *The Core of the Bible.* Harper Torchbook.

Theodore H. Gaster, *The Dead Sea Scriptures.* Doubleday Anchor.

Edgar J. Goodspeed, *A Life of Jesus.* Harper Torchbook.

Dom Aelred Graham, *The Christ of Catholicism.* Doubleday Image.

Gilbert Murray, *Five Stages of Greek Religion.* Doubleday Anchor.

Chapter 2

Adolf Deissmann, *Paul: A Study in Social and Religious History.* Harper Torchbook.

C. H. Dodd, *The Meaning of Paul for Today.* Meridian Living Age.

Chapter 3

Jacob Burckhardt, *The Age of Constantine the Great.* Doubleday Anchor.

Charles Norris Cochrane, *Christianity and Classical Culture.* Oxford Galaxy

Edward Gibbon, *The Decline and Fall of the Roman Empire.* Viking Portable; also in two volumes under different titles in Harper Torchbook.

F. C. Grant, *Ancient Roman Religion.* Liberal Arts Press Library of Religion.

F. C. Grant, *Hellenistic Religions: The Age of Syncretism.* Liberal Arts Press Library of Religion.

W. K. C. Guthrie, *The Greeks and Their Gods.* Doubleday Anchor.

Jane Harrison, *Prolegomena to the Study of Greek Religion.* Meridian.

Helen Waddell, *The Desert Fathers.* University of Michigan Ann Arbor.

Chapter 4

Robert Grant, *Gnosticism.* Liberal Arts Press Library of Religion.

Adolf Harnack, *Outlines of the History of Dogma.* Beacon.

Adolf Harnack, *What Is Christianity?* Harper Torchbook.

Edwin Hatch, *The Influence of Greek Ideas on Christianity.* Harper Torchbook.

Dorothy Sayers, *The Mind of the Maker.* Meridian Living Age.

Chapter 5

St. Augustine, *The City of God.* 2 vols. Hafner.

Christopher Dawson, *The Making of Europe.* Meridian.

W. P. Ker, *The Dark Ages.* New American Library Mentor.

Chapter 6

G. G. Coulton, *Medieval Fate and Symbolism and The Fate of Medieval Art.* Harper Torchbook.

Christopher Dawson, *Religion and the Rise of Western Culture.* Doubleday Image.

C. H. Haskins, *The Rise of Universities.* Cornell University Press Great Seal.

C. H. Haskins, *The Renaissance of the Twelfth Century.* Meridian.

Arnold Hauser, *The Social History of Art,* Vol. I. Knopf Vintage.

Emile Malê, *The Gothic Image.* Harper Torchbook.

Emile Malê, *Religious Art.* Noonday.

Erwin Panofsky, *Gothic Architecture and Scholasticism.* Meridian.

Henry Osborn Taylor, *The Emergence of Christian Culture in the West* and *The Classical Heritage of the Middle Ages*. Harper Torchbook.

Chapter 7

Steven Runciman, *Byzantine Civilization*. Meridian.

Chapter 8

Jeanne Ancelet-Hustache, *Master Eckhart and the Rhineland Mystics,* Harper Men of Wisdom.

St. Thomas Aquinas, *On the Truth of the Catholic Faith.* Several volumes. Doubleday Image.

St. Augustine, *An Augustine Synthesis* (Przywara) Harper Torchbook.

M. C. D'Arcy and others, *St. Augustine.* Meridian.

Anne Fremantle, *The Age of Belief: The Medieval Philosophers.* New American Library Mentor.

Johan Huizinga, *The Waning of the Middle Ages.* Doubleday Anchor.

W. R. Inge, *Christian Mysticism.* Meridian Living Age.

Thomas a Kempis, *The Imitation of Christ.* Doubleday Image.

Henri Marrou, *St. Augustine.* Harper Men of Wisdom.

Maurice de Wulf, *An Introduction to Scholastic Philosophy.* Dover.

Chapter 9

Jacob Burckhardt, *The Civilization of the Renaissance in Italy.* 2 vols. Harper Torchbook.

Chapter 10

Roland H. Bainton, *Here I Stand, a Life of Martin Luther.* New American Library Mentor.

Heinrich Boehmer, *Martin Luther: Road to Reformation.* Meridian Living Age.

Johan Huizinga, *Erasmus and the Age of Reformation.* Harper Torchbook.

Chapter 11

Roland H. Bainton, *The Age of the Reformation.* Anvil.

Roland H. Bainton, *The Reformation of the Sixteenth Century.* Beacon.

Chapter 12

Roland H. Bainton, *The Travail of Religious Liberty*. Harper Torchbook.

William Haller, *The Rise of Puritanism*. Harper Torchbook.

James Hastings Nichols, *A Short Primer for Protestants*. Association Reflection.

R. H. Tawney, *Religion and the Rise of Capitalism*. New American Library Mentor.

Chapter 13

Perry Miller, *The American Puritans*. Doubleday Anchor.

Thomas Wertenbaker, *The Puritan Oligarchy*. Grosset & Dunlap Universal Library.

Chapter 14

Isaiah Berlin, *The Age of Enlightenment*. New American Library Mentor.

Crane Brinton, *The Shaping of the Modern Mind*. New American Library Mentor.

J. B. Bury, *The Idea of Progress*. Dover.

Ernst Cassirer, *Philosophy of the Enlightenment*. Beacon.

Stuart Hampshire; *The Age of Reason*. New American Library Mentor.

Richard Hofstadter, *Social Darwinism in American Thought*. Beacon.

David Hume, *Dialogues Concerning Natural Religion*. Hafner.

Søren Kierkegaard, *The Attack upon Christendom*. Beacon.

Alexandre Koyré, *From the Closed World to the Infinite Universe*. Harper Torchbook.

Friedrich Schleiermacher, *On Religion: Speeches to Its Cultured Despisers*. Harper Torchbook.

Ernst Troeltsch, *Protestantism and Progress*. Beacon.

Chapter 15

John Tracy Ellis, *American Catholicism*. University of Chicago Phoenix.

Etienne Gilson, *The Church Speaks to the Modern World*. Doubleday Image.

Terence P. McLaughlin, *The Church and the Reconstruction of the Modern World*. Doubleday Image.

H. Richard Niebuhr, *The Social Sources of Denominationalism*. Meridian Living Age.

Alexis De Tocqueville, *Democracy in America*. Knopf Vintage. 2 vols.

Stanley Stuber, *Denominations—How We Got Them*. Association Reflection.

Chapter 16

G. K. A. Bell, *The Kingship of Christ*. Penguin.

Karl Barth, *The Word of God and the Word of Man*. Harper Torchbook.

Nicolas Berdyaev, *The Beginning and the End*. Harper Torchbook.

Elmer T. Clark, *The Small Sects in America*. Abingdon Apex.

Martin D'Arcy, *Communism and Christianity*. Penguin.

F. H. Heinemann, *Existentialism and the Modern Predicament*. Harper Torchbook.

George Hunt, *Ten Makers of Modern Protestant Thought*. Association Reflection.

Allan A. Hunter, *Christians in the Arena*. Fellowship.

Karl Jaspers and Rudolf Bultmann, *Myth and Christianity*. Noonday.

Joseph Wood Krutch, *The Modern Temper*, Harcourt, Brace Harvest.

Stephen Neill, *Christian Faith Today*. Pelican.

Reinhold Niebuhr, *An Interpretation of Christian Ethics*. Meridian Living Age.

Leo Rosten, *The Religions of America*. Simon and Schuster.

Paul Tillich, *The Protestant Era*. University of Chicago Phoenix.

Paul Tillich, *The Religious Situation*. Meridian Living Age.

INDEX

Abelard, Peter, 134, 136, 155, 158, 171f.
Abu Bakr, 148
acoimetai, 69
Acts of the Apostles, The, 29f., 33f., 38, 41, 66, 76
Act of Succession, 232
Act of Uniformity, 233f.
Adam, Karl, 154, 182, 346
Adam of St. Victor, 136
Adoptionism, 90
Aeterni patris (Leo XIII), 303
Aetius, 124
Agricola, Johannes, 242
Agricola, Michael, 260
Aidan, 126f.
Ailly, Peter d', 192
Alacoque, Margaret Mary, 291
Alaric, 102, 123
Albert, Archbishop of Magdeburg, 210
Albertus Magnus, 118, 172, 174f.
Albigensis, 117
Alcala, University of, 188
Alcuin, 133
Alexander VI, Pope, 200, 202
Alexander VIII, Pope, 278
Alexandrian theology, 89, 154
Ambedkar, 336
Ambrose of Milan, 53, 89, 125, 161f., 168
Ameaux, Pierre, 246
American Bible Society, 328
American Board of Commissioners for Foreign Missions, 329
American Sunday School Union, 328
American Tract Society, 328
Amiens, 135
Anabaptism, Anabaptists, 228, 236, 241, 287
Anacletus, 76
Anagni, 100
Andersson, Lars, 260
Andreae, John, 264
Anglican bodies, 75
Anglo-Catholicism, 101
Annas, 21, 24
Anselm, 109, 155, 170ff., 300, 302
Ansgar, 129, 132
Anthimus, 147
Antioch, Council, 142, 164
Antiochian or Antiochene theology, 89, 92, 154
Antiochus Epiphanes, 21
Antiquities, The, 28
Apocalypse, 21
Apocalypse, The, 58, 61, 72, 100
Apocrypha, 72
Apollinarius, Apollinarianism, 92f., 146
Apology, The (Tertullian), 60f.
Apostles' Creed, 75
Apthartodocetae, 146

Arius, Arianism, 90f., 93, 104, 124f.
Aristotle, Aristotelianism, 58, 173, 175, 301
Arminius, Arminianism, 42, 264, 332
Arnauld, Antoine, 264
Arnold of Brescia, 110
Arsenius, 145
Arthur (son of Henry VII of England), 197
Athanasius, 67, 72, 91f., 170
Athenagoras, 83
Auden, W. H., 354
Augsburg Confession, 232, 244
Augsburg, Diet of, 199, 237
Augsburg, Peace of, 243f., 262f.
Augustine, 42, 51, 65, 84, 89, 94, 99, 102ff., 125, 127, 141, 156, 168, 173ff., 183, 200, 206, 273, 300
Augustine of Canterbury, 114, 126, 130
Augustus Caesar, 20, 22
Aulen, Gustav, 171
Avenir, L', 304
Averroism, 174
Avicenna, 174
Avignon, 191
Avvakum, 254
Azariah, V. S., 336f.

Bacon, Francis, 297
Baptist Mission Society, 328
Baptists, 237
Babylonian Captivity of the Church, The, 216, 231
Barmen Declaration, 350
Barnabas, 44ff.
Barnabas, Epistle of, 72, 83
Barth, Karl, 16, 42, 308f., 351, 353
Baruch (Justin), 79
Basel, Council, 88, 193
Basel Society, 323
Basil of Caesarea, 69
Basilides, 80
Baur, Ferdinand Christian, 308
Baxter, Richard, 298
Beaton, Cardinal, 240
Beck, Tobias, 309
Bede, 126
Beecher, Lyman, 288f., 332
Belgian Congregation of the Immaculate Heart of Mary, 327
Belgic Confession, 237
Benedict of Aniane, 116
Benedict of Nursia, Benedictinism, 113, 114
Berdyaev, Nicholas, 345
Berengar of Tours, 169, 173
Berkeley, George, 296, 298
Bernard of Clairvaux, 117, 172, 174, 209, 302
Berno of Baume, 115
Berquin, Louis de, 221
Beza, Theodore, 247, 261
Biel, Gabriel, 207

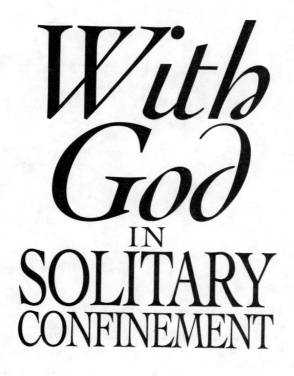

With God

IN
SOLITARY
CONFINEMENT

Richard Wurmbrand

Living Sacrifice Book Company
Bartlesville, Oklahoma

With God in Solitary Confinement
©1969 by The Voice of the Martyrs, Inc.

Published by Living Sacrifice Book Company, P O Box 2273,
Bartlesville OK 74005-2273.

Library of Congress Cataloging-in-Publication Data
Wurmbrand, Richard.
    With God in solitary confinement / Richard Wurmbrand.
        p.   cm.
    ISBN 0-88264-002-X (pbk.) : 7.00
    1. Persecution–Romania–Sermons. 2. Political prisoners–
Romania–Religious life–Sermons. 3. Jewish Christians–
Persecutions–Sermons. 4. Sermons, English. I. Title.
BR1608.R8W848   1993
272'.9'092–dc20   93-31630
                                                                CIP